UNITY LIBRARY & ARCHIVES

0 0051 0090428 8

"I have been involved in the Unity movement for over twenty-five years and am thoroughly knowledgeable of its origin and history. But it wasn't until I read Neal Vahle's biography, *The Spiritual Journey of Charles Fillmore: Discovering the Power Within*, that I truly felt the passion that permeated the mind and heart of Unity's co-founder. Vahle does a remarkable job of transporting the reader into the stream of 'zeal and enthusiasm' that Charles Fillmore resonated with into his ninety-fourth year."

—**Reverend Duke Tufty, minister and chairman of the board,**
Unity School of Christianity

"This book is an authoritative biography of Charles Fillmore, co-founder of the Unity School of Christianity. It provides an in-depth treatment of Fillmore's 'New Thought' antecedents and contemporary religious influences. The book is a tribute to Fillmore's enduring, but little understood, influence."

—**Vern Barnet, D. Min., columnist for the *Kansas City Star* and**
founder of the Kansas City Interfaith Council

"Neal Vahle's new biography of Charles Fillmore reveals him as the truly fascinating character that he was. Vahle places him squarely in his place and time and in doing so unveils deep insights not only about the man and his work, but also about the social and religious climate of his day . . . I recommend this book highly as the best and most accurate yet written about my great-grandfather."

—**Reverend Connie Fillmore Bazzy,**
former president of the Unity School of Christianity

"This book introduces the reader to one of the most fascinating personalities in American religion, who together with his wife Myrtle, created the world-wide Unity movement. The remarkable success of Unity is rooted in the eclectic, pragmatic, non-dogmatic, intense mystical outlook of its founders."

—**Joseph P. Schulz, director of the Center for Religious Studies, emeritus,**
University of Missouri-Kansas City

"Neal Vahle's dynamic biography of Charles Fillmore captures his metaphysical thought and spiritual insight. Vahle's work provides further clarification to the words and reflections of Charles Fillmore and motivates the reader to !
filled spiritual life."

—**Reverend Gregory C. Guice, minister and member of the board of dii**
Unity School of

"Neal Vahle's biography of Charles Fillmore contributes greatly to the n
literature. It not only provides an in-depth look at the life and teachings

Fillmore; the book also summarizes the contributions and teachings of other related metaphysical teachers/healers . . . It is goldmine of historical information."

—Charlotte Shelton, president and CEO of the Unity School of Christianity

"This new biography of Unity's cofounder Charles Fillmore has plenty in it to surprise fans of New Thought philosophy. Neal Vahle's research has provided us with fascinating insights into Unity and New Thought's origins . . . This is an important contribution to American religious history."

—Reverend Michael A. Maday, former editor of *Unity House* and anthologist of *New Thought for a New Millennium* and *Angels Sing in Me*

"An absorbing study! Neal Vahle has collected in one volume the essence of Charles Fillmore's thinking and the major sources that formed the beginning of the Unity Movement. Unity and New Thought ministers, teachers, researchers and students will find a wealth of new perspectives here, bringing alive the people and modes of thought that influenced Charles Fillmore."

—Reverend Philip White, former editor of *Unity Magazine* and dean of education of the Unity School of Christianity

"Neal Vahle has captured the essence, the core of the underpinnings of the New Thought movement through his comprehensive and in-depth biography of the life and writings of Charles Fillmore. The book provides a touching personal story of Charles Fillmore's dedication to the growth and development of the Unity movement. This comprehensive and passionate work is required reading for those who want to understand how the New Thought movement grew and developed, and for those who want to get a better idea of the place that New Thought occupies in the spirituality of today."

—Reverend Richard Mantei, minister and member of the board of directors, Unity School of Christianity

"This book is invaluable. With great clarity it sums up the evolution of the Unity and Metaphysical movements as seen through the eyes of Charles Fillmore, a modern mystic."

—Walter Starcke, author of seven books including *The Double Thread*, *It's All God*, and *The Gospel of Relativity*

"Neal Vahle's chronicle of my grandfather's remarkable journey truly captures the amazing spirit of this very unusual man. This biography, in addition to his two other works, *Torch-Bearer to Light the Way* and *The Unity Movement,* makes Vahle the premier historian of the Unity movement and a major contributor to the history of New Thought."

—Reverend Rosemary Fillmore Rhea, founder, director, and host of *The Daily Word* television show and co-producer of *The Word from Unity*

The SPIRITUAL JOURNEY of CHARLES FILLMORE

The SPIRITUAL JOURNEY *Of* CHARLES FILLMORE

Discovering the Power Within

NEAL VAHLE

Unity Library & Archives
1901 NW Blue Parkway
Unity Village, MO 64065

Templeton Foundation Press
West Conshohocken, Pennsylvania

Templeton Foundation Press
300 Conshohocken State Road, Suite 670
West Conshohocken, PA 19428
www.templetonpress.org

© 2008 by Neal Vahle   06/08
mH

All rights reserved. No part of this book may be used or reproduced, stored in a retrieval system, or transmitted in any form or by any means, electronic, mechanical, photocopying, recording, or otherwise, without the written permission of Templeton Foundation Press.

Templeton Foundation Press helps intellectual leaders and others learn about science research on aspects of realities, invisible and intangible. Spiritual realities include unlimited love, accelerating creativity, worship, and the benefits of purpose in persons and in the cosmos.

Designed and Typeset by ION Graphic Design Works

Library of Congress Cataloging-in-Publication Data

Vahle, Neal.
  The spiritual journey of Charles Fillmore : discovering the power
within / Neal Vahle.
      p. cm.
  Includes bibliographical references and index.
  ISBN-13: 978-1-59947-140-2 (pbk. : alk. paper)
  ISBN-10: 1-59947-140-X (pbk. : alk. paper) 1. Fillmore, Charles,
1854-1948. 2. Christian biography. 3. Unity School of Christianity.
I. Title.
  BX9890.U58F546 2008
  289.9'7092—dc22
  [B]
                          2008002794

Printed in the United States of America

08 09 10 11 12 13   10 9 8 7 6 5 4 3 2 1

Contents

PREFACE

I t is now thirteen years since I began this biography of Charles Fillmore. It has taken much study over many years for me to appreciate fully his many talents and gifts, as well as the strength of his character. The path that led me to Charles Fillmore began in 1990 when I began work on the biography of Ernest Holmes, the founder of the United Church of Religious Science and the creator of the philosophy of Science of the Mind. While working on *Open at the Top: The Life of Ernest Holmes*, published in 1992, I observed how Science of the Mind grew out of New Thought, a nineteenth-century metaphysical philosophy and healing movement that drew upon, among others, the work of Emanuel Swedenborg, Ralph Waldo Emerson, Franz Anton Mesmer, and Warren Felt Evans. The origins and development of New Thought intrigued me, so I began looking for another major figure in the New Thought movement whose work merited a biography. As I searched the literature, it became evident that Charles Fillmore was a prime candidate, as he had written nine books, all dealing with metaphysical healing, and he drew upon the best of the nineteenth-century metaphysical authors. He had also cofounded, with his wife Myrtle, the largest of the New Thought orga-nizations in the United States, the Unity School of Christianity, located at Unity Village, in metropolitan Kansas City, Missouri.

Unity School officials, when they learned of my interest in working on a biography of Charles Fillmore, welcomed me to the school and gave me permission to conduct research in the Unity Archives, which contained the works of all the leading figures in the Unity movement. After eighteen months of work and with the project about half complete, I realized that I needed to write a chapter dealing with the contribution of Myrtle Fillmore. Myrtle was known for her work as a teacher and healer and was the editor of

Wee Wisdom magazine. However, she had written very little for publication about the Unity spiritual teaching. She had been known, however, as a prolific letter-writer, engaging in extensive correspondence with people who had written to her for prayer or spiritual healing.

I was astounded to find, preserved in the archives, copies of over two thousand letters written by Myrtle during the three years before she died in 1931. These letters were often several pages long and contained not only prayer, affirmations, and spiritual advice but also explanations of aspects of the Unity teaching that pertained to the particular spiritual challenges faced by her correspondent. I discovered in these letters the entire Unity teaching. In addition, it was presented in a clear, straightforward, and easily understandable manner. The writing was much more forceful and direct than that of Charles and contained the kind of intimacy that only letters can provide.

The letters demonstrated that Myrtle was as important a figure as Charles in articulating the Unity message and that she played an equal role with Charles in the development of the Unity movement. I decided at that time to postpone the biography of Charles and write a biography of Myrtle. That book, *Torch-bearer to Light the Way: The Life of Myrtle Fillmore*, was published in 1996.

Upon the book's completion, Connie Fillmore Bazzy, president of Unity School of Christianity, invited me to research and write the history of the Unity movement from its beginnings in 1889 through the end of the twentieth century. That work took four years to complete and was published by Templeton Foundation Press in 2002 as *The Unity Movement: Its Evolution and Spiritual Teaching*.

My return to the biography of Charles Fillmore was again postponed when, after completion of the manuscript in 2000, I was asked by Connie Fillmore Bazzy to become the editor and publishing director of *Unity Magazine*. Only after completing my tenure as editor in September 2005 was I able to resume work on the biography of Charles Fillmore. Since a considerable amount of research and writing had been completed in the early 1990s, I assumed that completing the biography would be a relatively easy task that would take only a short amount of time.

It soon became evident that my previous research was incomplete and that the writing needed major revision. I also began to see Charles in a new and more appreciative light. I had not realized how conversant he was, as a thirty-five-year-old without formal education, with the spiritual literature of the day as well as with the classics of world literature. I had not seen that the basic elements of the Unity teaching were already developed in his mind in 1889 when he began editing and writing for *Modern Thought* magazine, the forerunner to *Unity Magazine*. Finally, I did not appreciate how capable he was as an organizer and how important his organizational ability was to the successful development of the Unity movement. This biography is a much fuller and more in-depth work than would have resulted had I continued with my original plan to complete a biography of Charles before focusing on Myrtle or on other Unity-related work.

ACKNOWLEDGMENTS

During the past fifteen years many people assisted me in my research and writing about the Unity Movement. Several of those whom I acknowledged in *Torch-bearer to Light the Way: The Life of Myrtle Fillmore* and *The Unity Movement: Its Evolution and Spiritual Teaching* contributed indirectly to this biography. I appreciate the work they did to set the stage for this work.

I give thanks to Vern Barnet, Gregory Guice, Michael Maday, Rosemary Fillmore Rhea, Joseph P. Schulz, Charlotte Shelton, Walter Starcke, Duke Tufty ,and Phillip White. Their deep knowledge of the Unity Movement, and the work of Charles Fillmore, enabled them to read the manuscript with a critical eye and give valuable comments. I am particularly grateful for the support of Connie Fillmore Bazzy. During her presidency of the Unity School of Christianity, she made it possible for me to conduct the research upon which much of this biography was based. She also read and gave advice on this manuscript.

Thanks are due to the Unity School archivist Eric Page, whose knowledge of the materials in the Fillmore collection facilitated my research. Carol Guion, who for many years was an editor at the Institute of Noetic Sciences, provided copyediting service. Natalie Lyons Silver and Mary Lou Bertucci at Templeton Foundation Press undertook the detailed editorial work required to get the manuscript ready for publication.

As I wrestled with the day-to-day problems of organization and writing style, my wife, Nancy, who is knowledgeable in spiritual literature, made suggestions that were useful in moving the work ahead. She also provided the emotional support that a writer who works in isolation often needs. That help was much appreciated.

INTRODUCTION

Charles Fillmore was a metaphysical teacher and healer, a writer and thinker who, from the beginning of his work in 1889 until his death in 1948, made a notable contribution to the development of spirituality and religion in America. Early in the twentieth century, he and his first wife, Myrtle, cofounded and organized the Unity School of Christianity in Kansas City, Missouri, an institution with a staff of four hundred, which continues to be devoted to spiritual teaching, healing, and publishing.

The teachings of Jesus, as he understood them, were central to the work of Charles Fillmore. As May Rowland, the longtime director of Silent Unity and close personal associate, said, "Charles Fillmore was a tremendous advocate of Jesus Christ." Shortly before he died, he questioned those who went to see him, "Do you know what the greatest teaching was that was ever given to man?" He hesitated when he asked that, and then he said, "It is Christ in you, the hope of glory." Then he told his visitors, "and don't forget it." Rowland reported that he signed all his letters, "Representative of Jesus Christ at large."[1] Charles at one time referred to himself as a minister "of the Gospel of Jesus Christ."[2]

Charles Fillmore set the tone for his spiritual work and his focus on the teachings of Jesus in the inaugural issue of *Modern Thought*—the magazine he began editing and publishing in 1889. He wrote, "The teaching of Christ rightly understood and applied will lead the human family back to Eden."[3] The prayer that he loved most, May Rowland recalled, was "Jesus is now here, raising me to his consciousness of eternal life."[4]

From the time Charles Fillmore began his editing and publishing in 1889 until he died in 1948, all of the issues of *Unity Magazine* and its predecessors have his writings in them. They took many forms—unsigned commentaries, editorials, publisher's notes, radio talks, sermons, and articles. He was a prolific writer.

The SPIRITUAL JOURNEY *of* CHARLES FILLMORE

Chapter 1

From Businessman to Spiritual Teacher

Growing Up in Rural Minnesota

Charles was born in 1854 on an Indian reservation near St. Cloud, Minnesota, to parents who came to the state as pioneers. During his youth, his father, Henry G. Fillmore, worked as a trader with the Chippewa Indians and as a farmer. His mother, Mary Georgiana Stone Fillmore, worked as a dressmaker.[1] His parents separated when he was seven. The family was small by pioneer standards; his only sibling was a younger brother, Norton, who at age ten ran away from home.[2]

Charles grew up in a society in which educational institutions were in their infancy. The little schooling available to him as a boy was interrupted by a physically disabling accident that had life-threatening consequences. A broken hip from an ice-skating accident and improper medical treatment left him disabled physically. He reported: "When I was ten my life was crossed by what the doctors pronounced a fatal illness. It began with what was at first diagnosed as rheumatism in the right leg, which gradually developed into tuberculosis of the hip."[3] His problem was made worse by improper medical treatment from incompetent medical practitioners in a frontier community.

> I was bled, leeched, cupped, lanced, seatoned, blistered and roweled. Six running sores were artificially produced on my leg to draw out the diseased condition which was presumed to be within. Physicians of different schools were employed and the last one always wondered how I ever pulled through alive under the treatment of the "quack" that preceded him; and as I look back at it now it's a miracle to me how I ever got away from them all the little bundle of bones and sinews which I found in my possession after they finished their experiments.[4]

3

The doctors told Charles that by the time he was forty he would be a helpless cripple in a wheelchair.[5] For several years Charles was so incapacitated that he could not lead a normal life. He explained:

> I managed after years to get on my feet, although my right leg was several inches shorter than the left, and I was to all appearances destined to chronic invalidism. I managed to get about on crutches and cane and attend school in a desultory way until I was eighteen.[6]

By the time Charles reached maturity, one leg was four inches shorter than the other and a leg brace to walk was required.[7]

Religion or spirituality played practically no part in his upbringing or in his early adulthood. Though a relative on his father's side, the Reverend Glezen Fillmore, was one of the early Methodist bishops in upstate New York, his parents apparently took little or no interest in religion. Nothing in Fillmore's description of his early life indicates that he attended religious services. Indeed, he said, "I wasn't at all religious."[8]

Business Interests in Texas and Colorado

As years passed, health improved, and, by the time he was twenty, he decided to leave Minnesota for Texas. Evidently, the move was in part because his parents maintained separate abodes: "As my mother and father were separated and without a permanent home, I became restless and wanted other surroundings."[9] In 1874 he went to Paris, Texas (then Caddo in Indian territory and now in Oklahoma), where he had a cousin. Shortly thereafter, he moved to Denison, Texas, where he lived for five years, working as a clerk in the freight office of the Missouri, Kansas and Texas Railway. His mother joined him in Denison and lived with him for most of the remaining fifty years of her life.

In 1879, Charles went to Leadville, Colorado, where he took a course in metallurgy, became a mining assayer, and settled in Gunnison City. Evidently, things did not work out in Colorado, as a letter written in 1880 to K. Murphy, a friend in Denison, indicated that life was better in Texas:

> I have not struck anything yet, and the prospects are not good for doing so either. These gold mining camps are mighty uncertain, and this one especially so. With the exception of Leadville, I have not seen a place since leaving Texas where as much business was done as in Denison.

This is the most desolate, barren region. Nothing grows but sage brush and cactus. Advise your friends to stay home if they wish to be happy.[10]

In 1877, before leaving Denison for Colorado, Charles met Myrtle Page, the woman who was to become his wife and partner in spiritual work. Myrtle came to Denison in 1876 from Clinton, Missouri, where she had been teaching in the local schools. She chose Texas for reasons of health, hoping to find relief from recurring bouts of tuberculosis. The two struck up only a brief acquaintance before Charles left for Colorado.

Little information is available about his contact with Myrtle between his leaving Texas in 1879 and his returning to marry her in Clinton, Missouri, in the early spring of 1881. Without a doubt, they corresponded, though no copies remain of their letters. The couple left for Colorado after their marriage and settled in Gunnison. When the mining boom broke later in the year, they moved to Pueblo, where Charles engaged in real estate. It was there that Lowell and Rickert, their first two sons, were born.

SETTLING IN KANSAS CITY

Charles was not ready to settle permanently in Pueblo and, in 1884, moved the family to Omaha, Nebraska. They stayed there for one year before moving on in 1885 to Kansas City. Charles attributed the constant moving to his search for his true calling:

> I never seemed satisfied with my surroundings nor at peace with my work, and the urge to go elsewhere was always with me. So I began looking for a location, without knowing exactly where to look. We broke our home in Pueblo in 1884, and we spent one winter in Omaha, Nebraska. However, there was a constant urge to go to Kansas City, and in the spring of that year we moved.[11]

After settling in Kansas City, Charles engaged in what he called "real estate plunging," acknowledging that he was "quite successful."[12] Though living in Kansas City, he continued to maintain a financial interest in the Zuni Mining Company, which operated silver mines in western Colorado, outside the town of Silverton. Charles traveled occasionally to Silverton to involve himself in the work. The investment was a valuable one, as in 1887 he was offered $75,000 for his share.

During the mid-1880s, Charles occupied himself with business affairs, having yet to develop an interest in religion. He indicated that his early religious education was "quite limited."[13] He also said that he was "not biased on the God question by an orthodox education," and that until his mid-thirties "God was an unknown factor in my conscious mind."[14] Nothing in Charles' background prior to 1889 indicated that he would give up his business career and devote his life to spiritual teaching and healing.

In 1886, he and Myrtle attended a series of lectures in Kansas City on spiritual healing given by a Christian Science practitioner from Chicago, Eugene B. Weeks. These lectures proved to be a turning point for Myrtle, who had suffered from tuberculosis since childhood. She began using healing practices learned in the lectures and, within a short time, recovered from the disease that had left her on death's door on a number of occasions. She then began using these healing principles in working with others. Charles reacted to the Weeks lectures in the way a busy Kansas City businessman might have been expected to react. "The doctrine," he said, "did not at first appeal to me."[15]

"OUR AIM IS TO CONVERT THE WORLD"

Nothing in Charles Fillmore's personal or professional background would indicate that, at age thirty-five, he had the ability to edit, write for, and publish spiritual magazines and, in the process, present a spiritual teaching that would make a major contribution to the developing nineteenth-century metaphysical healing movement. Nor would it have seemed possible that he would later write books that helped shape the course of religion in twentieth-century America.

Growing up in Minnesota, Charles received no formal education: he never completed grade school or high school. As an adult, he supported himself and his family in fields outside editing and publishing—work that presumably fully occupied his time.

It seemed likely that the contents of *Modern Thought* magazine, published monthly beginning in April 1889, would reflect the qualities of an untrained, uninformed, superficial mind, considering Charles' limited educational and professional background. Charles might be credited with being audacious but also faulted for being in over his head. Yet the range and depth of Charles Fillmore's knowledge is surprising, as revealed in the first issues of *Modern Thought* and then in the magazines that succeeded it—*Christian Science Thought*, *Thought*, and *Unity*. He demonstrated an amazing command of the literature, from the classics of Plato, Aristotle, and Socrates to the works of William Shakespeare, William Ellery Channing, Leo Tolstoy, and Mark Twain. He had read widely in the works of the major spiritual writers of the eighteenth and nineteenth centuries, including Emanuel Swedenborg, Franz Anton Mesmer, Ralph Waldo Emerson, James Russell Lowell, Mary Baker Eddy, Warren Felt Evans, Emma Curtis Hopkins, and Ursula Gestefeld.

Charles had also delved into the literature of the occult, including hermetic philosophy, theosophy, Rosicrucianism, and spiritualism. He was well versed in the Bible as well as the works of John Wesley and John Calvin, and he was very familiar with traditional Christian teachings. In addition, he had read the Bhagavad Gita as well as writings on Buddhism.

How did Charles amass this knowledge? We can only surmise how he acquired it. During his boyhood, after being injured in a skating accident, he was housebound and unable to attend school. However, he was able to work with a tutor who lived in St. Cloud, Minnesota, a woman by the name of Caroline (Mrs. Edgar) Taylor. She was college-educated, which was unusual for that time, and noted for her interest in classical literature. Mrs. Taylor introduced him to classics, sparked his interest in reading, taught him the rules of grammar, and gave him writing exercises.[16] Charles' phenomenal ability to synthesize, integrate, and retain the material he read can attributed to only one thing—a brilliant mind.

Charles indicated in a biographical sketch later in life that he was "self-taught."[17] He must have been a voracious reader throughout his adult years to have amassed the information that was at his fingertips when he began publishing *Modern Thought*.

Charles believed he had a mission to present a new spiritual doctrine to humankind. He stated in the inaugural issue of *Modern Thought* that the magazine would be devoted "to the development of man's devotional nature."[18] "Our aim," he said, "is to spread all over this Great West, the good which we know lies in wait for those willing to receive it."[19] Men and women needed to have a better understanding of spiritual truth: "The world must be reformed; the work is ours and we must not shrink from it."[20]

Charles told readers that the magazine would not be "an organ of any school of thought" or committed to any one doctrine, spiritual point of view, or religion. Rather, it would be of interest to "all honest souls earnestly seeking spiritual light." He believed the magazine would be of particular interest to "the independent Christian or any independent thinker on any line of spiritual philosophy or science."[21]

Charles was convinced that the religious beliefs held by traditional Christians, both Catholic and Protestant, were in large measure erroneous and were in part responsible for humankind's lack of spiritual development. Fundamentalist ministers who preach "hell-fire" and "wail over the sins of the world" had done much to poison the minds of their listeners.[22] Belief in Jesus as the Savior had caused many Christians to focus on the afterlife rather than living in the here and now. He wrote, "Thousands of so-called Christians are looking forward to death, when God is to save them into life ever lasting."[23] Christians lacked self-responsibility and often saw themselves as victims. Charles observed that "Christians have leaned on others and are consequently like children in real spiritual power."[24]

Charles saw an even bigger problem with people with no religion at all, people who had succumbed to the materialism that existed in nineteenth-century American society. He observed that, when people accumulated wealth, they tended to forget the needs of other less well-off members of society: "The moment man comes into earthly possessions his tendency is to selfishness, and that is the one great evil to be done away with."[25] Materialists were not aware that manifesting the divine inner presence was a life-changing possibility. In their ignorance, they worshiped a false god. As he noted in *Christian Science Thought*, "The most devoted worshipers at the shrine of Materialism admit that their goddess is a melancholy, dark visaged dame, continually threatening them with her cruel and vindictive temper."[26]

Charles recognized that the task he set before himself was large. "The question is," he indicated, "how can we best help humanity out of the darkness of mistaken concepts?"[27] Rather than focus on human weakness, he wanted to address human strengths, particularly the divinity he saw in all of humanity. His task was "to save men from themselves by uncovering the possibilities for good latent in every human soul—possibilities grand beyond comprehension."[28] His most bold statement regarding his mission was made in September 1891 in *Thought* magazine, where he wrote, "Our aim is to convert the world."[29]

Chapter 2

Co-creator of the Basic Unity Teaching

Introduction

By the time he was preparing the inaugural issue of *Modern Thought* for publication, Charles had already formulated many of the spiritual ideas that would ultimately become the Basic Unity Teaching. These teachings focused on spiritual truth, the nature of God, the laws of man's being, manifesting the Divine within, and the spiritual practices that facilitated it. These practices included the use of intuition; strong faith; powerful ideas, thoughts, and words; affirmations and denials; going into the silence, prayer, and divine love. In addition, the Basic Unity Teaching also contained doctrinal statements on bodily regeneration, human perfectibility, the afterlife, reincarnation, and the practice of metaphysical healing. Brief commentaries were made by Charles in these writings on the merits of political, social, and economic reform.

Charles ultimately came to characterize the Basic Unity Teaching as "Practical Christianity." In answering questions in 1895 of readers of *Unity* about the doctrine, Charles explained how the name was chosen:

We are frequently asked, "Is this doctrine you promulgate through your publications Christian Science, Divine Science, Mental Science or what?" To such inquiries we reply, "We are not attached to any School, and our teaching is not formulated. We are guided by the Spirit of Truth." We have readers among all the schools of thought and we find good in them all, yet we cannot say that we are an exponent of any. If our doctrine were nameable we should prefer to call it *Practical Christianity*.[1]

The name "Unity" was ultimately chosen not only as the name of the magazine, but as the name of the movement he and Myrtle cofounded. The name came to him as an inspiration received while meditating. Charles and Myrtle and a few students had met one evening in 1891 to pray in the silence. Suddenly, the name *Unity* flashed across Charles' mind. "That's it!" he cried out. "*Unity!* That's the name for our work, the name we have been looking for."[2]

The contents of *Modern Thought* and its successor magazines contained articles by well-known spiritual writers of the day. At the beginning or at the end of an article, Charles often included his own ideas or editorial comments. He also expressed his opinions in unsigned columns called "Notes and Comments" and "Questions and Answers." I was struck by the clarity with which these short pieces were written. Charles was specific, to the point, and did not ramble, as he did later in his articles and books. He did not equivocate and was forceful in putting forth his point of view.

It seems ironic that Charles' articles and books lack the readability of these early writings. I have discussed Charles' writing with many people in Unity. No one in my acquaintance finds his books and articles easy to read. His writing is frequently disjointed, disorganized, and scatter-shot. Sometimes his writing is so abstract that it is incomprehensible. He wrote in a stream-of-consciousness manner, as if he was in a meditative state when he wrote. He repeats himself continually, making the same points over and over, using slightly different language each time.

Nevertheless, it is important to note that, while Charles' writing lacked clarity, it was not lacking in content, although the reader may expend a large amount of time and a good deal of effort to find it. Unfortunately, Charles was unable to reach the level of clarity in published works that he did when pressed to answer questions or required to make a short commentary in a limited amount of space. He needed a good editor; he never had one.

Charles indicated that the first step in spiritual development was the capacity to know and understand "spiritual truth." It was necessary for everyone to lay a foundation that is "deep and strong in spiritual understanding."[3] As Charles described it, "We seek to set men free through an understanding of the Truth of their own powers." Quoting scripture, he once wrote, "Ye shall know the Truth and the Truth shall set you free."[4]

Charles observed that Jesus had stated again and again, "by parable and precept, the necessity of spiritual understanding and the power which accompanies it."[5] The need to know and understand was critical. In this essay, he continued, "We can afford to make any sacrifice to bring about the development of the pearl of great price—spiritual understanding."[6]

Charles equated spiritual truth for the Unity student as knowing and understanding the elements of the Basic Unity Teaching.

THE NATURE OF GOD

Charles' views on the nature of God formed the basis upon which his doctrine was developed. He acknowledged that God was "Omnipotent, Omniscient, and Omnipresent."[7]

Nevertheless, he did not see God as many traditional Christians viewed God—as "a mighty king, decreeing the destiny of man with an iron hand, from which anger is dispensed more freely than love."[8] Over and over again, Charles indicated that God dwelled within humankind, that men and women were made in the image and likeness of God.[9] For example, in an early issue of *Unity*, he wrote that "God is not an exclusive being, nor does he dwell in an inaccessible place apart from his creations. He is around you, about you, within you, without you. You are God yourself."[10]

Charles continually referred to God as Spirit, "not 'a Spirit,' but just Spirit—everywhere present Intelligence. . . . God is Spirit and man is Spirit, of the same character as God."[11] Charles indicated that Jesus used the same language when referring to God:

> "God is Spirit," is the most important statement Jesus ever made. . . .
> Remember, God is the invisible Spirit everywhere present—the Living
> Well of Truth within you. Not absent for a moment of our existence,
> but nearer and dearer than your father, mother, brother or sister. "Ye
> are the temple of the living God."[12]

Charles believed that the idea of God's existence within humankind was becoming accepted by more and more people. "The belief that the Supreme Source of All-Power, God, is outside yourself," he observed, "is weakening."[13] The traditional Christian view of God as personal was also on the way out, as he noted: "Hell has been wiped out and now the personal God is about to lose his throne."[14]

God, according to Charles, did not operate personally in the universe but as "Principle." "In order to get on in the study of Truth, it is necessary," he indicated, "that we have clear understanding of God as principle." God was not a living God. Rather, "God is life, God is love, God is Wisdom, God is Substance."[15]

In defining God as principle, he wrote:

God as Principle is unchanging and does remain forever uncognizant of and unmoved by the changing things of time and sense. It is true that God—as Principle—does not feel pain, is not moved by the cries of the children of men for help. . . . God is Principle, but God is Person also. Principle becomes personified the moment It comes to dwell in eternal manifestation in a human body.[16]

Charles recognized that, while he had definite views on the nature of God, it was not possible to totally define God. He said, "To describe God is to give him limitation, hence he could not be given a fairer designation than I am that I am."[17]

THE LAWS OF MAN'S BEING

Charles believed that the universe operated according to "Laws of Man's Being." Cause and effect was the primary law. He explained, "There are no accidents in the laws of Being. 'As a man sows, so shall he reap' is another way of saying that for every cause there is an adequate effect. This law of sequence is the balance wheel of the universe."[18]

Every human action or human thought functioned under a specific law of man's being. The list was lengthy. Some of the laws he referred to in his early writing included the perfect primal creative law, the law of demand and supply, the law of responsibility, the law of existence, the law of mental projecture, the law of mind, universal law, the law of Good or God, the law of seed time and harvest, and the law of manifestation. He did not always focus on the specific law that governed a situation in human thought or action, referring to it simply as "the law."[19]

He indicated that the law of man's being was operative at all times in everyone's life, without exceptions. "You are using the law every moment," he said.[20] "No one was exempt from these laws and no one could escape the consequences of failing to obey them," he wrote elsewhere.[21]

Men and women needed to know, understand, and make effective use of the laws that governed their existence. These laws were "open to the discovery" by everyone. "It is so important," he said, "that you should know the law and use it. . . . If you are not doing so with intelligence it is disastrous to your happiness."[22] The consequences of failure to make intelligent use of the law were hazardous: "To be ignorant of mind and its laws is to be a child playing with fire, or a man manipulating powerful chemicals without knowing their relation to one another."[23]

In describing how thoughts operated under the law, he said:

You think, and your thoughts take form as environments, your bodily condition, your health, your finances, your intelligence, your energy, your domestic and social relations, in fact everything connected with your life is the result of your own thinking. . . . Your thought is the creative and destructive force in the world in which you live.[24]

Charles was particularly mindful of the effects of negative thought on the life circumstances of those who harbored them: "If you hold thoughts of envy, malice, jealousy, lust, anger, pride, hypocrisy, hate or fear, your body will show forth disease and you will be subject to accidents and all the destructive agencies which such thoughts call about you."[25]

Given the importance of personal thought on human development, Charles presented a pessimistic assessment of humanity's level of spiritual attainment: "From within, out of the hearts of men, proceed evil thoughts, adulteries, fornications, murders, thefts, covetousness, wickedness, deceit, lasciviousness, an evil eye, blasphemy, pride, foolishness—all these evil things come from within, and defile man."[26]

Charles advised Unity students to be constantly aware of their thoughts. "Always remember that the thoughts you send out are pregnant with power and will sooner or later produce effects."[27] Because of this, good things happened in life when the mind was focused on positive outcomes. When you see "only the good, the pure, the perfect, the just, the true . . . then the Divine Principle of Life, Love and Truth will manifest in all you do."[28]

Manifesting the Divine Within

Charles recognized that, while the power of the Divine lies within humankind, most men and women had not manifested that power. The "Indwelling Presence" was latent within them, existing in potential only. Men and women could manifest the inner Divinity or the Christ within by (1) understanding spiritual truth, (2) living in accordance with the laws of man's being, and (3) undertaking the spiritual practices contained in the Basic Unity Teachings.

Charles used the term "the Christ within" to characterize the inner presence of God in the human soul because he believed that Jesus had manifested that presence in greater depth than any other human being. "Jesus Christ more fully voiced this nearness of God to man than any of the prophets," said Charles, "and his words are correspondingly vivified with that inner fire and life."[29]

A favorite saying of Charles' was taken from St. Paul: "Christ in us the hope of glory"[30] (Col. 1:27). In the June 1889 issue of *Modern Thought* he used this phrase for the first time in print. He repeated it many times throughout his teaching career and on his deathbed. Charles viewed Jesus as fully human, a man with a highly developed spiritual consciousness who provided others with a glimpse of the "perfect ideal."[31]

Charles indicated:

Jesus Christ recognized that he was not an exceptional man, nor did he have superhuman abilities. He simply recognized his place in the Godhead and developed powers in himself which are dormant within each one of us. He said, "Ye shall do these and greater." If he had been an exceptional creation or the possessor of powers not given to all men, why should he claim that we should exceed him?[32]

By his life and work and by claiming "Divinity for himself and all men," Jesus set an example for all to follow.[33]

Now the truth is that we all desire to be just what Jesus Christ was in every way. We want to heal the sick, raise the dead, cast out demons, provide for our needs instantly and without the "sweat of our brow," and above all be certain of immortality. . . .[34] The fact that Jesus of Nazareth had manifested the powers of the Christos, or spiritual man, is of vital importance to every soul. Not only is it important as an example, showing the possibilities latent within each of us, but . . . he bridged the way or formed a connecting link between humanity and God. [35]

Charles was convinced that Jesus had presented "the clearest presentation of Divine Science that has ever been given the world"[36] and that his teaching, "rightly understood and applied," would enable humankind to reach its full divine potential.[37] Because Jesus taught and set an example for all to follow, it was now possible for men and women to manifest the "Christ Principle."[38]

Charles believed that "the Christ within every soul" was attainable by everyone who did the necessary spiritual work. He was optimistic about humankind's chances. Why? Because, he said, "You are all Gods, and Sons of the Most high."[39]

As men and women manifested the Christ within, they demonstrated spiritual truth. These demonstrations included physical and psychological health, prosperity, and success in work and relationships. Those who fully manifested the Indwelling Presence regenerated their bodies. Charles considered these demonstrations of spiritual truth and as living proof of the correctness of the Basic Unity Teachings. Charles called this teaching "The Truth" because of his conviction that the truth had been discovered about how men and women could manifest the divine potential that was inherent in their nature.

SPIRITUAL PRACTICE

The Christ within was manifested through spiritual practice. These practices included the use of intuition, strong faith, powerful ideas, thoughts and words, affirmations and denials, going into the silence, prayer, and persistence until the work was accomplished. In a sermon at the Unity auditorium in 1911, Charles said, "We are here as Christians to learn how to handle our minds."[40]

1. The Use of Intuition

It was through intuition that men and women were able to know and understand spiritual truth and make contact with the Christ within. Intuition, according to Charles, represented the "direct knowing capacity of the mind."[41]

It was the faculty "that unites us to the divine being, the channel through which we hold direct communion with God,"[42] and it helped us determine right from wrong: "We are not competent to pass judgment upon any line of thought, until the soul within us has by experience proved its truth or falsity."[43]

Intuition came to him as an extremely compelling inner voice. "Our 'still small voice' is always so nearly right that we tremble when we go contrary to its suggestions."[44] When men and women gained the ability to tap into this inner knowing, major changes would take place "in the most minute details of our affairs": "Health takes the place of disease. The moral nature is also renovated and the vicious become more virtuous in thought and act. . . . Material things finally surrender their hard sway and the poor find themselves in better condition financially."[45] Human conduct would improve if men and women sought guidance from the inner witness. Charles said:

> Submit every thought and motive to the Lord and let that inner monitor decide upon their legitimacy. . . . You will get the pure inspiration of the Spirit that will move you to do the right and just, regardless of circumstances of a personal nature.[46]

Intuition was more reliable than the analytical mind in determining spiritual truth. Charles indicated that, through intuition, "we are all impelled to do things by a higher power."[47] Yet he was distressed by what he perceived as humanity's lack of appreciation of the power of intuition: "How few there are who recognize intuition as an essential to spiritual growth. . . . Few there be who are willing to acknowledge the existence of such a faculty."[48]

The human intellect, according to Charles, could not compare with the intuition as a determiner of spiritual truth. "The spirit of intuition," he said, "is found to be pure reason. . . . It leads to an apprehension of truth of which the intellect does not dream."[49] Those who relied on the intellect alone, however, "believe in what is proven to them by analogy on the external plane."[50] "Intellectualism," as he called it, had its limitations: "We look at the intellect, or sense mind, as a piece of mechanism with a scope a littler broader than a modern threshing machine or corn sheller, but no more competent to do work outside of its sphere than are these crude machines."[51]

2. Strong Faith

Charles recognized that faith was required if we were to be able to accept the truth of the reality of the divine inner presence. Through "faith in Spirit, we receive the higher ideas, and entertain them as if they were realities instead of 'figments of the imagination.'"[52]

Charles believed that, if Jesus and his disciples did "marvelous things" through faith, then we can also do them. "All that is required," he indicated, "is persistence in the use of faith until we make connection with the higher realms of consciousness."[53] The key factor was the depth of the believer's faith in the Inner Presence: "The essential factors in every demonstration is their active faith in the omnipotent and all present God. . . . [There are] powerful mental currents that go forth from one firmly grounded in faith."[54]

As with apprehending spiritual truth and creating a better life, intuition, rather than reason, played an important role in the development of faith. Our faith grew as we trusted the information received through the use of intuition:

> The world looks upon faith as a kind of blind believing without cause
> or reason, and the man or woman on the cold intellectual plane can
> get no conception of pure faith because it is not born of human rea-
> son. Faith is not the result of blind belief, but comes from an exer-
> cise of the intuitive or pure reasoning faculty, which is dormant to a
> degree in those who depend entirely on intellectualism.[55]

He indicated that faith was not something "born full-formed into the consciousness." It took time for it to deepen. "It has its stages of growth."[56]

Faith required the use of good judgment. It was wrong, for example, to ask for things out of the realm of possibility. "You must have reasonable faith in the possibility of your asking be answered."[57] If you don't believe your request can be accomplished, you should not ask: "People say to us, 'If the Spirit works so easily I'll just ask for a million dollars right away.' This is foolish because there is not in the mind a grain of faith that sees the probability of accomplishment."[58]

3. Powerful Ideas, Thoughts, and Words

The mind operated through ideas, thoughts, and words, and, if used properly, these were vehicles for spiritual advancement. "Mind evolves ideas," he said, "and ideas express themselves through thoughts and words."[59]

Transformation began with the ideas men and women hold in their minds:

> If your ideas are not God-like you may rest assured that you are not thinking at all, notwithstanding you may be doing that which the world calls thinking. If your ideas are not filling the world with health and harmony you may know that you are dead in the upper story. If your ideas are not raising the dead and casting out demons you may know that you are among the demons of ignorance and dead in iniquity. If your ideas are not resurrecting your body and filling it full of the elixir of life, you may put it down that you are not living though you walk the streets and discuss the crops, the money market and the weather.[60]

Positive thoughts were as important as powerful ideas. In Charles' mind, thought could literally move mountains; he put no limitation on it. He indicated that the fundamental basis of the whole metaphysical philosophy is epitomized in one short passage of scripture: "As a man thinketh so is he."[61]

Given the power of thoughts and ideas, it is not surprising that men and women should be very careful with the words they used.[62] He indicated that the Bible dwelled upon the power of the word "from Genesis to Revelation."[63] God "created by the power of the word." Words of truth, he indicated, "when spoken by one full of the spirit of love become active agents in awakening to spiritual life the dormant faculties in other men and women."[64]

4. Affirmations and Denials

Affirmations and denials dealt with ideas, thoughts, and words and were powerful tools. One of the best ways to demonstrate the Christ Within was through their use. An affirmation, Charles said, is "a concentrated thought for good."[65] Affirmations were stated in the present tense and consisted of "words of Truth," words which Charles believed were "alive with Divine Life."[66] Charles indicated that because affirmations expressed "those desirable qualities which we know to be potential in Infinite Mind," they had the power to manifest the Christ within.[67] A particularly powerful affirmation that directed the mind inward was "God is Spirit"—"I am Spirit"—"I live, move and have my being in God."[68] "Affirmations were of great value," Charles said, because "in them inhere the primal law of all manifestation."[69]

Affirmations that evoked the name of Jesus were particularly effective: "When you make this affirmation ['I am Jesus Christ'] you begin to think spiritually—you feel an interior anointing and it dawns upon you that you are just what Jesus of Nazareth was, the anointed of God."[70] Jesus' sayings were also powerful. "I am" statements of truth appear throughout his teachings. Charles publicized many of them. He urged his readers to "keep your eye steadily to the front where is blazoned in letters of light, 'I *am* the way, I *am* the Truth, I *am* the Life.'"[71]

Affirmations were most effective when repeated regularly throughout the day. "Many people go to sleep with affirmations and petitions active in mind," Charles wrote, "and awaken themselves during the night repeating the words."[72] He told his readers to "hold in mind and affirm day after day that 'I am Life.' [It] will call into expression that principle of action until it suffuses every faculty."[73]

Affirmations consisted of positive thoughts that brought positive results:

If you persistently think thoughts of truth, regardless of contemporary material seeming, the picture will sooner or later appear just as you formulate it in your mind. The persistent holding in the mind of the universal intelligent principle which is God is a potent power working through you for the good.[74]

Denials were as important as affirmations in manifesting the Christ within. Charles believed there was "deep philosophy involved in the denial of negative things." Denials purified the mind by eliminating "the gross material concepts with which we have encompassed ourselves."[75] Charles indicated that denials dealt with "those false appearances of which we wish to be rid."[76] Negative thoughts were prime targets. It was possible to "cast out by denial all undesirable thoughts."[77]

Denials could be made in several ways. Charles indicated that it was not always necessary to say "I deny so and so." A denial could encompass a much deeper meaning. "The conscious acknowledgement that you have been mistaken in your conclusions is a denial. The admission of sin and the prayer of forgiveness is a denial."[78]

5. Going into the Silence

Charles believed that meditation opened the door to the mind. He quoted the New Testament as the source for its practice. The words "enter into the closet or private room," Charles indicated, meant "to go within."[79] It was in the silence that the still small voice could be heard.

Charles believed, based on his own experience in meditation, that it was in the silence that one made closest contact with the divine inner presence. Good things happened as a result. He said:

> All manifestation of life originates in the silence. . . . The thoughts that rise up in you and come to the surface in deed and act, are they not from the silence? Do you take a step or lift a hand that has not its motive from the depths of the mighty sea of throbbing life within your own being? Then why look to the external for that which comes only from the silence within?[80]

The meditative state offered a fertile space from which to make affirmations. Life circumstances often improved when affirming in the silence. He stressed this even late in his life:

> We do not promise that one can become prosperous overnight by sitting in the silence and affirming our prosperity thought, but marvelous demonstrations often result from the practice of the silence. . . . God is interested in your health and finances, and you can become secure in both if you make proper contact with his kingdom, which is the Mind.[81]

Charles urged readers of *Modern Thought* to meditate and gave simple instructions: "Try to set aside a few moments each day and retire to a place where you can, without being disturbed, commune with your higher self. . . . The attitude of aspiration and desire for help should precede every sitting."[82] He was aware that those who had never meditated would find it difficult to believe in its efficacy, but, throughout his life, he urged them to go slowly and trust.

Those who have experienced the peace and the power of the deep silence can appreciate how difficult it is to explain this experience to one who has never had it. The realm that we touch and begin to explore when we get very still mentally and give our whole attention to the inner consciousness is developed by degrees.[83]

6. Prayer

Prayers were often most effective when the mind was quiet and in a state of meditation. Charles quoted from the words of Jesus when he said, "When thou prayest enter into the retired place of thee, and lock the door of thee, and pray thou to the Father of thee, to thee in the secret" (Matt. 6:6).[84] Charles explained how results were attained when we "pray . . . to the Father in secret": "When one acquires this ability to make mental contact with the Father, with creative Spirit, one's thought force is increased tremendously and more is accomplished in a few moments than in a life time of [prayers of petition]."[85]

Those who made prayer a regular practice got the best results. The Christian metaphysician prays persistently, as he explained in the July 1894 issue of *Thought*: "His life is a perpetual prayer and he ceases not day or night" because "he knows that he is dealing with creative forces and he aims to regulate all the affairs of his life by his prayers. He depends on his prayers to bring him health, peace and plenty."[86] Moreover, those who were faithful in their prayers lived their lives in accord with the law of manifestation: "If you continually think and say, 'I am well,' 'I have plenty,' 'I am at peace with all men,' health and success will come to you."[87] Affirmative prayers were much more beneficial than prayers of petition to God, as he indicated in another issue of *Thought*: "Never ask God to grant you favors, but steadily affirm that all things are granted you now."[88]

Prayers that worked best took the form of praise, blessings, and thanksgiving. Prayers of supplication or petition had little chance of connecting with the Christ within. He made a clear distinction between prayers of petition and affirmative prayer:

> Are you begging some distant God to give you light, or are you praising the light in your very presence? One is praying for something we have not; the other is praying as if we had "already received." Thus we

see that praising and thanksgiving is the only key that will open the door for Spirit to reveal itself in our consciousness.[89]

"True prayer," Charles observed, "the prayer that gives thanks as if we had 'already received,' is the highest affirmation, and it is used by Christian metaphysicians universally."[90]

7. Divine Love

A heart filled with love—love for self and for others—was required for realizing the Divine within. In his earliest teaching—in the May 1889 issue of *Modern Thought*—Charles first indicated the importance of love: "Love is the power that moves the world, and the sooner mankind finds out and takes advantage of its resistless currents, the sooner will prosperity, happiness and harmony come to all.[91] He used superlatives to indicate its importance: "Love is the supreme faculty and is exalted above all. . . . Love occupies the highest place in consciousness."[92]

It was important to send out loving thoughts to everyone. We cut ourselves off from the loving center within us when we failed to do so. Charles urged people to "see everybody and everything as they really are, Pure Spirit, and send them your strongest thoughts of love." He believed there was "an immutable law lying back of this," and that law was "God is love and love is manifest as life."[93]

Throughout his writings, Fillmore equated God with love. One of his clearest statements was made in November 1896, in *Unity* magazine: "If we persist in thinking loving thoughts and speaking loving words we are sure to bring into our experience the feeling of that great love that is beyond description—the very love of God."[94] Indeed, Charles believed that men and women would become more fully conscious of the Divinity within when divine love was truly present in their lives:

> When love the universal magnet is brought into action into the consciousness of the race, it will change all our methods of support and supply. It will harmonize all the forces of nature and the discords that now infest the earth and air will disappear. . . . This mighty magnet is a quality of God that is expressed through man and it cannot be suppressed by any outside force.[95]

Charles recommended the use of affirmations to increase the power of love. He suggested that we declare silently to ourselves, "You are the abode of love. You are filled and thrilled with the magnetic force which she uses to do her work."[96]

Charles considered it likely that, if Unity students failed to demonstrate health or prosperity in their lives, it was probably due to lack of love:

> Many who have found the law of true thinking and its effect wonder why supply does not come to them after months and years of holding thoughts of bounty. It is because they have not developed love. They have formed the right image in mind, but the magnet that draws the storehouse of Being has not been set going.[97]

8. Persistence

Charles was aware from the beginning of his work that demonstrating truth took patience and persistence. It did not happen overnight. He encouraged Unity students to follow the example of Jesus, even at the end of his life: "Jesus was the most successful demonstrator of prayer of whom we have any record, and he urged patience in prayer. If at first you don't succeed, try, try again."[98]

Effort was required on a daily basis. He urged his students to "think every day of the goodness of God until his presence shines around you, which it certainly will if you persist."[99] When Charles received complaints from people who reported lack of success in their spiritual work, he responded by counseling them not to give up:

> How often we hear people complain that they have long followed instructions on "denials" and "affirmations" and "prayed as if they had already received," yet lack the understanding. . . . It does not make any difference how long you have sought the Lord, nor how "barren" the results. Keep right on.[100]

Charles knew that most people were unaccustomed to metaphysical spiritual practice. Those whose grew up with the teachings of traditional Christianity needed to adopt a new and unfamiliar spiritual mind-set and could not expect immediate results:

> The Spirit of Truth does not come into consciousness at one fell swoop, but it is a gradual inflowing; first a little trickling stream

springing up from the depths within, which must be welcomed by the prayer of thanksgiving unto the Father. Then its volume will increase gradually from day to day and year to year.[101]

Beginners in metaphysical practice and those who were prone to negative thought needed to take the teaching one step at a time. He counseled:

Never be discouraged because the evidences of your words do not show forth quickly. You may have been saying for years "I'm sick," or "I can't," or your disabilities may be the erroneous thoughts of generation after generation of ignorant ancestors, and you cannot, therefore, reasonably expect instantaneous recovery.[102]

Transformation required constant effort—work without immediate reward. Yet, results could be ultimately expected: "Radical changes for the better are the rule, and perfect health and satisfaction is always the reward for those who persist."[103]

Bodily Regeneration

Charles believed that, if men and women fully manifested the Christ within, they could regenerate the cells of their bodies, live far beyond the normal life span, and overcome physical death. In April 1889, in the inaugural issue of *Modern Thought* magazine, he expressed confidence in the ability of humans to regenerate their bodies, predicting:

This society will produce individual members who, through soul concentration, will have so spiritualized the atoms of their bodies as to be able to make themselves visible or invisible at will; and who will have the power to live upon this earth plane any length of time they may desire. They will do all the works of merit recorded in the Bible, and many others not now dreamed of.... These spiritual powers are latent in all and must ultimately be unfolded in all, for we are children of the one God.[104]

It was on the teachings of Jesus that Charles based his belief that human beings would be able "to lay down and take up the physical body at will":

Jesus Christ said that he could lay down his life or take it up and demonstrated his ability to do so. He also said that those who followed him were to do even greater things, and why should we doubt the final victory of man over the last enemy—death.[105]

Though scripture indicated that Jesus had been tried by a Roman judge, condemned to death, and forced to carry the cross to Mount Calvary where he was crucified, Charles did not believe that Jesus actually died on the cross. "The popular thought, based on Theology, that Jesus died upon the cross for our sins," Charles noted, "is not reasonable nor true,"[106] he stated in the May 1905 issue of *Unity* and then elaborated:

It is quite evident that theology hasn't understood the true character of Jesus' death. Instead of dying upon the cross like the two thieves that were crucified with Him, He simply passed through the human consciousness of death and came out fully alive on the other side. The bodies of the robbers were turned to clay, while that of Jesus became alive again, and was glorified.[107]

In the same article, Charles asserted that Jesus "still lives in the spiritual ethers of this world and is in constant contact with those who raise their thoughts to Him in prayer."[108] In another issue of *Unity*, he cited his own experience, indicating that he had made personal contact with Jesus and that others have had similar experiences:

Jesus did not die nor has He gone away. He said He would continue to be here always. We should not doubt His word. Paul saw Him and talked with Him several times years after He had sublimated his body. He told Paul to go ahead with his work, that He would stand by him and uphold him. He is a power in the world's thought today. He is right here in our midst fully alive. I have talked with many people who declare they have seen Jesus; some conversed with Him mentally. I have also seen Him, and felt His presence many times.[109]

Charles believed that it was of vital importance to humankind that "Jesus of Nazareth lived and manifested the Power of the Christos, or spiritual man," which he saw as "an example, showing the possibilities latent within each of us." For Charles, Jesus "bridged the way or formed a connecting link, between humanity and God.[110]

Those who chose to follow a spiritual path that led to bodily regeneration needed to follow the example of Jesus. They needed to engage fully in metaphysical spiritual practices—accessing intuition, meditating, and employing affirmations and denials. They also needed to conserve their sexual energy, "the elixir of life" as Charles called it, and refrain from sexual involvements: "Those who desire to come into closest unity with the Spirit of Truth and construct here on earth the true temple of God—a regenerated body—must abstain from sex relations."[111]

Charles' ideas on bodily regeneration were not original but had been known to those who had in the past delved deeply into metaphysics, as he acknowledged in November 1889:

> The medical world has stumbled onto the fact that the fires of life are centered in the sex nature of all forms. It is not a modern discovery but has been known to the wise of all ages and taught by modern metaphysicians for years. . . . Were this matter fully understood by the human family and proper conservation of the sex force practiced, all forms of disease would disappear and the life of man be lengthened hundreds of years.[112]

He then proceeded to describe the physiology of regeneration as he understood it: "This seed is the point where is concentrated the life force. . . . This seed when conserved is thrown back into the nervous system and there becomes the highest attenuation of matter in the body tangible to the human eye."[113]

Charles believed that married couples who refrained from sexual relations, as a part of an effort to regenerate their bodies, would enhance the quality of the marital relationships:

> This does not mean that the true marriage between man and woman shall be done away with. This marriage is of the soul and not of the flesh—in fact the flesh has not part in it whatsoever. If all persons who are now living inharmoniously, as husband and wife on the animal plane, would cease the indulgence of this carnal man and through the power of the loving work invoke the sweet spirit of purity, their homes would soon be turned into havens of harmony. Poverty, discord, and disease would drop away and the energy and full life of youth would return to them.[114]

In the same article, he continued with advice for men who might have difficulty living up to such a high standard:

If the thought of sex comes into your mind silently deny it and affirm both for yourself and her your true being—Pure Spirit. Do not, under any circumstances condemn the sex nature but firmly say to it, "I will show you a more excellent way." In all your relations with your wife be as brother to sister, or better, as the very angels in heaven.[115]

Charles was so convinced of the importance of bodily regeneration that he made an exceedingly strong claim, saying: "The only salvation for the human family lies in the conservation of the sex force."[116] He lamented the fact that many men and women did not see the importance of the practice.

HUMAN PERFECTIBILITY

Charles presented a pessimistic assessment of humankind's current level of spiritual attainment. Although he believed that, given humanity's latent inner divinity, men and women would ultimately reach the level of spiritual perfection attained by Jesus, he recognized that most men and women did not have an understanding of "Truth" and had not developed their inborn spiritual gifts. Nevertheless, he was confident that "truth will be poured into the souls of men" and the insights of metaphysics would soon become widely understood and accepted.[117] Humanity would then take a great leap forward, and human perfection would ultimately be attained. Charles said he had received information in his own meditations that confirmed the ultimate destiny of humankind:

I have been shown by Spirit, in ways not necessary here to explain, that . . . societies of people trained in mental harmony will form the basis of a new mentality on this planet, and that out of this will be constructed that harmonious civilization called the "New Jerusalem."[118]

Charles' optimism about future human possibilities was no more clearly expressed than in the following passage:

We are now in the dawn of a millennium, the old is passing away, the new is being ushered in. . . . Stupendous changes are about to be made in our social, religious and governmental affairs in a very few years. A new race is being born which will see the affairs of men from the mental instead of the material plane. Wrong must go out. Right must take its place. . . . The last days are upon us, the New Jerusalem is already builded in the heavens ready to descend upon the earth.[119]

The Afterlife

Charles was sure that life existed after physical death. "I know that man does not die—that he lives right on, sometimes in a natural body, sometimes in an astral body and sometimes in no body at all."[120] His experience with spiritualism probably provided him with these strong convictions. As he wrote in an issue of *Modern Thought*, "The evidence of man's existence after death in individual form closely resembling the one used on this mundane sphere is overwhelming in its array of facts,"[121] indicating that many people were convinced of the existence of an afterlife: "This planet now has its millions who absolutely know that man lives and has his body after death of the physical."[122]

Reincarnation

In 1889, when Charles began his editing and publishing work, he was not yet ready to commit himself to the doctrine of reincarnation. Nevertheless, he was seriously considering it and, in February 1890, ran an article in *Modern Thought* by J. D. Buck, M.D., that argued the case for it. He told his readers that "each must judge for himself whether Dr. Buck proves his case."[123]

By 1892, Charles had evidence that convinced him of the validity of the doctrine. It evidently came to him in meditation that, in a past life, he had been the Apostle Paul. Charles used the third person to relate his discovery:

> He who once manifested as Paul the Apostle is now expressing himself through another form right here in America. . . . Paul lived over thirty years in his present form, a plain American citizen, before he knew he was the same ego that had once expressed itself in flesh as Saul, the Jewish zealot; afterwards the Christian pioneer.[124]

Based on his reading of scripture, Charles concluded that Paul had not yet achieved a high level of spiritual attainment, asserting, "A calm unbiased perusal of Paul's history, as recorded in his writings, will convince anyone . . . that he lacked much of being the saint that the church thinks of him."[125] Charles reflected on how he saw himself now that he believed that in a past life he had been St. Paul. He said, "He who once manifested as Paul is only now getting a practical understanding of the scientific laws underlying the so-called miracles of the religious world."[126]

By 1894, Charles was convinced that those who had not regenerated their bodies experience "many lives and many deaths." He had concluded that "the death of the body in one generation is but an incident in the history of the soul."[127] By 1895, he indicated that reincarnation was a part of the law of cause and effect. In referring to the failure to regenerate the body, he wrote, "When you refuse to receive this baptism of the Holy Ghost your flesh is not quickened and must eventually go back to dust; and you are again sent to school to learn the lesson in another earthly experience ages hence. This is the law."[128]

For the remainder of his teaching career, Charles continued to believe that men and women would reincarnate if they failed to regenerate their bodies:

> God is no respecter of persons: there is but one universal law for all men. . . . We have lived and died in sense-thought numerous times and will continue to do so until we overcome sin, sickness and death, and raise our body to the place of the fourth dimension of Jesus Christ. The great men and women of past ages are the great men and women of today. As Shakespeare says, we all are merely actors in a great world drama, each one playing many parts.[129]

Social, Political, and Economic Reform

The period of the 1890s and the early twentieth century was one of social, political, and economic unrest in the United States. The Industrial Revolution, which took place in the United States in the nineteenth century, had widened the gap between rich and poor, leaving farmers and laboring groups suffering from an unbridled capitalist economic system that had few governmental controls. The Populist and Progressive movements, which pressed for reform in the nation's economic, political, and governmental institutions, gathered strength during this period.

Charles was not in sympathy with the reformers, concluding that they were doing more harm than good. He saw the problem as lying with the individual rather than with institutions. "Divine Science," he said, "deals with the individual, first, last and always. It is a science of the *unit*—it does not attempt to unravel the moral, social or governmental tangle by making new laws or laying down rules of action."[130] The solution lay with the individual person. "Get the unit right, that is get your self right," he said, and "the tangle will take care of itself."

The problem lay in the minds of much of the nation's populace—specifically in men and women's greed, malice, selfishness, and other forms of negativity—rather than in the capitalist economic system or in the nation's governmental institutions:

All this clamoring for *rules* of action; what to do in a specific case of sickness, how best to administer charity, how to deal with vice, what class of legislation will quickest suppress prevalent social evils and remedy finances, and so on through the list, are one and all attempts to purify a stream polluted at its fountain head. That fountain head is the thinking faculty of humanity.[131]

The nation's problems would be resolved when "each and every man, woman and child learn this law of thought formation and mental cleansing." He believed that reformers caused more problems than they resolved: "The so-called reformers do build up in their own imaginations mountains of sin, poverty and discord, and through the mental currents which they send forth [add] to the burdens of those whom they ignorantly seek to help."[132]

Charles did not believe that those engaged in spiritual work should involve themselves in the political affairs of the nation. He saw no reason, he wrote,

why he whose work is on the plane of the spiritual should go out on the street and argue politics. This is where many metaphysicians are being led away from the proper sphere. They see that Spirit is at work in the minds of men as never before and conclude that in order to help they should, for a time at least, give attention to party politics. This is error.[133]

Traditional Christianity and the Basic Unity Teaching: Some Important Distinctions

From the beginning of his public work in 1889, Charles was highly critical of traditional Christianity, both Protestant and Catholic. While he had great respect and appreciation for the teachings in the Bible, viewing it as "a rich storehouse of higher astronomy," he saw problems with the way traditional Christianity interpreted it. Most Christians considered it to be literally true.

As a consequence, the Bible was cited as the authority for "far reaching dogmas" that were full of errors. He saw the Bible as "veiled in symbol"; thus, it required careful reading. He believed it could be accurately interpreted only "by the illuminated."[134]

Charles criticized traditional Christianity for failing to engage in metaphysical healing, for portraying Jesus as the Savior of humankind, and for its inept leadership and stifling organizational structures. "None of it," he said, "is the pure Christianity of Jesus Christ."[135]

Throughout the seventy years of his teaching, Charles used strong language to distinguish the Basic Unity Teachings from those of traditional Christianity. He concluded that traditional Christianity had failed to present its adherents with the truth about the life, teaching, and mission of Jesus, as the quotations below from his teachings indicate:

Regarding the Nature of God:

- The Jews believed Jehovah to be a God of vengeance—a kind of Jack-the-Giant-Killer, "who was angry with the wicked every day." The orthodox Christian world of today has this same concept of God, and you can on any Sunday hear God's likes and dislikes described by the average minister of the gospel. You will observe that these ministers invariably invest God with the parts and passions of an unusually arbitrary and unreasonable man. . . . Thus it has grown to be a race belief that God is a kind of Russian Czar.[136]

- The Christian church has personalized God, enthroned him in a sky heaven, and imagined him a temperamental autocrat who can be cajoled and persuaded to change his mind, who gets furiously angry with the wicked every day and condemns millions of his ignorant children to an eternal hell of fire and brimstone.[137]

Regarding the Divine Within:

- Christianity has been misunderstood from the very beginning. Instead of teaching men how to live here and now, with this earth as their future home, Christianity has emphasized the joys of life in a faraway heaven after death. Jesus did not teach this, and all the Scriptures that tell about heaven as a place are wrong translations. "The Kingdom of God is within you." Jesus taught the unity of the heavenly and the earthly in the present consciousness.[138]

- A favorite phrase with church people is "Give God the glory," and the idea that God requires praise and adulation. This is far from the truth. The real secret is that the inner spirit of man is God, and by praising the power of the spirit within himself man is in a measure bringing out and exercising his own faculties.[139]

- Religion is looking for the mighty Creator away off in some distant heaven, right in the fact of the distinct teaching of Jesus that God is Spirit and that his kingdom is within man.[140]

Regarding Metaphysical Healing:

- Christian ministers of this age do not heal the sick by laying on hands, raise the dead, see visions, work miracles. . . . To the modern Christian such works are lost arts. . . . Hence it is evident that the Christian church has not recognized the whole truth taught by Jesus.[141]

- The great need of the Christian church today is a better understanding and application of spiritual laws by its ministers. They are standing in the shoes of the Pharisees of old, depending for salvation on their literal study of the Scriptures. . . . The fact is that Christianity, as taught today by its ministers, ignores its greatest asset—the healing of the sick. Instead of encouraging faith in God as the source of health, the dominant trend in Christian literature and the Christian ministry is to weaken that faith.[142]

Regarding Misinterpretation of the Teachings of Jesus:

- The church has strayed from the system taught by Christ and the apostles, in making a dead letter of scripture supplemented by their stereotyped creeds, their lifeless formulas and arbitrary rules, the guide of men's souls. Thus the blind have led the blind, until all have fallen into the ditch of materialism and sensualism. . . . In sundering the conscious vital connection between men's souls and the upper world, the church has lost its power, and is like a plant in a barren soil, stunted and withered by long continued drought. . . . The spiritual gifts enumerated by Paul (1 Cor. 12:1–11), among which was the power of healing, have disappeared and instead of it we have a dry creed and a dryer ritual.[143]

- The pure doctrine of Jesus Christ has never been popular with those who like formality and rites in religion. . . . Pure Christianity was literally killed in less than three hundred years after the Crucifixion. What is called Christianity is a combination of paganism, Israelitism, and the letter of Jesus' doctrine without the spirit. This heterogeneous mass became acceptable because it was sanctioned by kings and enforced as the church of the state. As it has a little from all the religions, it offered balm to the forced worshipers from each sect, and thus quickly became popular. It is not the doctrine of Jesus Christ, however, and never has been, in any of its many forms and sects.[144]

Regarding the Doctrine of the Trinity:

- The doctrine of the Trinity is often a stumbling block, because we find it difficult to understand how three persons can be one. Three persons cannot be one, and theology will always be a mystery until theologians become metaphysicians.[145]

Regarding the Afterlife:

- He [the traditional Christian] has looked upon his religion as having to do with the salvation of his soul—a sort of school in which he is coached in catechism and creed and prepared to go to a place called heaven after death.[146]

- No one should be deluded with the vague assumption that there is a place in the skies or on some far away planet, called heaven. There is not the shadow of a foundation in either the old or new Testaments for such doctrine.[147]

Regarding Church Organization:

- The church says it is the plan of salvation for men which is set forth in their dogmas and creeds. But that plan, that formulation of doctrine, those creeds and dogmas, were set up three hundred years after Jesus taught and demonstrated. There is no authority from him or his disciples for them. They are the work of men who had an industry to sustain, known as the church; and a privileged class of people to provide for, called the clergy . . . hence the church creed and church government. This was the Catholic Church, and the Protestant Church is its off-spring. All that the Protestants count dear as doctrine, they borrowed from the Catholics, who patched it together from early Christianity and paganism. None of it is the pure Christianity of Jesus Christ.[148]

- There is a degeneracy in the church that is most patent, for either the spirit of God was poured out upon men in Bible times, or else the whole thing is a fiction. Three-fourths of the church's adherents have outgrown its creeds and long for a religion in harmony with the progress of the age.[149]

Chapter 3

Co-creator of the Doctrine of the Twelve Powers

The Evolution of the Teaching

"Twelve Powers" are the words Charles Fillmore used to describe the human attributes that men and women needed to develop in order to manifest the Christ within and to regenerate their physical bodies. He also called the Twelve Powers the "faculties of the mind." The names he gave them are spiritual understanding, wisdom, faith, divine love, imagination, will, zeal, power, strength, elimination or renunciation, order, and life.

Charles began developing his doctrine of the Twelve Powers in articles in *Thought* and *Unity* magazines in the mid-1890s. However, it was not until 1930, thirty-five years later, that he presented the doctrine in book form as *The Twelve Powers of Man*.

Charles began publishing his ideas on the Twelve Powers for the first time in the October 1894 issue of *Thought*. His description was sketchy as it was clear that he was in the process of developing his thoughts on the subject: "The Grand Man, Christ, has twelve powers, represented in the history of Jesus by the twelve disciples. So each of us has twelve powers to make manifest, to bring out and use."[1] In the June 1895 issue of *Thought*, he wrote, "Man has twelve great faculties or powers of manifestation, and each has a focal point in the body through which it manifest,"[2] but did not go into detail to describe the powers. In the August 1895 issue of *Thought*, he further stated that the Twelve Powers "represent twelve factors that enter into the expression of man's life problem," indicating that every scriptural writer has referred to "the twelve great powers of man" though they might be "disguised under many symbols."[3] As examples, he cited the twelve tribes of Israel and the twelve disciples of Jesus. Again, he gave few details to describe the powers themselves.

Next, in the February 1896 issue of *Unity*, he repeated that Jesus' twelve apostles represented the Twelve Powers. Again, the discussion was incomplete and included information that he would later discard. For example, he would never again state that "every one of our faculties is a living being. Our twelve powers are twelve persons living, breathing, and acting in our own mental consciousness."[4]

Charles advanced his discussion of the powers in November 1896, writing, "It is man who through his word calls these powers into activity that he may manifest God." This was a point he would continue to make as he built the doctrine. He identified the names of the apostles with the powers. "Andrew represents Strength, James represents Judgment. . . . John is love, Peter, the thinker."[5] As time passed, he continued to identify the powers with each of the apostles.

Finally, in the January 1897 issue of *Unity*, Charles provided a description of the doctrine that he would continue to use: "Man in this state of existence has established twelve states of consciousness, which have centers in the body. . . . When these centers are all properly developed and work harmoniously, we have a man after the type of Jesus."[6] In this statement, Charles presented a key point in the doctrine: the spiritual seeker who is able to develop all Twelve Powers will have raised his or her consciousness to the level of Jesus and will demonstrate the powers in the same manner as Jesus did. In June 1897, he acknowledged that Jesus was the only one to his knowledge who had awakened the Twelve Powers: "It is only the Christ-man who has all his faculties equally brought out and balanced, and we know so far of but one such man. All others have been but partially developed and are consequently open to faults of thought and judgment."[7]

Brief items would appear from time to time in *Unity* magazine, each giving a glimpse of the doctrine as Charles developed it. It seems probable that he was receiving information during his periods of meditation that enabled him to move ahead with the descriptions. In February 1898, he indicated that he was still in the process of understanding the doctrine, writing: "Only when we know the workings of all the faculties on three planes of consciousness: Spirit, soul and body, can we fathom the intricate processes of man's mind in the regenerative birth as symbolized by the life of Jesus."[8] From 1898 to 1909, when he published his first book *Christian Healing*, Charles would on occasion briefly describe in *Unity* magazine one of the powers. Included were descriptions of love, power, imagination, wisdom, life, and spiritual understanding.

Christian Healing itself has information on several of the Twelve Powers but no general description of the doctrine. Without a comprehensive overview, the reader had no idea of what Charles meant when statements like the following were made:

- This formative power of thought requires distinctive faculties, which is called the "imagination."[9]

- Good judgment, like all other faculties of the mind, is developed from Principle.[10]

- The twelve faculties of the mind must be massed at the great brain center called the solar plexis.[11]

- As man develops in understanding, his imagination is the first of his latent faculties to quicken.[12]

Charles' limitations as a writer were painfully evident in his treatment of the Twelve Powers in *Christian Healing*. He assumes that the reader has knowledge that may have been provided in previous issues of *Unity* magazine but was nowhere to be found in this book.

For the next decade (1910–1920), Charles did not attempt in writing to outline the general theory that lay behind his doctrine. Then, in the April 1920 issue of *Unity*, he indicated his intention to provide an in-depth treatment of the subject:

> It was announced in *Unity* over a quarter of a century ago, that Jesus represented in his life and teaching the type of man passing from the nature to the divine state of being, and that the calling of his twelve disciples symbolized the call into activity of the twelve latent faculties of man. . . . There has been a widespread call among metaphysicians for a book giving in detail the steps man goes through in passing from the natural to the divine consciousness. . . . To this end

we have decided to devote a whole year of *Unity* magazine to the explanation of the spiritual meaning of the twelve disciples.[13]

In the February 1920 issue of *Unity,* Charles for the first time provided an outline of the twelve disciples, the faculties they represent, and "the cell-centers" at which they preside. These are listed below:

- Faith—Peter—center of the brain

- Strength—Andrew—loins

- Discrimination or Judgment—James, son of Zebedee—pit of stomach

- Love—John—back of heart

- Power—Philip—root of tongue

- Imagination—Bartholomew—between the eyes

- Understanding—Thomas—front of brain

- Will—Matthew—center front brain

- Order—James, son of Alphaeus—navel

- Zeal—Simon the Canaanite—back of the head, medulla

- Renunciation or elimination—Thaddeus—lower part of back

- Appropriation or life conserver—Judas—generative function.[14]

The 1920 volume of *Unity* magazine provided the most comprehensive treatment up to that time of the doctrine of the Twelve Powers. Charles gave every indication that he was ready to publish the teaching in a book.

However, his next book, *Talks on Truth,* published in 1926, did not provide a treatment of the Twelve Powers. *Talks on Truth* contained a restatement of the Basic Unity Teaching. Passing references were made to the Twelve Powers, as in *Christian Healing,* but no general description of the doctrine.

In 1929 Charles again began addressing in *Unity* magazine the doctrine of the Twelve Powers. The treatment was more in depth, as several issues of the magazine were devoted to the subject. Finally, in 1930, Charles presented the doctrine in book form in *The Twelve Powers of Man.*

In the introduction to the book, Charles pointed out that the doctrine of the Twelve Powers was not for the beginning metaphysical student. It was aimed at advanced practitioners, those who were serious about regenerating their bodies and overcoming the death of the body. He defined regeneration as consisting "of the gradual refinement of the man of flesh into the man of Spirit."

Jesus provided the example for all to follow. Charles indicated that the book described how the powers were "expressed and developed"[15] and dealt with "the attainments necessary for man before he can follow Jesus in this phase of his regeneration."[16]

Charles believed that men and women would regenerate their physical bodies when they were able to manifest fully the Christ mind. "The way," he said, "is through the Christ consciousness, which Jesus demonstrated."[17] A complete transformation of the entire person was required. "Eternal life," he said, "can be regained only through the resurrecting power of the Christ Mind in the individual."[18]

Presented below is probably the clearest statement Charles made tying the regeneration process to the manifestation of the Christ consciousness:

> This resurrecting process is now going on in many people. It is a gradual change that brings about a complete transformation of the body through renewal of the mind. Spirit, soul, and body become unified with Christ mind and body and soul become immortal and incorruptible. In this way death is overcome.[19]

Charles indicated that the twelve faculties were in weakened condition in most men and women because they had succumbed to negative thought, sleep-walked through life, and lacked spiritual understanding. Men and women needed "to get control of these centers"[20] and awaken them in appropriate ways. He explained, "What we are all aiming at is restitution—a perfect balancing of all our faculties which have fallen into inharmonious action through ages of wrong thinking."[21] Awakening the faculties was essential, Charles indicated, "in the development of the perfect man."[22]

Charles indicated that the twelve faculties were located at different places in the human body. He noted that each "has a focal point in the body through which it manifests."[23] Self-observation had led him to conclude that thought manifested itself from each of these body centers, not just from the brain itself. Man "has established twelve states of consciousness which have centers in his body."[24] Each of these "twelve great centers of action," he explained, "works through an aggregation of cells that physiology calls a ganglionic center."[25] If men and women wanted to awaken these centers and make them functional, they needed to undertake the necessary spiritual practices.

The Twelve Faculties or Powers

1. Spiritual Understanding

Charles indicated that spiritual understanding was the starting point for anyone who wanted to develop the Twelve Powers. "The earnest desire to understand spiritual things," he said, "will open the way and revelation within and without will follow."[26] He recognized that intellectual understanding almost always preceded spiritual understanding. "Intellectual understanding comes first in the soul's development," he said, "then a deeper understanding of the principles follows, until the whole man ripens into wisdom."[27]

Charles believed that, through spiritual understanding, men and women could see the validity of bodily regeneration. "Spiritual understanding shows," he said, "that the resurrection of the body from death is not to be confined to Jesus, but is for all men who comprehend Truth and apply it as Jesus applied it."[28]

2. Wisdom

Charles' description of the faculty of wisdom indicated that he viewed it as related to spiritual understanding. He explained, "Wisdom is the power that lighteth every man that cometh into the world, and without it man is not man but a tempest-tossed barque that continually seeks but never reaches port. The quality of Wisdom is necessary to the adjustment of many conflicting questions of existence."[29]

One needed to look inside for wisdom; as he said, "Look not abroad for power or wisdom. Seek at home. There, in the silent recesses of your own soul, you will find the pearl of great price. The well of living water must spring up in you."[30]

3. Faith

In Charles' view, faith was the key element in enabling men and women to accept the reality of the Indwelling Presence. Throughout his written works, Charles focused on the nature of faith and the importance of developing it. He observed, "The development of the faith faculty in the mind is as necessary to the work in spiritual principles as is the development of the mathematical faculty in the worker in mathematics. Neither of these faculties comes at a bound fully formed into consciousness, but both grow by cultivation."[31]

4. Divine Love

Charles attached the utmost importance to divine love because he felt that, to manifest the Christ within and regenerate the body, this pure form of love must be in the consciousness of every seeker after truth:

> Through the joining of the creative forces of Spirit by souls attuned in love the new body in Christ is speedily formed. . . . Regeneration is not possible without love. . . . No man can in his own might attain this exalted estate, but through the love of God, demonstrated by Jesus.[32]

Human love, particularly romantic love, needed to be supported by the other faculties, specifically wisdom and understanding. He observed:

> The most mysterious part of man's nature is the heart. As the seat of affections it is the center of forces that are difficult to harmonize. Love is of itself blind. It is a force, an energy, a wild, untamed cyclone of energies, swaying us this way and that way, until we are dazed and weary of the struggle. We learn by experience that *love must be directed* by wisdom. If we give up blindly to the impulses suggested by our loves we shall suffer many downfalls.[33]

5. Imagination

Charles viewed the imaginative faculty as being extremely powerful. It created the outer reality in which people lived their lives. "That there is a limit to the ability of the mind is unthinkable," he declared. "What a man imagines he can do, he can do."[34] Earlier, he had written concerning this subject, "You may attain to everything you can imagine. If you imagine it possible to God, it is also possible to you. Whatever possibility your mind conceives, that is for you to attain."[35]

6. Will

In the August 1920 issue of *Unity*, Charles discussed the volition, the power to choose, as "the focal point around which all action centers."[36] He indicated that the faculties of will and understanding worked in conjunction with each other, for the two, along with the imagination, were physiologically located in the same place in the front brain.[37] He noted, "The will and the understanding are very closely related; the understanding comprehending all our speculative, and the will all our active, powers."[38] Charles indicated that as men and women developed spiritual understanding, it was easier for them to manifest the power of will. As he stated in an earlier issue of *Unity*, "Man can balance his will and understanding, and when he does this he will always do the right thing at the right time. Nearly every mistake is the result of will acting without the cooperation of his brother, understanding."[39]

7. Zeal

Charles defined zeal as "the affirmative impulse of existence; its command is 'Go Forward.'"[40] He observed that many beginners in the study and practice of "Truth" expected immediate gratification. "Many fail," Charles observed, "because they are not patient. They want results at once."[41] He often stressed that success required time and effort. He cautioned, "A man cannot expect his ideas to be transformed at once by the Spirit of God. He must be patient and receptive to the Word, and await the result."[42]

Charles felt that humankind's lack of spiritual development made it unrealistic to expect immediate results in developing the Twelve Powers. Success would come, however, to those who were zealous enough to keep practicing in spite of apparent failure: thus, he advised, "Think every day of the goodness of God until His presence shines around you, which it certainly will if you persist."[43]

8. Power

To Charles, words were the product of the power center, a faculty that lay in the throat. "The throat controls all the vibratory energies of the organism," he observed. "Every word that goes forth receives its specific character from the power faculty."[44] He cited the Bible as the authority for the power of words, writing, "If the word of God created all that was created, it follows that everything must be subject to transformation through the power of the word on its plane of formation."[45]

Men and women who fully employed the power of words took an important step in raising their spiritual consciousness. The power faculty, Charles declared, "swings open all the doors of soul and body. . . . One can feel the power of unity with the higher self, [through] the vibrator center in the throat quicker than in any other way."[46]

A highly developed faculty of spiritual understanding coupled with strong faith provided words with an even stronger impact: "Words, to be vital, strong, nourishing and helpful, must have back of them a broad, comprehensive comprehension of Truth. One must think about God as the Source of life and strength, and then his words will go forth with life and strength."[47]

9. Strength

Located in the small of the back, the faculty of strength, Charles stated, "represents the all-around stability that lies at the foundation of every true character."[48] The strength that Charles refers to here was, as he stated in a previous issue of *Unity*, "not physical strength alone, but mental and spiritual strength."[49] Men and women, he indicated, should focus on becoming "steadfast, strong and steady in thought," so as to develop "mastery of the spiritual over the material."[50]

Charles indicated that men and women who developed this faculty demonstrated the "strength-giving attitudes" of joy and gladness. Charles also indicated that, with the faculty of strength, men and women could more easily overcome thoughts of "timidity and fear" as well as mental weakness.[51]

10. Elimination or Renunciation

The faculty of elimination or renunciation is located, according to Charles, in the lower part of the back near the base of the spinal column. It was primarily concerned with eliminating offensive thoughts. He indicated, "There must be a renunciation or letting go of the old thoughts before the new can find place in consciousness. . . . Living old thoughts over and over keeps the inlet of new thoughts closed."[52]

11. Order

Charles provided little information on the faculty of "order," and his only writing on the subject lacked clarity. His most extensive treatment of this subject, entitled "Spiritual Law and Order," published in *The Twelve Powers of Man* and in the February 1930 issue of *Unity*, rambled from one unrelated subject to another without providing a coherent treatment of the topic. Order does not seem to possess mental attributes inherent in humankind and in the other eleven faculties. As a result, the observer might easily conclude that order did not qualify as a "faculty of the mind."

12. Life

Charles placed great stress on the need to develop the "focal life center" in the process of regeneration. When the life faculty was fully developed, the physical bodies of men and women would be transformed from the material to the spiritual plane of existence.

In order to develop the "focal life center" and regenerate the physical body, Charles believed it necessary to conserve the seminal fluid that was normally discharged during sexual intercourse. This fluid, in his view, contained powerful life-giving properties and must remain in the body to facilitate the regenerative process. He stated:

> When the seminal substance in the organism is conserved and retained the nerves are charged with a force that physiologists have named *Vitamine*. This is another name for spiritual energy, which runs like lightning through an organism well-charged with the virgin substance of the soul. . . . In the conservation of this pure substance of life is held the secret of body rejuvenation, physical resurrection

and the final perpetuation of the whole organism in its transmuted purity.[53]

It followed that men and women must refrain from sexual relations so as to conserve the "seminal substance" and make it available to revitalize the body. He commented, "Those who desire to come into closest unity with the Spirit of Truth and construct here on earth the true temple of God—a regenerated body—must abstain from the sex relation."[54]

Developing the Twelve Powers

Charles indicated that a variety of spiritual practices should be used to develop the Twelve Powers. Gaining control of the mind was essential. Affirmations as well as denials produced positive states of consciousness, so essential in the development of each of the powers. Prayer—when it took the form of praise, thanksgiving, and blessing—also helped. Meditation calmed the mind and provided the setting for experiencing the Christ Consciousness.

Affirmations and Denials

Charles believed that affirmations provided men and women with the clarity of thought needed to develop the latent potential in each of the twelve faculties. He recommended that a half an hour each day be spent "in silent or audible affirmation."[55] Specific affirmations should be used, worded to have the greatest effect in developing "the centers," as he called the individual faculties. "Keep this up," he urged, "until you have all the centers *alive* and under your mental direction." He acknowledged it was not an easy task. "This requires persistence and patience," he noted, "but it is the only way to get control of the body and renew it."[56]

Charles indicated that developing the life faculty required more work than did the other eleven faculties, declaring:

> We must concentrate, we must bend every energy along the line of life, acknowledging life, speaking life, thinking life. If anything comes up that opposes it, we must dismiss it, deny it; the thought of the absence of life does not belong where life is.[57]

Charles was convinced that the most powerful affirmations were cloaked in "I Am" statements of Truth. "Metaphysicians," he observed, "have learned by experience the power of words and thoughts sent forth in the name of the Supreme I Am."[58]

Charles viewed the "I Am" as the "Central Identity" of every human being. The "I Am," he observed, "is the metaphysical name of the spiritual self,"[59] and he stated that the use of the "I Am" had its basis in Scripture.[60]

Denials were as important as affirmations in developing the life faculty. The sex drive needed to be controlled. Charles indicated that denials helped. "Persistently deny the carnal belief in sex," he urged. "This can be done only by the power of the word."[61]

Prayer and Meditation

Prayer and meditation were a necessary means of awakening the faculties. In his book *The Twelve Powers*, Charles wrote that these powers were developed, "from patient and persistent spiritual study, prayer and meditation."[62] The power of prayer and meditation should not be underestimated: "The dynamic energy that man releases through prayer, meditation and the higher activities of his mind are very great."[63] He indicated that prayer was one form of "asking, seeking and knocking" and that it should be done repeatedly.[64] "No one ever attained spiritual consciousness without striving for it."[65] Prayers of supplication or petition had little chance of activating the Twelve Powers because these prayers failed to create the required mental state.

THE TWELVE POWERS DOCTRINE AND THE BASIC UNITY TEACHINGS: A COMPARISON

The two teachings have a great deal in common. Both consider the basic goal of spiritual life and practice to be the manifesting of the Indwelling Presence or the Christ Consciousness. Both consider the regeneration of the physical body to be vitally important. The spiritual practices required to attain the Christ mind are the same: accessing intuition, meditation, prayer, and the use of affirmations and denials. The essential faculties contained in the Twelve Powers doctrine are presented in the Basic Unity Teaching as human attributes—attributes that the spiritual seeker needs to develop to access the Christ Consciousness. These attributes include spiritual understanding, strong faith, divine love, powerful ideas, thoughts and words, a focus on the process of bodily regeneration, and persistence in doing the required spiritual work.

The difference in the teachings lies more in semantics than in content. In summary, the Twelve Powers doctrine adds little that is new to the Basic Unity Teachings. It is another way—a more difficult-to-comprehend way, in my opinion—of formulating that teaching.

Charles had been teaching for forty-one years and had reached the age of seventy-five before bringing out *The Twelve Powers of Man*. Since the book and the Twelve Powers deal primarily with regeneration of the body, it may be assumed that he decided that he needed to present a more convincing statement or a better case for the validity of the regenerative process. He had been at work regenerating his own body from age thirty-five, so regeneration had been the major focus of his life. He may have felt that a more definitive presentation was needed than had heretofore been given in the Basic Unity Teaching.

In the eighteen years that he lived following the publication of *The Twelve Powers*, Charles wrote extensively in books and in *Unity* magazine. Articles by Charles appeared in almost every issue of *Unity* until just before his death. However, not one article dealt with the Twelve Powers. Only brief mention was made of the faculties in a few of the articles. During that time period, Charles also wrote six books. Three of those books—*Prosperity* (1936), *Jesus Christ Heals* (1939), and *The Atom Smashing Power of Mind* (1948)—are restatements of the Basic Unity Teaching and make only brief mention of the Twelve Powers. *Mysteries of Genesis* (1936) is a book of biblical interpretation that contains sections dealing with the faculties. *Mysteries of John* (1946) is another book of biblical interpretation containing only a few references to the faculties.

If the Twelve Powers was so essential to his teachings—and many people in the Unity movement consider them to be—why did Charles wait thirty-five years from the time he began teaching to place the doctrine in book form, and why did he fail to reinforce the doctrine in his post-1930 writings? It is now my opinion that he was more comfortable with the Basic Unity Teachings than with the Twelve Powers doctrine. I believe he came to view the Basic

Unity Teachings as the best and most comprehensive statement of spiritual truth.

In my book *The Unity Movement: Its Evolution and Spiritual Teaching* (2002), I indicated that there were two versions of the Unity teachings, one based on the Twelve Powers of man, the rubric under which Charles and Myrtle Fillmore organized their teaching, and another presented by H. Emilie Cady and Lowell Fillmore, which contained the Basic Unity Teachings. I no longer believe that interpretation to be correct. A more accurate statement would be the following: the Basic Unity Teachings are at the heart of Charles Fillmore's work. The Twelve Powers doctrine was an amplification or restructuring of a teaching that he had been presenting for many years.

Chapter 4

Sources of Charles Fillmore's Spiritual Teaching

Introduction

Charles often acknowledged that the spiritual ideas expressed in the Basic Unity Teaching were not original with him or with Myrtle. He said:

> We have been readers among all schools of thought and we find good in all of them. . . . We do not claim to have discovered any new truths, nor have had any special revelation of truth. There is truth in every religion. It is my privilege to take Truth from any source, put it into my religion, and make it a fundamental rule of action in my life.[1]

In developing the Basic Unity Teaching, Charles drew most heavily upon the work of Ralph Waldo Emerson, Emma Curtis Hopkins, Warren Felt Evans, and hermetic philosophy. While theosophy and the work of Mary Baker Eddy influenced Charles, neither was a primary source of his work. Phineas P. Quimby is considered by some scholars to be the father of the modern metaphysical healing movement, therefore having influenced at least indirectly the Fillmores' work.[2] In 1889, at the beginning of Charles' teaching, he had little or no knowledge of Quimby. From 1895, when a brief biography of Quimby appeared, until the *Quimby Manuscripts* were published in 1921, Charles had only unreliable secondhand knowledge of Quimby's work. As a result, Quimby's influence over the content of Charles' teaching or his healing methods appears to have been marginal at best.

RALPH WALDO EMERSON

Charles Fillmore drew heavily on the works of the world-renowned American transcendentalist Ralph Waldo Emerson (1803–1882). Charles considered Emerson to be "the greatest spiritual teacher America ever had."[3] Almost every issue of *Modern Thought* and its successor magazines had quotations from Emerson. Charles had ringing praise for his teaching. He expressed his indebtedness to Emerson by stating, "All students of metaphysics should read Emerson. His writings contain the essence of all the higher thoughts that are now being so lavishly given the world through Christian Science, Metaphysics, Theosophy and the various systems of soul culture."[4] Indeed, Charles credited Emerson with formulating the truths from which he and other metaphysicians drew their teachings, saying, "Emerson anticipates the modern school of metaphysics and gave voice in his essays to all the truths which have formulated into Divine Science. His writings are growing more popular daily and no metaphysical student should be without this volume of his works."[5]

The teachings of Ralph Waldo Emerson, shown below in excerpts from his writings, are also found in the works of Charles Fillmore.

Regarding the Nature of God:

- God must be sought within, not without.[6]

- Let man then learn the revelation of all nature, and all thought to his heart; this, namely; that the highest dwells with him, that the sources of nature are in his own mind.[7]

Regarding the Laws of Being:

- Cause and effect, means and ends, seed and fruit, cannot be severed; for the effect already blooms in the cause, the end preexists in the means, the fruit in the seed.[8]

- These laws execute themselves. They are out of time, out of space, and not subject to circumstance. .... He who does a good deed is instantly enlarged. He who does a mean deed is by the action itself contracted.[9]

Regarding Jesus and the Christ Within:

- I believe in the "still small voice" and that voice is the Christ within us.[10]

- Jesus is an instructor of man. . . . He teaches us how to become like God.[11]

Understanding Spiritual Truth:

- It was a grand sentence of Emanuel Swedenborg, which would alone indicate the greatness of that man's perception—"It is no proof of a man's understanding to be able to affirm whatever he pleases; but to be able to discern that what is true is true, and that what is false is false— that is the mark of character and intelligence."[12] (See Appendix A for more information on the contribution of Emanuel Swedenborg.)

Regarding Intuition:

- A man should learn to detect and watch that gleam of light which flashes across his mind from within, more than the luster of the firmament of bards and sages.[13]

- Residing within each individual, this intuitive capacity breathes life into religions because it provides insight into the relationship of the human spirit to the one mind indwelling in all things.[14]

Regarding Faith:

- To believe your own thought, to believe what is true for you in your private heart is true for all men—that is genius.[15]

Regarding the Power of Ideas, Thoughts, and Words:

- The ideas in every man's mind make him what he is. His whole life is spent in efforts to create outside of him a state of things that conform to his inward thought.[16]

- The reality of things is thought. . . . It is the secret of power. All superiority is this, or related to this.[17]

- Speak what you think now in hard words and tomorrow speak what tomorrow thinks in hard words again, though it contradict everything you said today.[18]

Regarding Meditation:

- If he would know what the Great God speaketh, he must "go into his closet and shut the door," as Jesus said. . . . When I sit in that Presence, who shall dare to come in.[19]

Regarding Prayer:

- Prayer is the contemplation of the facts of life from the highest point of view. It is the soliloquy of a beholding a jubilant soul. It is the spirit of God pronouncing his works good.[20]

- Prayer as a means to effect a private end is meanness and theft. It supposes dualism and not unity with nature and consciousness.[21]

Regarding Divine Love:

- The whole universe is saturated with love, and the devils in hell are happy in that they love mischief.[22]

Regarding Traditional Christianity:

- Historical Christianity has fallen into the error that corrupts all attempts to communicate religion. As it appears to us, and as it has appeared for ages, it is not the doctrine of the soul, but an exaggeration of the personal, the positive, the ritual. It has dwelt, it dwells, with noxious exaggeration about the *person* of Jesus.[23]

Regarding Metaphysical Healing:

While Charles acknowledged his indebtedness, both spiritually and intellectually, to Emerson, he found Emerson's teaching lacking in one major area: he faulted Emerson for not applying his teaching to metaphysical healing. He felt that had Emerson done so, he would have used the teaching to heal himself physically:

> Emerson doubtless teaches in a different language everything that Jesus does but he did not step boldly out and affirm to the impotent man in himself, "Be thou healed," consequently he did not get the result of his understanding in the healing of his own body.[24]

(See Appendix B for further information on the contribution of Ralph Waldo Emerson.)

EMMA CURTIS HOPKINS

Emma Curtis Hopkins (c. 1845–1924) came to Kansas City for the first time in January 1890 to teach a primary course in Christian Science. Hopkins' teaching was sponsored in Kansas City by the Kansas City College of Christian Science, whose director, Dr. J. S. Thacher, was a friend of Charles Fillmore. Thacher sponsored teachers known as Christian Science dissidents, of which Hopkins was one.[25] Prior to her becoming an independent teacher, she had been a student and close associate of Mary Baker Eddy but had broken with Eddy and relocated to Chicago where she was teaching her own brand of the doctrine.

Charles was acquainted with Hopkins' written work, which consisted of a pamphlet entitled *Who Carry Signs?* as well as several lessons in Christian Science. These publications had been offered for sale, with a variety of other metaphysical publications, in *Modern Thought* magazine, beginning with its inaugural issue in April 1889.

Charles was also aware of her reputation as a teacher and spiritual healer. In an announcement in *Modern Thought* magazine in November 1889, Charles gave her work a strong endorsement. He urged readers to attend her classes which were to begin in Kansas City in January:

Everyone who has a desire to know more of this wonderful philosophy should embrace this opportunity of listening to Mrs. Hopkins. In many instances those who enter her classes confirmed invalids, come out at the end of the course perfectly well. She dwells so continually of the spirit that her very presence heals. These are not the claims of an enthusiast, but the carefully sifted testimony of scores of her students. Certain persons have the faculty of imparting knowledge of this great principle more readily than others and Mrs. Hopkins is one in whom this faculty is especially developed.[26]

Hopkins did not disappoint. After attending her class in Kansas City, Charles was enthusiastic about her personal qualities, her ability to heal, and her teaching, as the following testimonial published in *Modern Thought* indicated:

Those who went to the class as the most vehement scoffers came out enthusiastic champions of truth. . . . It is safe to say that this course of lectures has given an impetus to the work in this city which will ultimate [*sic*] in the freedom of every mind from the thralldom of sin, sickness and death, and open the way for the new heaven and earth.[27]

Hopkins returned to Kansas City for another series of lectures in March 1890. Again the Fillmores attended, and again they were touched by her presence and the content of her message. Charles reported, "The prominent characteristic of Mrs. Hopkins is her charity. She has such a broad generous grasp on Truth, her reading is so extensive and her knowledge so thorough that she charms and disarms the most prejudiced."[28]

The Fillmores attended her classes in the summer of 1890 in Kansas City and in Chicago in December. They completed Hopkins' metaphysical curriculum and were ordained by her as ministers in December 1890. Charles expressed his admiration for Hopkins and indicated the contribution she had made to his own understanding of spiritual principles, writing: "I have taken lessons in Christian Science and metaphysics from many teachers and many schools, and from all have received good, but there is one teacher who pointed the way so clearly that under her tutelage I made the most rapid advancement in understanding."[29]

There are several commonalities in the teachings of Emma Curtis Hopkins and of Charles Fillmore. These include teachings on divine law; manifesting the Christ mind; faith; the power of ideas, thoughts, and words; affirmations and denials; prayer; divine love; and the practice of metaphysical healing. The similarities are shown below in quotes from Hopkins' writing.

Manifesting the Christ Mind:

- If you repeat the name of Jesus Christ you will, step by step, come into His quality of mind. Then you will step by step, become cognizant of the divine nature charging through you.[30]

Regarding Divine Law:

In several passages in her work *High Mysticism*, Hopkins referred to the need to observe divine law. She called it "the law of soul life,"[31] "the law of mind,"[32] "mystical law,"[33] "the law of cause and effect,"[34] "the divine law of action," and "the divine law of cure."[35]

Regarding the Power of Thoughts, Ideas, and Words:

- Ideas have living messages.[36]

- We are entirely built up and moved by our thoughts. . . . The world in which we live is the exact record of our thoughts.[37]

- Could God, the principle of thought and speech, invest His people with a richer heritage than the power of the word? Is there anything more majestic than this great principle of every word being full of divine potency?[38]

Regarding Affirmations and Denials:

- Try the denials of metaphysical reasoning and see if you do not feel a new freedom.[39]

- Successful men and women along any line have borne about within their own minds strong, native affirmations.[40]

Regarding Faith:

- Words do not cure unless we have faith in them, faith is the curative principle.[41]

Regarding Prayer:

- The only difference between our prayer in the Truth and the old orthodox prayers is that we pray as if we had already received the blessings.[42]

Regarding Divine Love:

- Whoever gets into the state of overflowing unquenchable love is manifesting Jesus Christ.[43]

Regarding the Twelve Powers:

- Mind is composed of twelve powers. When mind exercises these twelve powers it has twelve characteristics, which shine like polished jewels. They may be a perfect foundation for the absolute demonstration of the Jesus Christ Spirit.[44]

Regarding Metaphysical Healing:

- Your mind holding firmly on to its denials and affirmations is certain to cure, though you do not lift a finger.[45]

While Hopkins' teaching and that of Charles Fillmore have many similarities, there are some important differences. Charles' ideas on the nature of God and on Jesus are significantly different from the views of Hopkins, who was a Trinitarian and, in many respects, true to her Congregationalist roots. She accepted the traditional Christian view of Jesus as part of the Godhead and born divine. She attributed personal qualities to Jesus as Savior, Redeemer, and Messiah and personal qualities to God the Father and God the Holy Spirit. Charles rejected the doctrine of the Trinity, considering Jesus as born human and not divine at birth. Charles believed that Jesus raised his consciousness, through spiritual practice during several lifetimes, to the level of the Divine. Hopkins never mentions reincarnation; as a traditional Christian, she probably would not have believed it. She never discussed meditation practice, nor does she indicate the importance of relying on intuition to gain spiritual understanding—all important parts of Charles' teaching. Finally, while she viewed overcoming death as a goal of spiritual practice, she does not discuss bodily regeneration. (See Appendix C for more information on the life and teaching of Emma Curtis Hopkins.)

WARREN FELT EVANS

Warren Felt Evans (1817–1889) was the first American writer to give literary form to the ideas and methods of spiritual healing. His book *Mental Cure*, published in 1869, is considered to be the first of all the New Thought books.[46] It was read widely in the United States and in Europe, went through several editions, and was published in several languages. Horatio Dresser, the early historian of New Thought (writing in 1919, fifty years after the book was published), considered it to be "still superior . . . to most of the New Thought literature of today."[47] Charles Braden, a widely respected authority on metaphysical movements in America, commented that Evans "was the only important figure, aside from Mrs. Eddy, who attempted to work out a consistent and philosophically supported system of metaphysical healing and mental healing after Quimby."[48]

Charles read all of Evans' books and was generous in his praise. In 1908, he commented:

> W. F. Evans is called "The Recording Angel of Metaphysics." He has hunted out all the vital issues in ancient and modern spiritual writing, and sifted them thoroughly. I have read the seven volumes which he has written and think them the most complete of all metaphysical compilations. He is not an original thinker, but knows the Truth when he sees it.[49]

Evans' book *Primitive Mind-Cure* drew special praise from Charles. He said, "This work is a complete exposition of the system of mental healing and contains a full instruction in the philosophy and practice of Mind Cure." Charles also said that all of Evans' works "commend themselves to thinking people everywhere. . . . They are the strongest works that have ever been published in substantiation of the supremacy of the Spirit."[50] Their theories and practices of metaphysical healing are also virtually the same.

Evans combined the work of Franz Anton Mesmer, who illustrated the beneficent impact of the mind on the body for purposes of health, with the spiritual teaching of Ralph Waldo Emerson, which addressed the value of becoming one with the divine Indwelling Presence. (See Appendix D for more information on the contribution of Franz Anton Mesmer.) Deepening the mental healing movement by demonstrating its spiritual basis, Evans provided the basis upon which Charles developed his teaching.

A comparison of the spiritual teaching of Warren Felt Evans with that of Charles Fillmore reveals remarkable similarities. Evans' teachings in the field of Christian metaphysics, shown below in excerpts from his writings, match the writings of Charles point by point with few exceptions.

Regarding the Nature of God:

- Each individual spirit is not God, but a god, and is possessed of all the attributes of its parent source among which are omniscience and omnipotence.[51]

- The internal man, in its highest degree, is divine, immortal and celestial.[52]

Regarding the Laws of Being:

- There is no departure from the laws of our nature, in other words, no miracles, but only the operation of higher law.[53]

- By an immutable law of our being, what we have sown we shall sometime reap.[54]

Regarding Jesus and the Christ Within:

- Of the real Self, the Christ within, we may always predicate perfect health and blessedness.[55]

- The Collective Man, the universal Divine Humanity, is the real Christ, of whom Jesus is an incarnation.[56]

Understanding Spiritual Truth:

- The man who can steadfastly think the truth in regard to his real being has the key that unlocks the handcuffs of his soul, and his mortal powers are set free.[57]

Regarding Intuition:

- In seeking spiritual knowledge we are to look only within.[58]

- The faculty of intuition . . . is the highest guide to truth within earth and heaven. It is the only faculty in man through which divine revelations come, or ever has come. By means of it we gain access to an interior and permanent region of knowledge, where are stored up all the truths which were ever known or can be known.[59]

Regarding Faith:

- Faith may be defined to be the power of perceiving spiritual realities that lie above and beyond the range of the senses, and a confidence in those higher truths.[60]

Regarding the Power of Ideas, Thoughts, and Words:

- Before things can exist in the sense-world, or as actualities, the ideas of them as subjective realities and typeforms must exist.[61]

- It is thought which shapes and governs worlds.[62]

- One of the principal mediums through which mind acts upon mind is that of words, spoken or written. Words are the representatives of ideas, the outward manifestation of thought, and the ultimation of hidden spiritual powers.[63]

Chapter 4

Regarding Affirmations:

- The most intense form of action in a psychological or curative effort upon ourselves or others is . . . a positive affirmation. It does not say "Be thou so and so," but rather . . . in its highest expression, "You are well."[64]

- It is our business only to think the truth and under proper conditions to affirm it verbally, and then to leave the truth to have everything its own way.[65]

Regarding Meditation:

- We should wait in the silence that lies at the heart of things for the "soundless word" that rise out of eternal Life. In the stillness of our own soul, we are to let it speak to us.[66]

Regarding Prayer:

- The most effectual prayer is wordless—the turning of a soul, conscious of its emptiness towards the boundless Life of the heavens and of nature.[67]

- Real prayer . . . is not a repetition of a form of words, but a certain receptive state and attitude of mind and heart of man.[68]

Regarding Divine Love:

- A love so great, so divine, as to be willing to lay down life itself, that others might have, and to bear the burdens and the pain of others.[69]

Regarding Human Perfectibility:

- The infant powers of the mind, and its latent, undeveloped faculties, shall sometime expand into full angelhood. The germ of divine life in man, which lies at the inmost center of our being, will sometime come to dominion, and have everything its own way in our inner and outer nature.[70]

Regarding Bodily Regeneration:

- When we attain the true Christian position of thought, and death becomes transformed into resurrection, or the ascent of the soul to a new and higher life on earth, then pain and disease disappear from consciousness. . . . In this resurrection day, the real man, the immortal self, comes forth from the sepulcher of the body, and lives eternal life on earth. . . . The Christ within must be allowed to reign in us until every enemy is put under his feet; and the last enemy that shall be destroyed is death.[71]

Regarding the Afterlife:

- It is a law as universal as the presence of God in nature, that out of what the world falsely calls death there is always evolved a higher form and order of life. There is not death. All is boundless, endless, omnipresent, omniactive life. . . . Death is an illusion or deceptive appearance.[72]

Regarding Traditional Christianity:

- We encounter at the outset in our instruction a great evil, and that has served to hold humanity down and prevent its rising from the lane of sense to the life of faith. I refer to the fact that the Church, Catholic and Protestant, has claimed a monopoly of the principle of faith. They have connected it with certain dogmas which are, to many intelligent minds, unreasonable, absurd, and incredible.[73]

Regarding Jesus as Healer:

- Jesus, the Christ, is the only physician who has ever given, theoretically and practically, due prominence to the spiritual side of human nature in the cure of disease. . . . He aimed to restore first the disordered mind to health and harmony and then through this the outward body.[74]

Regarding Metaphysical Practice:

- We look away from the surface of a patient's being, become blind to the disease which has its seat only there, and recognize his unchanging, undying spiritual self alone, which is included in the Christ and is one with the manifested God.[75]

- The science of modern times has never appreciated the power of intense *thought* directed to a person with a beneficent end or healing intention.[76]

Regarding the Role of the Metaphysical Practitioner:

- The Christian method of cure is essentially a system of instruction. The doctor is the teacher, as the word itself implies. His aim is to bring the patient into his own mode of thought and feeling . . . by which is signified a complete inversion of a person's way of thinking, the turning of the subject of it from the life of sense to the dominion of spirit. If it is not this, it is of no great value.[77]

- It should be our aim and wish, not merely to impress our thoughts upon a patient's mind, but to lift him from a lower to a higher plane of thought. . . . To elevate a patient from the plane of sense, "the horrible pit and miry clay," into the spiritual realm of his being, is to place him beyond the reach of all possible maladies.[78]

Regarding the Responsibilities of the Patient:

- It must be kept in mind that this method of cure which was practiced by Jesus implies in the patient a DESIRE to be saved, and a *predisposition to believe*. Where these exist, the cure is easy. Where they do not exist, little can be done, and it is a waste of time and energy to undertake impossibilities.[79]

- When a man is convinced of his error and rejects it as an evil which is contrary to the divine Will, which is the same as the Infinite Goodness and thus changes his mind or way of thinking in regard to it, and purposes to think and live differently, he has repented and come into an attitude of mind toward the hurtful error and evil that renders the remission, or the putting away the sin from him, possible.[80]

Regarding Absent Healing:

- If the mental rapport is established, which is the most important thing, it may be three feet or three hundred miles. Nearness and distance in the realm of spirit are not estimated in feet, in miles, and leagues, but in states of interiors.[81]

Regarding Allopathic Medicine:

- Many a person has been doctored into the graveyard, by treating him for a disease he never had and thus administering the wrong medicines.[82]

- The system of drug medication has had and still has its uses. But is there not a higher and more efficient method of cure? Does drug medication belong to Christianity? Did Jesus and the Apostles deal in pills and potions? And did they not cure even organic diseases? While not discarding true medical science, may we not learn more at the feet of Jesus?[83]

The areas of divergence in the teachings of Evans and Charles Fillmore are relatively small. Evans believed that, with a certain few patients, hypnosis was helpful. Fillmore did not employ hypnosis. Evans also saw some benefit in hands-on healing, though he used it rarely. Hands-on healing was not a part of the Unity teaching. Evans was receptive to Western medical practices, whereas Charles was leery of them. Evans did not address the doctrine of reincarnation, indicating that it was not a part of his teaching; Charles Fillmore accepted the doctrine. (For further information on the life and work of Warren Felt Evans, see Appendix E.)

HERMETIC PHILOSOPHY

Charles indicated that, from the time he was a youth, he had an interest in the occult.[84] The occult deals with supernatural influences or powers often hidden or known only to an initiated few and is viewed with suspicion by most of the religious and secular world, which categorize it with magic and witch-craft. Charles, however, found great value in occult teachings, stating: "The various occult phenomena now so common have always been known to a few in every age, who had graduated out of the sense plane, but were regarded with superstitious fear by the masses."[85]

Charles identified himself as "a student of many schools of occultism." He observed that many people "poopoo as fairy tales" the phenomena of the occult. However, he said, "those who have taken even a slight peep behind the material shadow will recognize them as among the possibilities latent in the human soul."[86] Of the occult philosophies, which included spiritualism, Rosicrucianism, theosophy, and hermetic philosophy, it was the last that he relied upon most heavily.

Hermetic philosophy had its origins in antiquity, in Egypt where Toth, god of wisdom and inventor of script, first made his appearance in the pyramid texts around 2500 BCE. Fifteen hundred years later, around 1000 BCE, Toth is regarded by the Greeks as their god Hermes, messenger between gods and humans.[87]

Hermes Trismegistus is the central figure in the hermetic writings and the supposed founder and namesake of hermeticism. Whoever or whatever he was, or even if he never existed at all, there is one characteristic universally associated with Hermes Trismegistus: Hermes is presented as a teacher figure or as an example.[88]

Hermetic writings tend to be either scientific or philosophical in nature. The philosophical writings interested Charles Fillmore.[89] The philosophical texts fall into six main groups: the *Framenta Hermetica*, the *Nag Hammadi Codex*, the *Stobaei Hermetic*, *The Definitions of Hermes Trismegistus for Ascelius*, the *Corpus Hermeticum*, and the *Asclepius*. The latter two are the best-known hermetic works, and some scholars consider them to represent the "foundational" writings of hermeticism.

For many years, these teachings were transmitted orally. They were put into written form somewhere between the first and sixth centuries CE and composed by anonymous authors. The Dutch hermetics scholar Cokkey van Limpt indicates that many of the texts originated in Alexandria, Egypt, which he described as "the Egyptian-Greek-Jewish-Christian melting pot of cultures." The texts offer, van Limpt indicated, "insights in the origin of the world and secrets of creation."[90]

The core of hermetic philosophy can be summarized in its seven basic principles:[91]

1. The principle of mentalism: all is mind; the universe is mental.

2. The principle of correspondence: As above, so below; as below, so above.

3. The principle of vibration: nothing rests; everything moves; every thing vibrates.

4. The principle of polarity: everything is dual; everything has its pair of opposites; extremes meet.

5. The principle of rhythm: everything flows, out and in; all is ebb and flow, action and reaction, advance and recoil.

6. The principle of cause and effect: every cause has its effect; every effect has its cause. everything happens according to law . . . nothing escapes the law.

7. The principle of gender: everything has its masculine and feminine principle.

Charles appears to have been well acquainted with hermetic philosophy and with the seven hermetic principles. He said, "I have always been drawn to the mysterious and the occult," taking "great interest in branches of Hermetic philosophy." As an indication of his interest in hermetic philosophy, he offered readers of *Modern Thought*, as a bonus for subscribing, a one year's free subscription to *The Hermetist*. This monthly magazine, which was published by the Hermetic Publishing Company in Chicago, focused on "teaching the Ancient Wisdom, and knowledge of the Occult, or hidden laws of nature."[92]

Charles commented often on aspects of hermeticism. In *Unity* magazine in October 1896, he indicated agreement with the principle of correspondence, stating, "It is an axiom of hermetic students that the above may be judged by the below, and the within by the without."[93] In the June 1891 issue of *Unity*, he indicated that he agreed with the principle of mentalism or mind:

An understanding of God or Universal Mind is a key to all scriptures and occult writings. . . . In all these scriptures and Hermetic accounts of creation an intimate relation is always held between God and Man or Mind and Thought or Principle and Perfect Idea.[94]

In a short piece in *Christian Science Thought* in October 1890, Fillmore described hermetic philosophy, presenting in a favorable light some of its major tenets:

It is recorded that over twenty-five thousand years ago certain Hermetic brotherhoods of the Orient had schools in secret temples far from habitations of men in mountain vastness. These temples were dedicated to the study of God or Primal Cause.[95]

He described how the powers or faculties attributed to the brotherhoods were attained through spiritual practice:

They found that in certain stages of high understanding, the result of systematic training along certain lines, they came into harmonious relations with this Primal Principle or First Cause, that they were themselves endowed with causing power. They found that by living right and thinking generously and unselfishly they awakened new faculties within themselves. They sought the good or God and through that universal law that like attracts like, good or God sought them.[96]

Charles indicated these ancient people awakened within themselves the indwelling Divine Presence and, by so doing, attained the same levels of spiritual understanding and consciousness that Jesus had manifested:

They also found that when they came into right relations with the principle of good that they had apparently supernatural powers. They found what Jesus Christ called the Kingdom of Heaven within and all things were thereby added unto them. They are said to have had the power to cause rain or sunshine, heat or cold and produce at will the flowers, fruits, and other products of the field. They could also bodily fly through the air, having acquired an understanding of that which lies back of gravity. They controlled all the elements by that word or thought and proved that we became like that which we study. They studied cause and became master of effects.[97]

Members of the hermetic brotherhoods lived their lives in accordance with divine law, discovered the power of thought and words, and engaged in metaphysical healing:

> They found that by coming into relations . . . with this invisible cause, that they were moved by it to give expression both in thought and speech to certain words, and that when those words were so expressed through them wonderful transformations occurred in their surroundings. The conditions which they had always supposed to be impossible of variation from the laws of nature, were, in the twinkling of an eye, set to naught. They had always believed that sickness, decay and death were a part of an immutable law. Yet they found certain words which in meaning were in harmony with the pivotal truth God or First Cause is Spirit and all good; healed the sick, made happy the sorrowful and filled the coffers of the poor.[98]

These brotherhoods were also aware that negative thought had a harmful effect on human conditions. They trained themselves to think only in ways that produced harmonious human conditions:

> They found that certain words or thoughts, that did not correspond to nor harmonize with the attributes of primal cause or good, produced conditions of inharmony in those who uttered them and in those about them. Under their expression people became sick, sorrowful and generally unhappy.[99]

In recent years, much has been written about Hermetic philosophy in the scholarly literature. Europeans, particularly the Dutch, have taken a deep interest. A Library of Hermetic Philosophy now exists in Amsterdam. In addition, Amsterdam University now has a chair of hermetic philosophy. One of the more in-depth accounts of hermetic philosophy is entitled *The Secret Science: Hermetic Philosophy, Book One*, written by Dario Salas Sommer, a South American who wrote under the pseudonym of John Baines. Dario Salas Sommer, director of the Institute of Hermetic Philosophy, which has centers in North and South America, Europe, and Russia, was interviewed by Jessica Rosemischer in the December–February 2005/06 issue of *What Is Enlightenment?* magazine. Sommer was described as having "rekindled a mystical teaching known as Hermeticism" and "revivified the essence of this teaching for a postmodern age."[100]

Hermetic philosophy, as described in Baines' *The Secret Science*, is similar in many respects to the Basic Unity Teaching as presented in the writings of Charles Fillmore. The areas of commonality include the nature of God and man; the laws of Being; intuition; Jesus; the divine within; the power of thought; affirmations and denials; Divine love; metaphysical healing; bodily regeneration; the afterlife; and reincarnation. The similarities are shown below in quotes from Baines' work:

Regarding the Nature of God:

- God is all. Everything that exists and everything that does not exist is within God.[101] When someone says, "I am who I am" it is Spirit manifesting itself.[102]

Regarding the Nature of Man:

- All the mystery of mysteries is hidden within man because he is the son of God and is essentially made in his image.[103]

Regarding the Divine Within:

- All that is within us is also outside of us and, therefore, he who conquers his internal nature is also able to achieve dominion over the external.[104]

- Without a doubt, instinctively the most profound desire and yearning of each human being is to unite with God—in other words, to find God within himself.[105] It is absurd to pretend to find God in the external. He is found within man.[106]

Regarding the Laws of Being:

- The law of cause and effect is what determines the path we will follow during life.[107]

- Nothing happens by chance. Everything happens according to the law.[108]

Regarding Intuition:

- [Everyone] may manifest in all its power the divine spark within himself, that is the part of the great universal mind that lives within him.[109]

Regarding Jesus:

- It was in Egypt where many spiritual supermen received directly from the priests, the science which enabled them to create themselves, or to regenerate, among these was Jesus himself . . . the super conscious son of the great universal Mind.[110]

Regarding Prayer:

- When he prays, man places himself in contact with the energy of God that is within him.[111]

Regarding Meditation:

- One should frequently meditate, concentrating one's thoughts on the heart. Meditate constantly on wisdom, love and truth.[112]

Regarding the Power of Thought:

- All is mind. We can understand the truth of the aphorism "as a man thinketh, so shall he be."[113]
- One who thinks he is persecuted by bad luck, for example, places himself in a state of negativity which breeds misfortune and misery.[114]

Regarding Affirmations:

- It is necessary to educate the imagination to have room only for beautiful, positive and optimistic thoughts: thoughts of success, peace and prosperity.[115]

Unity Library & Archives
1901 NW Blue Parkway
Unity Village, MO 64065

- All the universe is mental creation, and we can therefore affirm that we exist within the mind of God.[116]

Regarding Denials:

- Because we all go through moments of crisis and difficult situations, we must train ourselves to consciously deny that which is negative or bad for us.[117]

Regarding Divine Love:

- The only way to find God is through the practice of the highest spiritual virtues, practicing love towards all human beings without distinction.[118]

Regarding Persistence:

- Success in life depends to a great extent on the will power of the individual, on one's capacity to persevere, to work hard when others falter, to overcome unpleasant situations, misery and failure.[119]

Regarding Metaphysical Healing:

- All that manifest later in the physical, originates in the soul. If man is ill, it is because his soul is sick.[120]

- Occult medicine begins, therefore, by altering the vibrations of the soul in order to destroy all that is negative which could, or already has, manifest itself as illness.[121]

Regarding Bodily Regeneration:

- For the initiate who has managed to reach total and complete dominion over matter, nothing is impossible, because he can rejuvenate his physical body and live on earth for a length of time that would seem incredible to the profane.[122]

- Through his mind, he will be able to modify his cellular structure, overcoming old age and death.[123]

Regarding Human Perfectibility:

- The day will come when the man will have attained perfect mastery of the mind, enabling him to materialize his thoughts, giving him the ability to achieve the integration of matter.[124]

Regarding the Afterlife:

- Nothing dies, everything passes into another state of existence.[125]

Regarding Reincarnation:

- Death is only the beginning of a new form of life. . . . For the true occultist, death only dignifies the shedding of one wrapping, to continue life in the invisible world and to return to earth in due course.[126]

THEOSOPHY

The teachings of Madame Helena Petrovna Blavatsky (1831–1891) and the early Theosophists became publicly available in the two decades before the Fillmores began their own work. The Fillmores' high regard for theosophical teachings was indicated in 1889 in reviews of literature in the first issue of *Modern Thought* magazine. No fewer than thirteen books on theosophy were recommended, including the landmark work by Madame Blavatsky, *Isis Unveiled*. In addition, a book entitled *Christian Theosophy* by John Hamlin Dewey was recommended as "one of the very best books on the subject" and given a lengthy review and highly praised. The periodical entitled *The Wilkins Letter on Theosophy* was suggested for all who wanted to learn theosophical doctrines.[127] Charles Fillmore acknowledged his own intellectual debt to theosophy when he commented: "I myself was a very earnest student of Theosophy and quite familiar with its literature, and found much truth therein. . . . I have studied [it] carefully, both from the exoteric and esoteric standpoints.[128]

The growth and development of the theosophical movement in the United States, Europe, and India in the late nineteenth century can be attributed in large part to the work of two disparate and unlikely middle-aged collaborators, Madame Helena Petrovna Blavatsky, a brilliant, captivating, and eccentric Russian émigré to the United States, and Henry Steel Olcott, a diligent, pragmatic, New York lawyer with family ties back to the Pilgrims. Blavatsky articulated the teaching in several books on the occult. Olcott's work as an administrator and organizer was essential to the development of the theosophical movement.

Blavatsky wrote prolifically. Her collected writings consist of a dozen volumes. Her two-volume masterwork, *The Secret Doctrine*, was published in 1888. It is a recasting of *Isis Unveiled*, making the development of the inner man the reason for human evolution.[129] It combined ideas from Asian religions within a cosmic framework that gave meaning to human destiny and is considered by some authorities to be the major work of occultism in the nineteenth century.[130] Her last book, *The Voice of Silence*, is a theosophical devotional classic that continues to be popular in the present day and had a significant effect on shaping the outlook of theosophy. Theosophists consider it to be the most widely read and beloved of all her writings.[131]

Theosophy has its roots in Eastern religion, Swedenborgianism, Mesmerism, transcendentalism, and spiritualism. Its teachings on karma and reincarnation can be found in Buddhism and Hinduism; its ideas on the afterlife come from Swedenborg; its beliefs in the positive impact of one mind upon another are no doubt derived from the work of Franz Anton Mesmer and his followers; its views on the immanence of God are transcendentalist ideas; and its effort to bridge the gap between science and religion and to acknowledge human evolution are also evident in spiritualism.

During the twentieth century, there were three separate theosophical organizations, two with headquarters in the United States and one in India. Membership peaked at 50,000 in the 1920s, most of which was in India. Worldwide membership as of 1980 was approximately 40,000. The activities of branches and centers include courses and lectures in theosophy; a publications program; and sponsorship of bookstores, libraries, and summer camps.

After the deaths of Blavatsky and Olcott, three twentieth-century spiritual teachers, Annie Besant, C. W. Leadbeater, and J. Krishnamurti, gained renown for their theosophical works.

Charles Fillmore would have agreed with many of the spiritual teachings of leading theosophists, including Madame Blavatsky and P. T. Pavri, a professor in the Sind National College in India.

Regarding a Personal God:

*   We reject the idea of a personal, or extra-cosmic and anthropomorphic God, who is but a gigantic shadow of Man. . . . The God of theology . . . is a bundle of contradictions.[132]

Regarding God as Principle:

*   [God is] an ever unknowable Principle.[133]

*   We believe in a Universal Divine Principle, the root of ALL, from which all proceeds, and within which all shall be absorbed at the end of the great cycle of being.[134]

Regarding the Immanence of God:

*   Our Deity is neither in a paradise, nor in a particular tree, building or mountain; it is everywhere, in every atom of the visible as of the invisible Cosmos; in, or over, and around every invisible atom and visible molecule.[135]

*   We call our "Father in Heaven" that deific essence of which we are cognizant in us, in our heart and spiritual consciousness, and which has nothing to do with the anthropomorphic conception we may form of it in our physical brain.[136]

Regarding the Power of Thought:

*   What you think upon, that you become.[137]

Regarding Prayer and Meditation:

- Meditation is silent and unuttered prayer ... the ardent turning of the soul toward the divine, not to ask for any particular good (as in the common meaning of prayer) but for good itself—for the universal Supreme Good.[138]

Regarding Reincarnation:

- Each man must pass through many lives, returning to earth again and again and dwelling each time in a different earthly body. ... When the experience of one life is assimilated, he returns to the earth for another life, in order to gain more.[139]

Regarding Karmic Law:

Charles disagreed with theosophical teachings regarding the law of karma. Charles said, "The Karmic law belongs to the same family as the orthodox devil and the consciousness of fear which it sets up is equally paralyzing in its effect."[140] Thus, the following statements by Madame Blavatsky on karmic law would have been rejected by Charles:

- Our philosophy teaches that Karmic punishment reaches the ego in its next incarnation.[141]

- Our philosophy has a doctrine of punishment as stern as that of the most rigid Calvinist, only far more philosophically consistent with absolute justice. No deed, not even a sinful thought, will go unpunished; the latter more severely even than the former, as thought has far more potential in creating evil results than even a deed.[142]

(For further information on theosophy and the teachings of Madame Blavatsky, see Appendix F.)

MARY BAKER EDDY

Of the nineteenth-century practitioners of mental healing, Mary Baker Eddy (1821–1910) was without a doubt the most successful, if success is measured in terms of impact on the largest number of people. At age forty-five in 1866, she reported she was divinely healed from a serious injury through an experience of being fully conscious of the divine Presence. Thereafter, she dedicated her life to divine healing, teaching the techniques she had learned, calling her work "Christian Science." Her book *Science and Health*, published initially in 1875, presented her teaching. By the year 2000, over eight million copies had been sold. An able organizer, she formed an association of practitioners, instituted a school of metaphysical healing, and founded a church.

Many people in Unity assume that Myrtle and Charles were in the spiritual lineage of Mary Baker Eddy, based on the fact that the Fillmores became mental healers after taking classes from Christian Science practitioners. While Charles and Myrtle studied with teachers who had been associated with Eddy, those teachers had separated themselves from Eddy's work and were teaching a brand of metaphysical healing they called Christian Science that was different in many respects from the Christian Science of Mary Baker Eddy.

In May 1889, in *Modern Thought*, at the beginning of his career as a spiritual teacher, Charles asked the question, "Is this Christian Science?" He answered by dissociating himself from the teaching: "Our views are not those of orthodox Christian Science" (by that he meant the Christian Science taught by Mary Baker Eddy). He acknowledged that he had studied Christian Science. "We have received instruction . . . have practiced its formulas . . . but have not been able to accept as truth all of its teachings."[143] Yet he was attracted to Christian Science, as he defined it: "We are partial and endorse Christian Science, and by Christian Science we mean all the metaphysical schools."[144] Mary Baker Eddy, who equated the term "Christian Science" with her own work, would have scoffed at the notion that "Christian Science" could include "all the metaphysical schools."

In April 1890, after studying Christian Science with Emma Curtis Hopkins, Charles changed the name of the *Modern Thought* magazine to *Christian Science Thought*. He explained that the new name more correctly described his teaching:

> The name *Modern Thought* was not an index to the Christian Science principles which the paper advocated and we were in consequence inundated by communications of a nature we did not care to publish, and were constantly obliged to explain our exact place in that great maelstrom of "modern thought." The new name does all this for us.

So to the public understanding, the name "Christian Science" stands for all the different schools of metaphysics, regardless of the technical differences by which their leaders distinguish them.[145]

For a few months after changing the name of the magazine, Charles appeared satisfied that the name "Christian Science" contained the basic contents of his doctrine. He defined Christian Science very simply. "Christian," he said, "pertains to Christ." "Science" he defined as "an orderly arrangement of ascertained truth." Charles found much that was positive in the teaching:

Had the people of the world any idea of the health, happiness, and satisfaction which results from this philosophy of Christ, they would willingly lay down their millions to possess it. It is the only philosophy that effectually solves the problem of life, and as a reform it so far exceeds all the partial measures now advocated that they pale into nothingness beside its all pervading light.[146]

In April 1891, after publishing an annual volume of *Christian Science Thought*, Charles again changed the name of the magazine. The new name was simply *Thought*. Charles had come to the conclusion that the name "Christian Science" created a false impression among readers. His reasoning was contained in a statement published in *Thought* by a Christian Science dissident, Joseph Adams.

In the mid-1880s, Adams had been a student of Mary Baker Eddy in Boston at the Massachusetts Medical College. Adams, like Emma Curtis Hopkins, distanced himself from Eddy and moved to Chicago where he taught Christian Science and edited a magazine entitled the *Chicago Christian Scientist*.[147] Adams wrote:

We find that as a matter of fact, after five years of study and experience, that the name Christian Science is misleading, and excites unnecessary prejudice and antagonism. The moment you use the word Christian Science to one who has not studied it, or had it explained to them, that very moment you invite inquiry. What is that? And you instantly generate in the mind a thought that Christian Science is something separate, distinct, apart from and antagonistic to the gospel of God. We know it is so. The moment I attempt to present Christian Science to those unfamiliar with it, they think it is something different from and opposed to the gospel of Jesus.[148]

Charles himself provided a more specific explanation as to why he no longer would edit and publish a magazine that was identified with Christian Science:

> A few of you have been with us from the first, when under the name *Modern Thought* our editor-in-chief gave forth his earliest conceptions of truth. Subsequently, to keep up with his expanding ideas of it, the name was changed to *Christian Science Thought*, but when the principles attached to that name became limited by the dogmas of creed and rules, the words "Christian Science" were dropped and the magazine became widely known as *Thought*.[149]

Charles would later explain why, as a Christian metaphysician, he should not be classified as a Christian Scientist:

> By many of those not acquainted with the distinctions of metaphysical thought, we are classed with Christian Scientists because we do healing. But we are radically different from them in nearly all of our expositions of Truth, and it is an error to class us with them in any way, except in the fundamental perceptions of the being of God, which are common to all religions.[150]

Charles had great respect for the work of Mary Baker Eddy but felt that she had compromised herself by engaging in the cult of personality. In July 1889, he wrote:

> There is not doubt but that the persistent claim by Mrs. Eddy of divine illumination has woven about this name a glamour of superiority. We must disabuse our minds of the belief that the great sea of health and harmony can be tapped and distributed in all its purity by those only who have assumed the name of Christian Science.[151]

Charles had reservations about the way Eddy handled her leadership role and the direction of the Christian Science movement:

> There is but one school entitled to the name "Christian Science" and those are the followers of Mrs. Eddy. . . . The fact remains that a definite creed has been adopted by a particular school, which the free

people do not accept, nor do they hold to the infallibility of Mrs. Eddy and her book, *Science and Health*.[152]

Christian Science as taught by Mary Baker Eddy and the Basic Unity Teaching as presented by Charles and Myrtle Fillmore treated many of the same spiritual topics.

These included the nature of the divine and human, spiritual truth, the role of Jesus, the power of thought, affirmations and denials, and metaphysical healing. There are some areas of agreement in their teachings. Charles would have agreed with the following statements made by Eddy:

Regarding God as Principle:

- God is the same yesterday, today, and forever. . . . He is unchangeable wisdom and love.[153]

Regarding the Power of Thought:

- As a man thinketh, so is he.[154]

- You must control evil thoughts, or they will control you.[155]

Regarding Death:

- The last enemy to be destroyed.[156]

Regarding Metaphysical Healing:

- [If the practitioner] reaches his patient through divine Love, the healing work will be accomplished in one visit.[157]

Regarding Absent Healing:

- [A practitioner may] heal cases without even having seen the individual.[158]

Regarding Allopathic Medicine:

- Material medicine substitutes drugs for the power of God . . . to heal the body.[159]

On the other hand, Charles would have taken exception to the following statements by Eddy. These are points of view that went to the heart of Eddy's teaching and were probably responsible for Charles' unwillingness to consider himself a Christian Scientist.

Regarding the Nature of God:

- We acknowledge and adore one supreme and infinite God. We acknowledge his son, Christ, and the host or divine Comforter.[160]

- I am strictly a theist, believe in one God, one Christ, the Messiah.[161]

- In your letter you spoke of your "divine self." Where do you find such a selfhood outside of God? . . . You can say your spiritual or God-like self, but divine self includes God, and man is not God.[162]

Regarding Jesus:

- Calvary enabled him to be the mediator, the way-shower between God and man.[163]

Regarding the Indwelling Presence:

- If the Spirit were once within the body, Spirit would be finite, and therefore could not be Spirit.[164]

Regarding Sin and Punishment:

- Divine Science reveals the necessity of suffering, either before or after death, to quench the love of sin. . . . Escape from punishment is not in accordance with God's government.[165]

- It is quite impossible for sinners to receive their full punishment this side of the grave.[166]

Regarding Metaphysical Healing:

- We should understand that the cause of disease obtains in the mortal human mind, and its cure comes from the immortal divine mind.[167]

- [Cures result] from taking up the cross and following Christ in the daily life.[168]

(See Appendix G for a description of Eddy's life and the relation of her work to Unity teaching.)

PHINEAS P. QUIMBY

In the literature of mental healing, Phineas P. Quimby (1802–1866), a native of Belfast, Maine, is considered to have been the originator of the mental-healing movement in the United States. Because of his influence over the work of Mary Baker Eddy, his connection with the work of Warren Felt Evans, and his indirect influence over students of Eddy who taught Charles and Myrtle the techniques of mental healing, including Emma Curtis Hopkins, Quimby is believed to have had an impact on the teaching and healing work of Charles Fillmore. Quimby was a clockmaker, inventor, and a man fully engaged in the scientific spirit of his time. He was one of many mid-nineteenth-century amateurs who became interested in the newly developed techniques of hypnotism and somnambulism, commonly known as Mesmerism. In 1838, at age thirty-six, Quimby learned the techniques from a traveling mesmerist and used them for purposes of mental healing.

Quimby was apparently very successful for many years in doing healing work with clients both locally and at a distance. According to Horatio Dresser, who edited Quimby's papers—Horatio was the son of Quimby students Julius and Annetta Dresser—Quimby recorded his experiences in letters to patients, in essays on disease and healing, and in commentaries on religious questions. These papers remained unpublished throughout the nineteenth century and did not appear until 1921 in published form as *The Quimby Manuscripts*.

Gillian Gill, in her excellent 1998 biography of Mary Baker Eddy, questions the authenticity of Horatio Dresser's editorial work. Gill indicates that Quimby was uneducated and incapable of putting this material into writing.

Gill, a Cambridge University doctorate who has taught at Harvard and Yale, points out that the Quimbyites have never been able to produce originals of Quimby's writings. The Quimby papers—Gill says they don't qualify as manuscripts—were produced by copyists who functioned "as stenographers, copy editors, (or) ghost writers."[169]

Nevertheless, it was on the strength of *The Quimby Manuscripts*, as edited by Dresser, that Quimby has been credited by J. Stillson Judah as "the forefather of mental science healing groups"[170] and by Charles Braden as "the original source of the New Thought movement."[171]

It is ironic that the world probably would have never known Phineas P. Quimby had it not been for the work of his most successful client, Mary Baker Eddy. Ralph W. Major, in *Faiths That Healed*, commented on the probability of Quimby's invisibility:

> Quimby's place in history, despite his great local success, would have been of no more importance than that of scores of successful healers, clairvoyants and magnetizers who flourished at that epoch, had it not been for one famous patient. This lady, unwittingly and certainly unwillingly, has made this niche for him.[172]

Quimby's writings were unavailable to Charles Fillmore when, in 1889, he began publishing *Modern Thought*. He was aware of a claim made in 1887 by Julius A. Dresser that Quimby had originated the modern system of mind healing. The pamphlet, according to Charles, "was very limited in scope and made but little impress upon the great tide of thought that had centered about *Science and Health* by Mary Baker Eddy."[173]

Charles gained greater awareness of the existence of Quimby's teaching in 1895 when a small book entitled *The Philosophy of P. P. Quimby* was published by Annetta Dresser. While the book contained only a short outline of Quimby's teaching, Charles accepted Annetta Dresser's claim that Quimby was the source of the Christian Science doctrines claimed by Mary Baker Eddy and published in her book *Science and Health*. Charles said, "The testimony here presented is so overwhelmingly in favor of Dr. Quimby as the originator of Mental Healing that no unprejudiced mind will for a moment doubt it."[174] Charles concluded from his reading of Dresser that "upon them [Quimby's teachings] were built up a religious sect of gigantic proportions whose literature is found in all parts of the civilized world."[175]

Charles was puzzled by the fact that Quimby's work, which had been completed in the years before his death in 1866, was not available in print for those interested in the literature of metaphysical healing. "Why the truths it contains," Charles said, "have been kept secret from the world these thirty years is a mystery."[176] Had Charles read the Quimby manuscripts and compared them with Eddy's teaching in *Science and Health*, he would have seen basic differences in the teachings.

Quimby's influence over the work of Charles Fillmore is in part based on the assumption that (1) *Science and Health* had a major impact on the development of the Unity Basic Teaching and (2) Mary Baker Eddy's teachings in *Science and Health* are based on the work of Quimby.

Two recent biographers of Mary Baker Eddy, Gilliam Gill and Robert Peel, after studying both *Science and Health* and *The Quimby Manuscripts*, find little similarity in these works. Neither Peel nor Gill agrees with Julius Dresser's assertion that Eddy plagiarized Quimby. Gill comments that there were "only general similarities" between their writings and that "any charge of plagiarism, particularly of the blatant kind . . . could never be upheld." Gill also indicates that Quimby and Eddy operated from different theological positions. "That Mary Baker Eddy's healing theology was based to any large extent on the Quimby manuscripts," Gill indicates, "is not only weak, but largely rigged."[177]

My reading of both *Science and Health* and *The Quimby Manuscripts*, as edited by Horatio Dresser, indicates that Eddy's efforts to change the beliefs of a client is similar in some respects to the approach taken by Quimby. There were major differences in their work—in the theological basis of their teachings and their approach to healing. Mary Baker Eddy remained true to her Calvinist Puritan upbringing, while Quimby rejected the tenets of traditional Christianity. His approach to the Divine was similar to that taken by Ralph Waldo Emerson and the transcendentalists. Eddy based her healing method on the ability of a practitioner to connect with an all-powerful transcendent God. Quimby, who indicated that he belonged to no religion, relied on reason to convince clients that their illness was a product of wrong thinking. Based on the above information, it would be difficult to conclude that Quimby's influence over Charles Fillmore comes through the work of Mary Baker Eddy and Christian Science.

Another group of writers conclude that Quimby's influence on Fillmore came through the writings of Warren Felt Evans. They base their view on the belief that Evans visited Quimby for two purposes: to be healed by him and to learn from him.

Evans himself, in all available published sources, never indicated that he sought relief from his ills by visiting Quimby for mental healing or to incorporate and pass on his teaching. Evans had a high regard for the work of Quimby, acknowledged his successes, and was generous in his praise but never indicated that he personally became a patient of Quimby. Evans commented:

> The late Dr. Quimby of Portland [was] one of the most successful healers of this or any age. . . . By a long succession of the most remarkable cures, effected by psychopathic remedies, [he] at the same time proved the truth of the theory and efficacy of that mode of treatment. Had he lived in a remote age or country, the wonderful facts which occurred in his practice would have now been deemed either mythical or miraculous. He seemed to reproduce the wonders of the Gospel history. But all this was only an exhibition of the force of suggestion, or the action of the law of faith, over a patient in the impressible condition.[178]

Evans, in an interview in 1888 with A. J. Swarts, a dissident former student of Mary Baker Eddy and editor of *Mental Science* magazine, indicated that he visited Quimby not for healing but to find out whether Quimby's healing practices were the same as those he had been using. Swarts reported:

> It is thought by some that he [Evans] formerly worked with P. P. Quimby. This is a mistake. . . . He told me recently that he was passing through Portland nearly twenty-five years ago, [and] that he called upon Dr. Quimby in the United States Hotel to ascertain his methods of treatment, and that he found them to be like those he had employed for some years.[179]

In spite of this testimony, the monographic literature in the field of New Thought indicates that Evans was healed by Quimby during two visits to the Portland metaphysician in 1863 and that, while being treated by Quimby, Evans learned the practice of mental healing. This interpretation is based on the testimony of Julius Dresser, who, as indicated above, studied with Quimby in the 1860s. Dresser asserted that Evans, like Eddy, learned the practice of mental healing from Quimby:

> Dr. Evans obtained his knowledge of Quimby mainly when he visited him as a patient, making two visits for that purpose about the year 1863, an interesting account of which I received from him at East Salisbury in the year 1876. So readily did he understand the explanation of Quimby, which his Swedenborgian faith enabled him to grasp the more quickly that he told Quimby at the second interview that he thought he could cure the sick in this way.[180]

The Dressers' son Horatio, who wrote extensively in the field of New Thought, reported that his father told him that Evans learned healing techniques from Quimby. Horatio Dresser explained:

> The impression I got from my father was that Dr. Evans' Swedenborgian beliefs and philosophical knowledge admirably fitted him to understand Dr. Quimby's theories and methods. It was evidently a case where a word to the wise was sufficient. Hence, Dr. Evans very soon concluded that he could heal in the same ways.[181]

William J. Leonard, author of a short biography of Evans that was published in 1905 in three issues of *Practical Ideals* magazine, relied on this testimony in concluding that Evans was a student of Quimby:

> When Dr. Evans learned the secret of Dr. Quimby's methods, we can easily believe that he was captivated by it, since he had long before come to believe that the healing works of Jesus were wrought through an understanding of mental and spiritual laws. He was there as a patient, Mr. Dresser tells us, but with what benefit to his health we are not told. That he drew out of Dr. Quimby all that he had in him to give with respect to his theories and methods we cannot for a moment doubt.[182]

New Thought commentators in the twentieth century have relied on the testimony of the Dressers to indicate Evans' indebtedness to Quimby. John H. Teahan, professor of religion at Rutgers University, reported:

> Evans suffered from poor health from a very early age. He wrote in 1864 that "my nervous system has been so prostrated that trembling seizes upon me in the performance of the simplest services." Such

chronic disorders prompted him to consult Phineas P. Quimby, who aided Evans in 1863 and 1864. Encouraged by Quimby to begin his own healing practice, Evans opened an office in Boston.[183]

Robert C. Fuller, in *Mesmerism and the American Cure of Souls*, echoed the conclusions of Teahan, Leonard, and the Dressers:

The progressive attenuation of mesmeric healing into a popular philosophy began with the New Thought's pioneer author, Warren Felt Evans. . . . A visit to Quimby in 1863 lifted his internal energies to a higher pitch and simultaneously provided him with a spiritual outlook broad enough to house his restless intellect. Quimby sensed that Evans possessed an above-average capability and encouraged him to set up his own practice of mental medicine.[184]

Fuller expanded upon these observations in 1999 in a profile of Evans written for the *American National Biography*:

In 1863 Evans visited the famed mental healer Phineas P. Quimby in Portland, Maine. Quimby's Mesmerism-based treatments not only cured him, but also provided the empirical evidence in support of a philosophy that advocated the power of mind spirit over matter. . . . Evans' healing practices were based squarely on Quimby's system, which combined mesmerized techniques that Quimby claimed were the true cause of all physical illness. Evans' chief significance is that he progressively developed Quimby's healing system into a distinctive worldview that combined idealistic philosophy, transcendental-inspired mysticism and a pantheism linked with the growing interest in Gnostic or occult interpretations of Christianity.[185]

The New Thought authors Leonard, Teahan, and Fuller appear to have been unaware that Swarts interviewed Evans, as the Swarts interview is not cited in any of their works. It is possible, had they known of Evans' own testimony, they would have been less inclined to rely so heavily on the recollections of Julius Dresser.

Information contained in the journals of Warren Felt Evans indicates that he was practicing mental healing prior to his meeting in 1863 with Quimby.

In a journal entry dated April 1, 1860, at a time when he was still serving as a Methodist minister, he wrote:

> My health is not yet adequate to the full work of this ministry. I long for strength to employ it in the work so dear to my heart. . . . I hope to regain my former power. The Lord is my strength. He is the health of my countenance and my God. I will find in Christ all that I need. He can cure every form of mental disease, and thus restore the body, for disease originates generally, if not always, in the mind.[186]

About one year later, Evans commented, "Through the blessings of God and in answer to prayer, my health is improved. I lay hold upon Christ as my life and as the health of my countenance and my God."[187] A journal entry on March 30, 1862, again shows how he was using mental healing practices:

> I have passed through a painful sickness, and am yet far from being fully restored. I have had some rich experiences of Divine things and some heavenly views. . . . God has given me an earnest spirit of supplication for some days past for restoration to health that I may be made the messenger of good to souls. My soul lives wholly from him and my body forms my soul. Hence in saving the soul he saves the body. That the body should be saved from an abnormal, disorderly condition by faith violates no law of nature, for it is the eternal order of God that faith saves the soul, and the body's life is derived wholly from the vital spirit it encloses.[188]

Another entry on August 11, 1862, again stressed the need for faith in healing:

> There is a faith to which the divine power always responds, "Go in faith, thy faith hath saved thee." With holy violence I laid hold upon Him who has become my salvation. I live because Christ lives. Here is the connection of cause and effect. I no longer live, but Christ liveth in me. I am dead and my life is hid with Christ in God. I feel myself saved—perfectly well, soul, spirit and body. The eleventh day of August [1862] is laid up in everlasting remembrance. From this time forth I live a life of faith. . . . I am saved on this eleventh day of August. All is well. Christ is bringing me up to a higher plane of divine life.[189]

Those who hold to the view that Evans was healed by Quimby and learned mental healing practices from him must be willing to accept the testimony of Julius Dresser. Dresser's discipleship of Quimby calls into question his credibility as an impartial witness—given his actions after the death of Quimby. Gillian Gill, who did research on the life of Dresser while working on her biography of Mary Baker Eddy, gives the following account:

> Following Phineas P. Quimby's death in 1866, Julius Dresser had given up all interest in mental healing. Employed in the 1860s as a journalist in Maine, he later moved to California, where he lived with his wife Annetta and only son Horatio until 1882 or 1883. At this point word of the new successes being reported by Christian Science somehow reached the Dressers, and they dropped everything and came east, fired, according to later New Thought accounts, by the desire to defend the memory and record of P. P. Quimby. And as far as I can see, by the intention to cash in on Mrs. Eddy's success. . . . By the end of 1882 Dresser had apparently decided to take up the mental healing business in earnest, and he saw Mrs. Eddy and her movement as his most dangerous rival in the field. In February 1883, therefore, Julius Dresser for the first time went public with accusations that Mrs. Eddy owed everything to Phineas P. Quimby, airing his views in a letter to the *Boston Post*.[190]

According to Gill, Eddy ultimately filed a complaint that Dresser plagiarized her work, and Dresser and A. J. Arens, another Eddy dissident, filed a countercomplaint in June 1883 arguing that Eddy had plagiarized Quimby's writings. Arens and Dresser did not have proof, as the only documents they could produce did not cover much of the theoretical ground covered in *Science and Health*. In addition, the documents were not written in Quimby's own handwriting but in Dresser's and that of his wife Annetta. Since Arens and Dresser could not present proof of what Quimby had actually written, Mrs. Eddy won her suit, and the defendants were forced to pay costs.[191]

It would be reasonable to assume that, if Dresser was attempting to discredit Eddy, so that Quimby could be seen as the founder of the mental healing movement in the United States, he might also have found it necessary to portray Evans as a student of Quimby and a proponent of his teachings. What better way to remove the credit from Evans, given the extent and popularity of Evans' writings in the late nineteenth century both in the United States and abroad?

A more accurate assessment of the origins of the mental healing movement was made by A. J. Swarts, who credited both Evans and Quimby. Swarts surmised that this movement, "in its modern development, originated with these two men, and that it is difficult to say which practiced it first."[192]

Assuming that Evans was as responsible as Quimby for the origins of the mental healing movement in the United States, the influence of Phineas P. Quimby on the teaching and healing work of Charles Fillmore cannot be traced through the writings of Warren Felt Evans.

Chapter 5

CHARLES, THE JESUS CHRIST STANDARD, AND NEW THOUGHT

INTRODUCTION

"New Thought" was the term used to describe the nineteenth-century metaphysical movement in which mental healing was the key feature. New Thought had its origins in the teachings of Emanuel Swedenborg, Franz Anton Mesmer, Ralph Waldo Emerson, Warren Felt Evans, Phineas P. Quimby, and Emma Curtis Hopkins.[1] Those who came to consider themselves as "New Thoughters," as they were sometimes called, might have at one time identified themselves with Liberal Christianity, Swedenborgianism, transcendentalism, theosophy, spiritualism, Christian Science, or the religions and philosophies of the East. They might also have used such terms as "Mental Science," "Mind Cure," "Practical Metaphysics," or "Divine Science" to describe their work.[2] New Thoughters were united in the belief that the inner or real self of men and women is divine.[3] They dissented from the common Christian view that men and women, though created in the image and likeness of God, did not share God's divine nature.[4]

UNITY AND THE ORGANIZATION OF THE NEW THOUGHT FEDERATION

Those who accepted New Thought ideas in the late nineteenth century in the United States were a disparate group, and no one organization on the regional or national scene met their needs. An organization called the International Metaphysical League, which attempted to serve as a clearinghouse, held conventions in various large cities in the 1890s, but it disappeared from the scene before the turn of the century. An attempt to organize at the national level did not begin in earnest until 1903. A Chicago group that called itself the Union New Thought Committee served as a catalyst. This committee, comprising representatives from several New Thought centers in Chicago, decided to bring together representatives from all New Thought organizations worldwide for the purpose of establishing a federation of like-minded groups.[5] Invitations went out to all individuals and organizations that engaged in mental healing, including Unity.

In addition to bringing groups together to discuss common goals and to receive inspiration from one another, one of the principal objectives of the meeting was to form an organization that served the needs of the member groups on an ongoing basis. Charles and Myrtle Fillmore, along with two members of their staff, Charles Edgar Prather and Jennie Croft, traveled to Chicago to attend the "International New Thought Convention," which was held November 17–20, 1903. Both Fillmores were on the program and presented papers. In response to the question "What Is New Thought?" the convention adopted a statement that, except for references to the role of Jesus, reflected the Fillmores' thinking on the nature of God and man. The statement read as follows:

- God—Universal Spirit, Mind, Principle, is omnipresent, omniscient, and omnipotent.

- Man is the individual expression of God, possessing inherently and capable of manifesting all the aspects of God.

- Man unfolds to a constantly expanding consciousness and manifestation of these aspects through right thinking and right living.

- The consciousness of harmony is Heaven, here and now, in the realization of which abide peace of mind and health of body.[6]

A committee was formed to discuss organizational issues and draft a resolution for the formation of a New Thought Federation. The resolution was presented for approval at the 1904 convention in St. Louis, October 25–28. The Fillmores were pleased with the results of the Chicago convention and believed that a federation of New Thought organizations was a positive step. In the December 1903 issue, *Unity* magazine commented:

Through experience it was found that the method of one would not, and could not, fulfill the ideals of another, yet permeating all were the same basic principles of universal law. Instead, then, of an organization with a creed or doctrine of its own, to which many could not fully subscribe, it was found that co-operation or federation, regardless of method or creed, was the one thing necessary for the proper advancement of the movement as a whole.[7]

The Fillmores returned to Kansas City believing that their work and that of the other soon-to-be members of the New Thought Federation had been very productive. *Unity* magazine reported that "Unity staff, consisting of Charles Fillmore, Myrtle Fillmore, Jennie H. Croft, and Charles E. Prather, returned to their several posts of duty filled with enthusiasm over the good accomplished by this gathering together of the exponents of so many different phases of the New Thought."[8]

The major work of the 1904 convention in St. Louis was the adoption of the constitution of the New Thought Federation and the appointment of a board of directors and officers. Article II spelled out the purposes of the federation:

> The purposes of the Federation are: To promote the better and wider knowledge and appreciation of the unity of all life, and to assist in the manifestation of this unity by means of cooperation, to stimulate faith in, and study of, the higher nature of man in its relation and application to health, happiness and character; to foster the New Thought movement in general; to publish such literature as may be found advisable.[9]

It was further indicated that membership in the organization did not require individuals or groups either to alter or give up their teaching. It was further explained, "In accomplishing these purposes, the Federation in nowise shall interfere with, infringe upon or be responsible for the teachings and interpretations of affiliating individuals or organizations."[10]

Charles' approval of the goals, purposes, and operating procedures of the federation was further indicated when he accepted appointment as a member of the board of directors of the new entity. Unity's participation in the activities of the New Thought Federation appears to have resulted in an increased involvement with New Thought groups in Kansas City. In November 1904,

Unity magazine reported that a "Union New Thought Service" was held at the Athenaeum Hall. Those who participated included, in addition to Charles, Henry Harrison Brown, president of the New Thought Federation, who was visiting from San Francisco; and Dr. D. L. Sullivan, vice president of the federation and a resident of Kansas City. *Unity* further reported that, "much interest is being taken in higher thought" and all New Thought centers in Kansas City are "working together in love and harmony."[11]

In March 1905, *Unity* reported on the opening of the New Thought Center in Cleveland, stating, "Unity extends congratulations and blessings to this new society and affirms unbounded success of the work." The magazine further reported that "the New Thought movement is gaining strength and power and new centers are being organized on all sides."[12]

Unity played a significant part in the 1905 convention of the newly formed New Thought Federation, for it helped to organize the meeting that was held from September 26 to September 29 in the small town of Nevada, Missouri, not far from Kansas City. As the convention drew to a close, *Unity*'s associate editor, Jennie Croft, in the October issue, reported on the benefits many people derived from attending:

> Thus closed the most successful convention in the history of the Federation, successful from every standpoint. The spirit of unity, harmony and love was most noticeable, and the enthusiasm awakened among the members to go home to work for the cause was marked.[13]

UNITY'S WITHDRAWAL FROM THE NEW THOUGHT FEDERATION

As 1905 drew to a close, Charles Fillmore began to harbor reservations about the desirability of Unity's continued participation in the New Thought Federation. In a long article, titled "New Thought: A Second Explanatory Lesson," in *Unity* magazine, Charles expressed his misgivings. He was primarily concerned about the contradictions he saw in the teachings, all of which were classified as "New Thought":

> New Thought is the common denominator of a complex and often contradictory mass of metaphysical doctrines which have sprung up

in the past few years. . . . What may be termed the Mental Science School holds that God is not a being of Love and Wisdom, but a force of attraction. They repudiate the Loving father proclaimed by Jesus Christ and hold that man is the highest form of self-consciousness in the universe.[14]

A basic problem, Charles indicated, was that many people who branded themselves as New Thoughters lacked discrimination in spiritual matters, as evidenced by the leaders they followed:

A large number of New Thoughters are not using spiritual discrimination nor spiritual independence, but are following the way pointed out by some enthusiastic half-truth discoverer. Thus there are sharp divisions based upon different understandings of the expositions of the Divine Law in New Thought circles.[15]

He found that disagreement existed even among New Thought people with a Christian orientation and expressed disappointment that common ground had not been reached:

There is another class of New Thought people who accept Christianity in its true sense and try to live up to the teachings of Jesus Christ. . . . There are a number of schools, passing under the general name of New Thought, that adhere to this Christian interpretation, yet even among them there are minor differences. Each teacher tinges with his mental bias the philosophy he promulgates. Not one seems yet to have attained that place where the revelation from the Spirit of Truth, promised by Jesus to his followers, is wholly transparent. For this reason disciples are never safe in accepting the teachings of any school as final.[16]

Moreover, people who were being introduced to New Thought teachings for the first time should be warned that much effort would be required to discover "the unadulterated truth." He continued:

It will be seen that the New Thought student has a broad field to select from, also that he should have his eyes open in order that he may know to choose the truth from the great mass of matter labeled as "New Thought."[17]

Finally, Charles admitted he had concluded that, in many respects, Unity teaching differed from that of other New Thought leaders and schools. As a result, he found it difficult to be an active participant in the work of the New Thought Federation:

> So far as the Society of Practical Christianity (the local Unity society in Kansas City) is concerned we must candidly say that its teachings differ widely from those of the majority of New Thought doctrines, and we do not feel at home in the average gathering under that name, although we try to harmonize with all truth seekers.[18]

Possibly as a result of his growing disenchantment with the group, Charles left the board of the federation. His name no longer appeared in 1906 on the roster of its board members.[19] While Charles expressed reservations about the desirability of Unity's continued participation in the federation, no decision was made to pull back in 1905. When it came time for the annual New Thought Convention to be held in Chicago, October 23–26, 1906, Unity students were encouraged to participate. *Unity* magazine suggested, "All who can, should attend and let their friends know. These are all speakers who are too well known to need any introduction, and you are sure of a treat."[20]

Charles and Myrtle attended the Chicago convention, along with other Unity staff. Charles' continuing reservations about the work of the federation were reflected in comments made in the December 1906 issue of *Unity* magazine after the adjournment of the convention. His principal complaint concerned the content of the teaching being presented under the "New Thought" label. A large percentage of the subject matter, he reported, "was far from New Thought as I understand it."[21] He also took issue with many of the teachings that were presented and could not defend them to Unity students:

> Quite a number of people who had taken our lessons last year asked me if I endorsed certain doctrines set forth by some of the speakers. I had to admit that I did not, yet they were accepted by the officials of the Convention without protest or explanation, and those unfamiliar with absolute Truth would naturally take for granted that they were New Thought teachings.[22]

The proceedings at the 1906 Chicago convention, Charles wrote, convinced him that he could no longer proceed under the "New Thought" label. The teachings were too far removed from "the Truth" as he saw it: "It dawned upon me that the name 'New Thought' has been appropriated by so many cults that had new theories to promulgate, that it has ceased to express what I conceived to be Absolute Truth."[23] Thus, it is not surprising, given his disillusionment, that Unity withdrew from the New Thought Federation. Charles defended the decision in the same article:

> The New Thought Federation is attempting to carry this load of thought diversity, and I can see no success in it. There are too many lines of thought to harmonize. When I hear what, to me, is rank error set forth by New Thought speakers, I protest and say, "If this is New Thought, then I must find a new name for my philosophy." In the face of these facts I have decided that I am no longer a New Thoughter. I have a standard of faith, which is true and logical, and I must conform to it in my teaching without compromise. We call it Practical Christianity, and under this name we shall henceforth do our work. [24]

In an editorial note in the January 1907 issue of *Unity*, Charles elaborated further on the misconceptions he perceived in the people who had enrolled as members of the federation. The principal difficulty, he said, was that many failed to accept "statements of truth" because they had not yet reached a high enough level of spiritual consciousness:

> What I saw as a hopeless task was the attempt to unify so many lines of individual thought, the basis of which was not in the absolute, but the relative, and must therefore always be disintegrating. There is but one foundation upon which we can have a permanent federation, and that is the One Absolute Mind. From that Mind, statements of truth can be formulated that will be accepted by all who are functioning in the top brain, where the super-consciousness has its seat of action. Those in whom the tide of life flows no higher than intellectual perception will not rise to this consciousness of the Absolute, hence we cannot expect them to accept its basis of the origin of things.[25]

Charles then restated a long-held belief that only those who committed their lives to the regeneration of the body could achieve advanced levels of spiritual consciousness. He was confident that more and more people would commit themselves to this ideal and that over time a sizable number would reach this advanced state. He continued in the same editorial:

> Only those who think purely and act virtuously in all ways, conserving the vitalities of mind and body, can rise and stay in the top brain, hence we may not get together a very large convention in the beginning, but it will come, and be a permanent federation of men who are truly seeking unselfishly to do the will of God.[26]

For several years after 1907, the pages of *Unity* magazine contained no information on the activities of the New Thought Federation or regarding its annual conventions. In April 1913, *Weekly Unity* broke the silence with the following announcement: "We are requested to announce that the New Thought Convention, to be held at Detroit, has changed the date of opening to June 16. We make this announcement for the information of our readers and not as a matter in which we are directly interested."[27] *Weekly Unity* then restated the position Unity had taken regarding its involvement in the activities of the New Thought Federation, again indicating that contradictions in the New Thought teaching had caused Unity to refrain from further participation:

> A number of years ago we decided that the holding of the New Thought conventions was unprofitable, and our views have not changed. Our work has grown much faster since we decided to stay at home and attend to it, and we are satisfied that the energy put into conventions would bring far greater returns to the cause, and the individuals concerned, if we expended it in local fields. Besides, the mass of contradictory statements presented at such gatherings is confusing the public as to the true character of the doctrines for which we stand.[28]

In April 1916, *Unity* magazine, in an editorial note presumably written by Charles, expressed misgivings about the current direction of the New Thought movement. Reference was also made to an earlier and happier time in the history of the movement when there was more general agreement on the content of the teaching:

> There was a time in the history of what is called New Thought when it had a standard of principles that were universally accepted by

its teachers. These principles were the expression of mind that had been illuminated by the inspiration of the untrammeled I Am. But there was neither head nor organization to New Thought, and of later years it has become a Babylon of voices crying in the wilderness. The name has been adopted by every kind of new doctrine, and has almost wholly lost the spiritual significance for which its early students regarded it. So do not take for granted that the name "New Thought" represents any defined spiritual doctrine.[29]

UNITY AND THE INTERNATIONAL NEW THOUGHT ALLIANCE

Three years later, in November 1919, with no prior indication that Unity's position had shifted regarding New Thought, it was announced that Unity had rejoined the International New Thought Alliance (the name the New Thought Federation had adopted in the interim) and that the I.N.T.A.'s Congress in 1919 would be held in Kansas City under Unity sponsorship. In a brief note entitled "Unity and the International New Thought Alliance," presumably written by Charles but not identified as such, the background of Unity's involvement was briefly traced:

> Early in the organization of I.N.T.A., Unity was active in its movements and represented in its program. However, as time went on, certain ideas were introduced into the Alliance which, from our point of view, were not in keeping with the Christ message, and we therefore withdrew from the organization.[30]

The note further indicated that officials of the I.N.T.A. had been striving to make the organization acceptable to Unity: "During the last few years there have been those in the Alliance who sought untiringly to eliminate from their programs and practices those things which had, in a sense, placed a stigma upon the name New Thought."[31] The result of these efforts was an acknowledgment that Christ was the head of the New Thought movement and its "invisible inspiration and guide." This was made official in 1919 by the action of the I.N.T.A. in its Cincinnati congress by the adoption of "Bulletin 17," which stated:

The universe is spiritual and we are spiritual beings. This is the Christ message to the twentieth century, and it is a message not so much of words but of works. To attain this, however, we must be clean, honest and trustworthy, and uphold the Christ standard in all things. Let us build our house upon this rock, and nothing can prevail against it. This is the vision and mission of the Alliance.[32]

Thus, based on I.N.T.A.'s action in adopting "the Jesus Christ Standard," Unity agreed to rejoin the alliance. In so doing, however, it was acknowledged that Unity was still not in agreement with a number of the teachings that were classified as "New Thought." The note continued:

The entrance of Unity into the New Thought Alliance does not mean that Unity endorses everything which has been and is now being taught under the name of New Thought. There are yet teachers who are giving forth ideas which are entirely inconsistent with the principles of Truth. Our action in this connection does indicate, however, that Unity believes in the spirit activating the International New Thought Alliance at this time, and that we propose to support this spirit in every way possible.[33]

The I.N.T.A. conference held in Kansas City, September 19–23, 1920, came off exceedingly well, from Unity's point of view. *Unity* magazine used words of high praise to characterize the proceedings and the impact of Unity's participation.

It is impossible for us to convey in words of exultation of spirit, the democratic camaraderie, the lovely accord which characterized all the proceedings of the Seventh International New Thought Alliance Congress. And why not this beautiful harmony? The spirit of the living Christ, active in all the business deliberations, the lectures, and the speeches, proved as ever, when invoked, a great, loving, brooding, harmonizing presence. . . . It is not too much to assume that the Unity spirit, which we have been cultivating at this center for years, came to perfect fruition at this Congress.[34]

The key to the success of the event, from the Unity perspective, was the emphasis placed on the role of Jesus Christ in the work of the I.N.T.A. The magazine reported:

The dominant note sounded by all the speakers was "conformity with the Christ standard." As the week went on and the sessions continued, one could in one's mind's eye see that gleaming banner, far-flung to the nations, inviting the weary, the disconsolate, the wretched, into the pure white light of the Christ self.[35]

It was considered remarkable that such a widely diverse group could join in acknowledgment of "the Jesus Christ Standard":

> It must be remembered that most of the different cults of the New Thought movement were represented at the Congress. Yet Jew, Gentile, Divine Scientist, Mental Scientist, Episcopal minister in the Immanuel movement, a pastor of the Universalist Church, even those who have been taught to heal by suggestion—these all proclaimed themselves as followers of the Jesus Christ standard as set by Unity over thirty years ago! Glory to His holy name.[36]

The relationship between Unity School of Christianity and the I.N.T.A. continued on a high note in 1921. The I.N.T.A. Congress held in Denver, July 17–24, 1921, was equally successful as that held under Unity sponsorship in Kansas City in 1920. After the convention, Charles, in remarks made at Unity headquarters to the Unity School staff and later published in the magazine *Unity* under the title "About the International New Thought Convention," gave his personal assessment of the progress that had been made as a result of Unity's involvement with the I.N.T.A. He explained:

> Many of you know that two years ago the Unity School here at Kansas City, through its President, decided to join the Alliance, and last year the Congress met at Kansas City.[37] . . . Many of our people thought we were getting along very well, and that it would be better not to go into any by-paths or make alliances with other movements so long as we were growing so rapidly. But we have always been classed with what is broadly termed the New Thought movement, and our sympathies have been with them in the advanced religious ideas which they are advocating. Consequently, when at the Cincinnati convention they adopted what is called the Jesus Christ Standard, we felt that we could no longer refuse to cooperate with them. As some of you doubtless know, in this move we have had to meet situations that

were not altogether harmonious, but on the whole, we are pleased to report that our work with them has been satisfactory, and that the fundamental doctrine for which we all stand is being furthered and more freely accepted by people everywhere as a result of our cooperation.[38]

Charles was particularly impressed by the spirit of cooperation that existed at the Congress and the goodwill that existed among all the participants. His remarks continued:

The peace, harmony, and love of the Christ Spirit were so apparent at the various meetings that many of the speakers commented on it. Lecturers and teachers representing every branch of New Thought were present, but the doctrines they set forth did not conflict in the least, and it was universally conceded that there had never been such perfect harmony at any convention before. This was proof that the Christ Spirit was present, and that we were working according to Divine Principle.[39]

Charles wrote that the convention in Denver was particularly successful because of the stress that had been placed on spiritual healing and was particularly pleased with the way convention presenters had addressed the subject, stating:

Unusual attention was given at this Congress to the practical application of public healing. Every meeting closed with healing demonstrations. . . . No attempt was made in these meetings to stimulate the emotional nature, and thereby get temporary results, as is the rule in most faith healing gatherings. Appeal was made directly to the understanding and realization of the truth that health is man's normal condition, and by having faith in the one omnipresent Life, Love, Substance Power, and Intelligence, man can come into such close relations with the source of health that he may be instantly restored. This feature of the Alliance is to be more fully brought out in future congresses.[40]

Finally, Charles also expressed pleasure with changes that had been made in the constitution of the alliance and expressed his belief that the I.N.T.A. would be even stronger if the word *Christian* were added to its name:

Quite a few changes were made in the constitution of the Alliance, and an open acknowledgement of Jesus Christ as the head of the movement, and the New Testament as its textbook was incorporated. The matter of adding the word "Christian" to the official name of the Alliance was brought up in the Plans Committee meeting, but it was decided to postpone the question until next year. Of course the Unity people thought that the word "Christian" added to the name of the Alliance would be notice to the world that it was a Christian organization.[41]

WITHDRAWAL FROM THE INTERNATIONAL NEW THOUGHT ALLIANCE

With no advanced warning and just five months after Charles' statement indicating that the Unity–I.N.T.A. relationship was flourishing, Unity, on March 22, 1922, withdrew from the International New Thought Alliance. The announcement that appeared in *Unity* magazine under the headline "Unity Withdraws From I.N.T.A." was short and gave few details as to the reasons for the action:

On March 7, 1922, a special meeting was called to consider the relationship of the Unity School of Practical Christianity with the International New Thought Alliance. Our directors, department heads and teachers were in attendance. It was unanimously voted, that, on account of the many protests received from our students against our membership in the I.N.T.A; and owing to the fact that the present methods of the Alliance make it virtually another metaphysical school rather than an association of schools, thereby rendering it impracticable for the Unity School to give time and support to it, the Unity School of Christianity resigned from the Alliance, the resignation to take effect at once.[42]

The brief announcement did not satisfy Unity students, and many wrote to the school asking for more information. Charles, in responding, acknowledged that the school had hoped to avoid a full disclosure, stating that "it had not been our intention to give publicly all the causes of the withdrawal from I.N.T.A."[43] The desire for more details on the part of Unity readers convinced him that it was necessary to provide a fuller explanation. Charles listed as a primary reason the I.N.T.A.'s refusal to add the word *Christian* to its name:

> The Unity School has from the beginning stood for certain religious ideals which the New Thought people have not adopted. We have proclaimed Jesus Christ as the head of our work, and have so notified the world by putting the word "Christian" into the name of our organization. This the I.N.T.A. has refused to do, although it claims to carry out Christian principles. When we advocated a change of name to include the word "Christian" the proposal was quickly hushed up in the executive board meeting. The argument was that, although I.N.T.A. was a Christian movement, it should not put anything in its name to antagonize non-Christians who might otherwise be induced to join.[44]

Second, Charles listed the I.N.T.A.'s refusal to adopt Unity teachings regarding the regeneration of the body. As a result, he felt Unity was hampered in presenting to the world the correct view of physical death and the afterlife:

> Unity teaches that the eternal life taught and demonstrated by Jesus is not gained by dying, but by refining the body until it becomes the undying habitation of the soul. This refinement of the body requires the renunciation of certain sense habits and appetites, such as the lust for meat, tobacco, stimulants, sex, coarse dances, and all pleasures that exalt sense above soul. Unity teaches that to gain the spiritual life man must sacrifice the animal life. "He that loseth his life for my sake shall find it." New Thought people do not advocate the renunciation of sense life in order to gain eternal life. They teach that man goes on to higher fields of action by dying. We hold that Christianity, rightly understood, teaches a science by which life can be attained here and now, and that dying is a loss instead of a gain.[45]

Because of these problems, he had concluded that only by being free from the New Thought connection could Unity properly put forth these teachings:

> Unity has certain ideals to carry forward, and it must have the greatest freedom in presenting them because they are revolutionary, and some of them, like eternal life here and now in the body, apparently visionary and beyond attainment. But these ideas are capable

of attainment, and admitted by progressive philosophers in various fields of physical science. Unity people are aiming to demonstrate these ideals, although the ideas may appear to be beyond present human achievement. . . . The Unity School found that it was hampered in the expression of its ideals through its intimate association with New Thought.[46]

Moreover, rather than being truly committed to it, the I.N.T.A. gave only lip service to "the Jesus Christ Standard," never fully accepting it as part of I.N.T.A. teaching:

We cooperated with the I.N.T.A. when that organization agreed to the Jesus Christ Standard, but we found that their concept of that standard was not ours, and they insisted that we should cooperate on the interpretation which they give to the ideas which we are working out. This hampered us instead of helped us. We must all in the end be set free, and Unity has declared its freedom from all organizations that advocate anything less than the highest idealism of Jesus.[47]

In his lengthy explanation, he also noted that confusion and consternation were experienced at Unity centers in the field when I.N.T.A. members were granted a forum at these centers and then presented teachings that contradicted those of Unity School:

New Thought requested the open platform at all Unity centers for its field lectures, because Unity was a member of the I.N.T.A. When this was granted and the lecturers opposed, as they nearly always did, the plain teachings of Jesus on these points, the congregations were confused and often dismayed at the apparent change of doctrine at the Unity center. It then required continued explanation and much effort on the part of Unity teachers to clear up points on which the two schools differed.[48]

Finally, Charles was particularly dismayed because, after Unity joined the I.N.T.A., the organization shifted its focus from being a federation of like-minded organizations to a school espousing a doctrine that on many points contradicted Unity teachings. As a result, a cooperative relationship devolved into a competitive one:

The I.N.T.A. directors are doubtless not aware of it, but they are making the Alliance another school of New Thought people, instead of a federation of schools that already exists. We were continually urged by the I.N.T.A. to cooperate in building up their school, which was working along lines parallel with Unity, yet so different in many respects that we did not harmonize with them. We see that the demand for a New Thought School has so crystallized around the I.N.T.A. that it will continue in spirit to be a school instead of an alliance of schools.... We have no objection whatever to the institution, but we do object to its trying at the same time to be a federation of institutions.... This and similar methods were pulling right away from the idea of a federation of schools for mutual benefit, causing many of our centers to complain of I.N.T.A. competition, instead of cooperation which we had expected.[49]

Unity's withdrawal from the I.N.T.A. in 1922 apparently ended official contact with the organization. In the two decades preceding World War II, Unity publications carried little information on I.N.T.A. activities. In October 1923, in a piece in *Unity* magazine, Charles emphasized the distancing from other New Thought groups when he declared, "We were also classed as New Thought people, Mental Scientists, and Theosophists, and so on, but none of these sufficiently emphasized the higher attributes of man, and we avoided any close affiliation with them."[50]

While most of the statements in the public record concerning Unity's relationship with New Thought groups were made by Charles, Myrtle evidently held views similar to his. Her thinking on the subject of New Thought was revealed in a letter written in 1928 to a Mrs. Kramer. Myrtle advised the woman, who apparently had involved herself with New Thought teachings, to let go of her attachment to ineffective teachings and devote herself to the teachings of Jesus. In her characteristically direct and forthright manner, Myrtle suggested:

Instead of thinking and saying "New Thought," would it not be better for you to think and speak of "God Thought"? It is not "New Thought," it is thought which is founded in the unchanging spiritual reality. "New Thought" lets one in for all sorts of conjectures and experiments and isms. To identify one's self with "New Thought" is to open the mind to the winds and waves of the race thought which is being built up. While to identify one's self with the Jesus Christ Standard of thinking which is made known in the individual's mind and heart through the action of the Holy Spirit, keeps one poised and freed and filled with Light.[51]

In the late 1930s, Charles, at a board meeting of Unity ministers, again restated the principal reasons for Unity's final departure from the I.N.T.A. The meetings recorder paraphrased Charles' remarks, commenting:

> Mr. Fillmore mentioned that in 1920 the Unity ministry in Kansas City joined the I.N.T.A. and soon after that they were invited to Kansas City for their meeting, but it was discovered that members of the organization were teaching ideas entirely opposite from what Unity teaches. . . . Also, certain (I.N.T.A.) members felt they should be allowed to present their teachings from Unity platforms. For this reason the Unity work in Kansas City immediately withdrew its membership from I.N.T.A.[52]

The recorder then appears to have quoted directly from Charles, who summed up his views, indicating:

> Since we have chosen the Unity way, it is our duty to stay true to the Jesus Christ teachings. . . . We should become so strong in our definite presentation of the Jesus Christ message that eventually all those leaders who are associated with I.N.T.A. will see this clearly.[53]

This last remark clearly reflects Charles' long-held hope that New Thought would ultimately incorporate into its teachings the Unity interpretation of the Jesus Christ message.

Chapter 6

REGENERATING THE
HUMAN BODY

The purpose of Charles' teachings—and why that teaching has been called "Practical Christianity"—was to demonstrate spiritual truth. Charles bluntly declared, "The object of Man's existence is to demonstrate the Truth of Being."[1] Charles was convinced that the time had come for men and women to realize the power of connecting with the divine within. He said, "The world is ready for demonstrations. The people are eagerly looking for those who can *prove* in actual works, the presence of the indwelling spirit."[2]

Charles Fillmore dedicated his life to demonstrating spiritual truth through bodily regeneration. He was convinced that, by applying the spiritual practices contained in the Basic Unity Teachings and the Twelve Powers doctrine, the cells of the human body could be renewed, body parts regenerated, youth restored, and illness overcome. In addition, it would no longer be necessary for humans to pass through physical death.

Charles was thirty-five years of age when he began the quest to regenerate his own body. At that time, he continued to suffer from the effects of a childhood leg injury. He testified that he was "a bodily wreck"[3] and still a "chronic invalid and seldom free from pain."[4] Believing now that bodily regeneration was possible, the first body part he sought to regenerate was his shortened leg. In a 1936 radio interview, he explained, "When I began to study what Jesus taught in the Bible about God as the source of life and health, I had faith that I could be healed"[5] and reported that, after he began the inner work, within a short time, he began to see progress:

I began to apply the healing principle to my own case with gratifying results. My chronic pains ceased and my hip healed and grew stronger and my leg lengthened until in a few years I could dispense with the steel extension that I had worn since I was a child.[6]

In 1898, in an article published in *Unity* magazine, Charles wrote that patience was required and that, while he had made significant progress, regeneration of the body required spiritual work over a significant period of time:

I am sure that I have made tremendous strides in spiritual unfoldment during the last ten years, yet the physical has not testified to the large degree which it surely will when the inner vibrations reach the outer crust, which is the flesh. There are various phases of spiritual and mental growth. Some people keep their thoughts centered on health, youth, beauty, money, things of this world generally, which quickens that mind that moves these ephemeral things to action and they get demonstrations according to their desires. Others go deeper and build from the center in integrity of character. This requires a reconstruction of the whole mental man and takes much longer to show forth in outward demonstration than health, youth, prosperity. This is the royal road that Jesus trod.[7]

In an interview in 1902 with Charles Brodie Patterson, editor of the well-respected metaphysical magazine *Mind*, Charles, now age forty-eight, reported major improvement:

The gradual healing of this diseased limb, and its growth to nearly normal size during the last ten years, has been to me, at least, one of the strongest proofs of the power of metaphysical treatment, especially in view of the fact that the physicians who attended me as a boy prophesied that when I reached the age of forty I would undoubtedly be a helpless cripple in a wheel-chair.[8]

He explained to Patterson the mental practice he employed to regenerate not only his diseased limb but his entire body, continuing:

I am transforming, through mental dynamics, the cells of my whole body, the ultimate of which will be immortality in the flesh. I have discovered that all the ganglion centres in the organism are in reality brains, who think thoughts in a measure independent of the central thinker, whose seat of action is usually confined to the head. In order to control these various brains I have found it necessary to project into them my conscious thought and fill them so full of true ideas that there is no room for the false. This task has not been a light one, and I have spent years in silent willing, denying and affirming, actually rebuilding every cell in my organism from centre to circumference. I would say that in this work I have been guided by an invisible intelligence, which I call the Holy Spirit. I have also found that the whole process is symbolically outlined in the life of Jesus Christ, and is what is technically called *regeneration.*[9]

A year later, in 1903, Charles described the actions he had taken to turn back the aging process. He reported:

About three years ago the belief in old age began to take hold of me. I was nearing the half century mark. I began to get wrinkled and gray, my knees tottered, and a great weakness came over me. I did not discern the cause at once but I found in my dreams I was associating with old people, and it gradually dawned on me that I was coming into this phase of race belief. Then I went to work with a vim. I repudiated the whole world of old age and decrepitude. I denied them any place in my mentality. I spent hours and hours silently affirming my unity with the Infinite Energy of the One True God. I absolutely refused to sympathize with old people in any way. I associated with the young, I danced with the boys, sang "coon" songs with them and for a time took on the thoughtless kid. In this way I "switched" the old age current of thought. Then I went deep down within my body and talked to the inner life centres. I told them with firmness and decision that I should never submit to the old age devil—that I was determined never to give in and that they might just as well give up first as last. Gradually I felt a new life current coming up from the Life Center. It was a faint little stream at first, and months went by before I got it to the surface. Now it is growing strong by leaps and bounds. My cheeks have filled out, the wrinkles and "crow feet" are gone, and I actually feel like the boy that *I am.* "God is not the God of the dead, but of the living."[10]

Four years later, in 1907, Charles, now past fifty, reported continuing progress in regenerating his leg:

> Through spiritual realization the leg has gradually lengthened, until now it is less than two inches short, and its shrunken muscles and flesh have been restored. I know this spiritual power will make it perfectly whole, although as men count time, I am over a half century in this body.[11]

In 1913, Charles again described the spiritual practice he engaged in to regenerate his body and the results that he observed:

> In my own case I can testify to a gradual physical renewal. I can feel the new life coursing through my nerves in living streams of energy. The energy I have learned to direct to the various organs of the body, and through daily practice of thought concentration I am renewing both mind and body. My skin is getting pink, as in youth, and my gray hair is changing at its roots to its natural color. I am satisfied that I shall overcome the disintegration of my organs and finally conquer death. As men count years I am nearly sixty, but I have for the past twenty years lived so constantly in the thought of perpetual life that I have no consciousness of loss of force or body energy.[12]

In 1920, Fillmore was sixty-six years old. He was not looking as young as he once did. When he observed his outer countenance, through pictures or looking into a mirror, he acknowledged that the cells of his outer body did not appear to be regenerating. He was disturbed by what he saw. He told himself, however, that his inner self was growing younger:

> The Spirit showed me several years ago that I must quit having my picture taken; that I must quit looking into the mirror and seeing myself as a murky imagination had formed me. I had within me the concept of a fine looking young man, but when I looked into the glass, or when I had my picture taken, he did not appear. And other people did not see him and they began to impress me with the thought of what they did see, and I had to meet the adversary of error both within and without. But I had a most vivid ideal of the character of the real man within and I am striving in all ways to bring him into visibility. I feel the vigor and life of youth in the inner man,

and claim day in and day out that I am young, strong, vigorous and free. But, if I should drop down for a single day to the consideration of myself as I appear, I would lose my grasp on that spiritual soul that is expanding and growing within me.[13]

Charles' concern for overcoming the death of his body was again expressed in 1924, when he indicated his faith in the teachings of Jesus as an important element in his spiritual work:

My body is not disintegrating. Why not? Because I am believing in God's life in me; I am affirming that life. I know that if I follow Jesus Christ in this respect I shall overcome death. I know that it is incumbent upon me to enter into the realization of the eternal life of the body and to teach the world that it is possible to overcome the great and last enemy, death.[14]

In a letter written to a friend in 1928, Myrtle Fillmore told how, through spiritual practice, Charles had overcome deafness in one ear:

Mr. Fillmore was once deaf in his right ear. And as soon as he saw that the life and intelligence in him was very active, and responsive to the direction of his mind, he began to work with his ears. He would give his undivided attention to God, and open his mind and hold it receptive to the ideas which he felt God had for him. He would declare that he was hearing mentally, through his ears. He would think of the abundant life which was flowing up from his life center and heart, through the glands of his neck, and into his ears. He would mentally see this life stream stimulating the nerves and cells there, and setting them into action. And one day, there was a great throbbing, and a rush of wax thrown out of his ear. And his hearing has been perfect ever since.[15]

One year later, Myrtle, in another letter to a longtime correspondent, indicated that Charles had still more work to do to heal his injured leg. In response to her friend's request that the Fillmores make a visit to California, Myrtle explained:

I have tried, ever so many times, to get him to join me in a lovely trip somewhere. But the dear man just doesn't like to get out among crowds; and really feels that he'd better wait until he has completed

his demonstration of healing his leg before going out, either for lecture work or pleasure.[16]

That same year, 1929, Charles, at age seventy-five, was asked by Unity
students, "Does Charles Fillmore expect to live forever?" His response indicated that he was still fully committed to regenerating his body and continuing to do the inner work:

> Because I have emphasized the eternal-life-in-the-body teaching of
> Jesus, the question is often asked by Unity readers. Some of them
> seem to think that I am either a fanatic or a joker if I take myself seri-
> ously in the hope that I shall with Jesus attain eternal life in the body.
> But the fact is that I am very serious about the matter and am striving
> earnestly to follow Jesus in the regeneration, which I am satisfied will
> result in a transformation of my body. I am renewing my mind and,
> at the same time, working out body transformation. As I study and
> apply the words of Jesus I cannot see any way to fulfill the law of God
> for man except through overcoming death. That death is the most
> dreaded enemy of the human race goes without argument. The Bible
> from Genesis to Revelation so teaches. . . . It seems to me that some-
> one should have initiative enough to make at least an attempt to raise
> his body to the Jesus Christ consciousness. Because none of the fol-
> lowers of Jesus has attained the victory over this terror of humanity
> does not prove it cannot be done. Every great forward movement
> of the race has been preceded by repeated failures. Every pioneer in
> untried fields has been called either a fool or a dreamer. So instead of
> ridiculing those who are striving to follow Jesus in the overcoming of
> death, we should encourage them to go forward, knowing as we must
> that they will finally attain the mastery—if not in this incarnation,
> then in the next, or the next. So do not throw cold water on me when
> I say that I am doing my best to follow Jesus in overcoming death
> of my body. I need your help, and the helpful thoughts of all loyal
> members of the brotherhood of Jesus Christ, in my battle against the
> most grievous enemy of mankind.[17]

Ten years later, in his mid-eighties, Charles again reflected on his longtime journey to transform his body and the current status of that effort:

I gradually acquired the ability to go into the silence, and from that source I received unexpected revelations and physical sensations. . . . I was informed by the Presence that I was beginning the body regeneration as taught by Jesus Christ. Neither physiology nor psychology offers a nomenclature describing it. The first sensation was in my forehead, a "crawly" feeling when I was affirming life. Then I found that I could produce this same feeling at the bottom of my feet and other nerve extremities by concentrating my attention at the place and silently affirming life. I spent several hours every day in this process and I found that I was releasing electronic forces sealed up in the nerves. This I have done for nearly fifty years until now I have what may be termed an electric body that is gradually replacing the physical.[18]

In 1938, when he was eighty-four, Charles was interviewed by Ralph Teener, a doctoral candidate at the University of Chicago, who was preparing a dissertation on the Unity movement. Teener, who was not a Unity student, was well aware of Charles' commitment to bodily regeneration. Teener's observations indicate that Charles still had much work to do to regenerate his hip:

Today, Mr. Fillmore is a quite interesting, humorous, white-haired man, some 84 years young. His right leg is much shorter than his left. He wears a higher heel on his right shoe and walks with a decided hitch. When in discussion, his mind is likely to wander from the point at issue. To a superficial observer, his teeth show dental work, certainly not of the "spiritual substance" kind. . . . He is almost retired from the business of Unity School, coming in from his country home to the headquarters only one or two afternoons each week.[19]

Charles was interviewed in 1942 at age eighty-eight by the religious historian Marcus Bach. A University of Iowa faculty member, Bach, who traveled to Kansas City for the meeting, found Charles to be an extremely lively, vital, and energetic man:

I first met Charles Fillmore in 1942 at Unity headquarters, 917 Tracy Avenue, in Kansas City. It was a rainy autumn morning, but the smallish, energetic man had utter disregard for the weather. He was bareheaded, exhilarated, it seemed to me, by the touch of the rain in his wisps of thin, white hair, and thrilled at the fact that his hands were opening the copper-grilled door to what might have been some celestial hideaway. His face was strong but gentle. Deep-set blue eyes and the confident hint of a smile had a way of saying that all was well with the world because all was well with him. His manner was that of a young man who had run through the rain catching the drops in his mouth, flushed with a sense of nature's friendly response. His ears were large, a fact I recalled particularly because of my impression that he did not really need them at all. As he sat at his rolltop desk and I on a cushioned kitchen chair in his modest office, his art of listening, as far as I was concerned, was psychic, as if interpreting the spirit of my questions rather than the spoken word. Had you been with me as we entered his office you might not have noticed that he limped slightly, and it would have stretched your credulity to believe that for twenty years and more he walked with the aid of a brace.[20]

In 1946, just two years before his death, Charles acknowledged that his leg was not yet fully healed, but it was still improving: "I do not claim that I have yet attained perfection, but I am on my way. My leg is still out of joint but it is improving as I continue to work under the direction and guidance of Spirit."[21]

Shortly before he died in 1948, Fillmore again gave an overview of the progress he had made in his work with his leg:

I can testify to my own healing of tuberculosis of the hip. . . . When I began to apply the spiritual treatment there was for a long time slight response in the leg, but I felt better, and I found that I began to hear with the right ear. Then gradually I noticed that I had more feeling in the leg. Then as years went by the ossified joint began to get limber, and the shrunken flesh filled out until the right leg was almost equal to the other. Then I discarded the core-and-steel extension and wore an ordinary shoe with a double heel about an inch in height. Now the leg is almost as large as the other, the muscles restored, and although the hip bone is not yet in the socket, I am certain that it soon will be and that I shall be made perfectly whole. I am giving minute details of my healing because it would be considered a medical impossibility and a miracle from a religious standpoint. However, I have watched the restoration year after year as I applied the power of thought, and I know it is under divine law. So I am satisfied that here is proof of a law that the mind builds the body and can restore it.[22]

In the summer of 1948, as he approached his ninety-fourth birthday, Charles was suffering from the effects of kidney failure. He recognized that the sixty-year effort to regenerate his body and overcome physical death was not going to succeed. He told a friend, "As for myself I would like to keep this body, but it seems that the lord of my being has decided otherwise, and I am ready to do what has to be done."[23]

As he neared the end, he said, "It looks like I'll have to go, but don't worry, I'll be back.... I am going to have a new body, anyway, and this time it's going to be a perfect body."[24]

Among his last words were, "Christ in you, the hope of Glory."[25]

Chapter 7

METAPHYSICAL HEALER

C harles Fillmore believed that, when people applied the principles of practical Christianity (the Basic Unity Teaching), positive changes occurred in their lives—in health, finances, and personal relationships.[1] Practical Christianity was about getting results. "We have a religion," he said, "that will demonstrate itself in the most minute details of our affairs."[2] Metaphysical healing was an area in which Charles earnestly pursued demonstrations of spiritual truth. He described metaphysical healing, or "mental healing" as he also called it, as "the healing power that inheres in rightly regulated thought-action,"[3] and further stated that

> metaphysical healing is a mental method of establishing health through an understanding of the fundamental principles of Being or Universal Life, and the working laws of its activities.[4] . . . the whole aim and object of mental healing is to set people free from the race opinions and beliefs which have become a habit of mind and surround them with the Spirit of Truth.[5]

Those who possessed the ability to manifest the Christ within and demonstrate spiritual truth were qualified to engage in the practice of metaphysical healing.

WORKING IN PERSON WITH CLIENTS

Beginning in 1887, Charles and Myrtle Fillmore engaged in the professional practice of metaphysical healing in offices in downtown Kansas City. They advertised themselves as "Teachers and Healers" with office hours of 10:00

a.m. to 4:00 p.m. daily, and each saw several clients a day.[6.] Charles explained the theory of metaphysical healing as he and Myrtle practiced it:

> We understand that the healing of the sick . . . is merely the setting to rights that which is. So all healing is a misnomer if by that is meant that we through an act of the will set in motion forces that build up that condition called health. No. We simply realize that which is already at hand and it shows forth. When you know that the kingdom of heaven is at hand, your patient is healed without resort on your part to denials and affirmations. These are simply to bring your ego out of its plane of sense into the plane of spirit—it is a process of breaking down mental partitions.[7]

Charles described how they treated patients who had not yet been exposed to the "Truth": "We let patients freely describe their disabilities at the first treatment, but always enter a silent mental protest or denial for each statement of error that they make. Their minds are also thus relieved of the disease pictures which they have been holding and the way opened for Truth."[8]

Charles indicated that they then advised their patients to stop focusing on the diseased conditions that had prompted them to seek help, as it would inhibit their recovery:

> We then caution them to make no further mention of their symptoms. During the recital we usually get a clue to the sin or mental error which lies back as cause to the whole trouble, and it is this that we deal with in effecting a cure, carefully blotting out of mind all physical appearances.[9]

The teaching part of the work was as important to the Fillmores as the healing part: "Every healer is first, last, and always a teacher, and has not done his duty toward his patient until he has told him plainly the cause of his ill-health, no matter how delicate the subject may be."[10] Charles believed that disease was "an evidence of wrong thinking." He explained:

> Thinking is generative—every thought clothes itself in a life form according to the character given it by the thinker. This being true it must follow that thoughts of health will produce microbes whose office is to build up healthy organisms, and thoughts of disease will produce microbes of disorder and destruction.[11]

He viewed it as the duty of the healer "to teach the patient the law of right mental action"[12] and indicated that the healer acted irresponsibly if he or she failed to instruct. In fact, to heal without instruction was a disservice to the client:

> If I heal one without instructing him as to the cause, I have deferred the lesson which the law was teaching him, and to that extent put him back in his understanding. Jesus said, "Go and sin no more." So we should be teaching always, and thus be in a position to tell the patient what line of thinking brought about the ill, so that he may avoid it in the future.[13]

Indeed, he was emphatic about the implications of the failure of the healer to teach. "If all the bodily ills of all the people in the world were healed instantly," he said, "they would soon be sick again, unless they were taught the Truth."[14]

Charles acknowledged that "a great deal of so-called spiritual healing" was hypnotism. "It is safe to say," he wrote in the July 1892 issue of *Unity*, "that all healing that is not followed by moral reformation is hypnotism." The healer should refuse to treat if a patient was not open to the truth, but simply wanted to be healed:

> The patient who will not listen to the doctrine and wants to be physically healed in order that he may continue his animal existence among the swine is not "drawn to the Father." And will not be treated by the conscientious practitioner. . . . If the patient refuses to be instructed, the healer is interfering with a retributive law, and simply deferring the judgment which is sure eventually to be visited upon the one who in his ignorance has separated himself in consciousness from the Universal Principle of Goodness.[15]

Charles explained how healings occurred with patients who were open to the teaching but were not sufficiently self-realized to be able to manifest the truth. The key is the level of consciousness of the practitioner: "Good healers always believe in the omnipresence of health and harmony, and through their imagining power the patient is awakened to the inner purification and finally rises to its expression outwardly."[16]

Charles pointed out, "Where the patient has gone so far as to be beyond taking up for himself the realization of God he can be helped by one who

knows the existence so strongly that *his realization* awakes the same perception in others." He emphasized that the work of the healer was merely a
temporary help, that the ultimate ability to heal lay in the patient's learning
spiritual truth: "Each must for himself know and realize the sustaining presence and power of that Universal Spirit ever waiting to gush forth within us
when we give it the Word of Acknowledgement."[17]

Charles warned that patients should not expect immediate results from
metaphysical healing. They needed to work at it and be persistent. "You cannot reasonably expect an instantaneous recovery. Yet radical changes for the
better are the rule, and perfect health and satisfaction is always the reward of
those who persist."[18] Moreover, he was insistent that, without a shift in consciousness on the part of the patient, no lasting results would be attained.
"There is not, never was and never will be," he said, "permanent healing in
anyone who has not reached that unity with the Father exemplified by Jesus
Christ."[19]

Over and over, Charles made the point that it was wrong to put the healing before the teaching. "We are not healers," he asserted in the August 1894
issue of *Unity*, "but ministers of the gospel of Jesus Christ and our one idea
should be to proclaim its Truths; letting the perfect results follow in harmony
and wholeness of body and affairs."[20] He further offered his own experience
with healing his own malformed leg as testimony to the fact that the application of these spiritual principles produced positive results: "I have demonstrated in my own case that just in proportion to my faithfulness to the
principles laid down have I been rewarded. I absolutely know that it works
every time the rule is honestly applied."[21]

ABSENT HEALING

From the beginning of their ministry in April 1889, the Fillmores viewed
absent healing as an important part of their work as metaphysical healers
and teachers. By absent healing, they meant the healing work that took place
when the patient or client was not physically in the presence of the practitioner. "Absent in body yet present in Spirit" is the way Myrtle characterized
absent healing in the inaugural issue of *Modern Thought* magazine.[22] It is the
Spirit, she said, "that does the treating and healing," and the Spirit was not

dependent on time or place. She wrote that she considered absent healing as "one of the noblest and beautiful phenomena that can be contemplated." She viewed it as a philosophy that was well supported by "facts, excellent evidences and testimonies from all quarters."[23] Charles participated in the creation of two organizations that engaged in the work of absent healing, the Society of Silent Unity and the Silent Unity Healing Department. The activities of these organizations are explored in the following chapter.

ALLOPATHIC MEDICINE

Charles had little confidence in allopathic medicine. The medical profession, he believed, had failed to devise remedies that could produce positive results. About medical doctors he said, "We know their medicines to be worse than useless in aiding suffering humanity."[24] On the ineffectiveness of the medical profession, he had this to say: "Medical therapeutics is now in a tangle more profound than all the other departments of the illusion combined. . . . Yet upon the outer thin ether just beyond the atmosphere, of this exceeding irregular and unstable nothing, *materia medica* bases its alleged science."[25]

Charles urged people not to follow the practices of the medical profession:

> You blindly grasp some medical potion, forgetting that you are yourself a laboratory and that all about you are the elements from which every concoction is primarily extracted. . . . What constructed your body in the first place? Was it a doctor, a magnetic battery, blue pills and quinine?[26]

Charles' antipathy toward medicine was most likely based on his own disastrous experiences with medical doctors as a young man. Allopathic medicine has made great strides since the nineteenth century when its practices often caused more harm than good. Important advances were made in the twentieth century, and Charles Fillmore most likely would have been more positive had he experienced Western medicine as it is practiced today.

Chapter 8

ORGANIZER OF
SPIRITUAL MINISTRIES

Many spiritual leaders who excel at teaching and writing are unable to organize around their work. As a result, their teaching lasts only as long as their books are read. Charles Fillmore's work has survived him because he was a gifted organizer. He thought in terms of organization, applied business principles to spiritual practice, and brought people together in organizations for carrying on spiritual work. As a result, spiritual ministries developed around the Basic Unity Teaching. These included metaphysical healing, publishing, spiritual education, and the establishment of Unity centers.

METAPHYSICAL HEALING

Healing others through prayer—physically, psychologically, and spiritually—has been central to Unity work from its earliest beginnings. In the spring of 1889, Charles and Myrtle Fillmore began praying with people, both individually and at a distance, as practitioners of what they ultimately called Christian metaphysical healing. In the early years, both Charles and Myrtle saw clients personally in their Kansas City healing rooms. As time passed and people from outside Kansas City wrote to them for help, they shifted their focus to "absent healing." Absent healing is the term used to describe the work of a spiritual healer when the client and healer are not in the same room at the time the healer does the work. Two groups that Charles organized, the Society of Silent Unity and the Silent Unity Healing Department, engaged in the practice of absent healing.

1. *The Society of Silent Unity*

The work of the Society of Silent Unity was begun in April 1890. Initially called the Society of Silent Help, the organization's name was changed in June 1891 to the Society of Silent Unity with the founding of *Unity* magazine. The Society's purpose was to foster the expansion of Charles and Myrtle's teaching and healing work beyond Kansas City.[1] *Unity* magazine was founded to provide spiritual advice and counsel to people who enrolled as members of the society.[2] The masthead of the inaugural issue of the magazine reflected the connection between the Society and the magazine, stating that *Unity* is "published by the Society of Silent Unity."[3] Leadership of the society was in the hands of the Fillmores since Charles and Myrtle were listed as its "Central Secretaries."

The Society's mission was spiritual rather than religious. The object and aim were to lead men and women to the God within them.[4] Charles and Myrtle clarified their intention regarding this work when they stated, "The only object and aim of this society is to get people to listen to that 'still small voice' and to know that God will lead them into all wisdom, health and happiness if they will but spend a few moments each day in His company."[5]

One of the main goals of the Society was to reach out to those who were unable to have "the benefit of personal healing or teaching."[6] Members of the society were encouraged to develop themselves spiritually by studying truth principles, by practicing meditation, and by doing healing work.[7]

Unity magazine was to play a major role in this effort. Its mission was to "have its columns devoted to the Society of Silent Unity and such points of Truth as are suitable for beginners,"[8] as the June 1894 issue proclaimed. In the 1890s, the Fillmores continually emphasized the connection between the society and the magazine, stating in the same issue, "We want all subscribers and members of Silent Unity to feel that they are equally interested with us in this good work."[9]

Membership in the society was open to "every soul in the Universe."[10] The only requirements were to sit in the silence at 9 p.m. each evening and to hold in mind an affirmation titled the "Class Thought," which was published in each issue of *Unity* magazine. The class thought was a central feature of the spiritual work assigned to members. Many of the class thoughts were for the purpose of connecting the member with the spirit of God within, as the following examples indicate:

"I am now manifesting the perfect harmony of Omnipotent Mind."[11]

"I am now conscious of thy indwelling Presence."[12]

"God wills through me to will and do that which ought to be done by me."[13]

Charles and Myrtle indicated that members needed to hold the class thought in mind daily at the regularly stated time. They continually stressed the importance of silent meditation and the need to make it a regular part of the day's activities. They were convinced that the Divine in the universe could be discovered by looking inward through meditative practice and used a variety of arguments to convince members, undoubtedly unaccustomed to meditative techniques, to take time out from a busy day for at least fifteen minutes to sit alone in silence:

All manifestations of life originate in the silence. Run over in your mind the main visible evidences of power and intelligence in the world of effects, from the delicate poise of the daisy to the mighty arms of silence that swing the planet out in space, and you will find that without exception they depend for existence upon that realm we call invisible. The thoughts that rise in you and come to the surface in deed and act, are they not from the silence? Do you take a step or lift a hand that has not its motive from the depths of that mighty sea of throbbing life within your own being? Then why look to the external for that which comes only from the silent within?[14]

Charles and Myrtle were concerned that members did not know how to engage in meditative practice. They recognized that most members were neophytes, so, on occasion, *Unity* magazine provided instructions on how to meditate. Periodic pep talks published in *Unity* magazine encouraged members to persist, have patience, and put in the time and effort required to get results. Most important of all, members needed to believe:

No one is picked up by the Spirit and carried to success on beds of roses. Only those who are faithful to the cooperative thought, and who trust in the spirit, and watch for the good, are helped. Let your asking be definite, and then be persistent in looking for fulfillment.[15]

In July 1892, Charles and Myrtle began encouraging those who had heretofore informally considered themselves members, because they participated in the 9 o'clock silences, to apply for formal entrance into the society. Those who sent in a personal written application would receive a certificate acknowledging their official membership in the Society of Silent Unity.

In October 1896 *Unity* magazine began publishing the numbers of people who had received certificates of membership. As of October 1, 1896, there were 6,124 people with certificates. The number grew to 7,500 in August 1900 and to 15,000 by January 1907. In 1909, shortly before the Unity movement began de-emphasizing the society's membership activities, the number of certified members totaled 16,000.[16]

2. *The Silent Unity Healing Department*

Growing up alongside the Society of Silent Unity in their Kansas City headquarters was the Silent Unity Healing Department. In their communications in *Unity* magazine with the members of the Society of Silent Unity, Charles and Myrtle Fillmore made it known they were available should members choose to write requesting help. The approach was low-key, and they did not actively solicit the work. They warned members that, because of their busy schedules, they "could not undertake to answer such letters personally." They did assure members, however, that they would "respond in the silence as Spirit directs."[17]

As the decade of the 1890s progressed, more and more members of the society wrote for healing. As workload increased, Charles and Myrtle engaged other Kansas City practitioners to handle some of the letter requests. A woman who identified herself as "Secretary McMahon" apparently was the first healer to be employed in the Silent Unity Healing Department. She wrote an article for *Unity* in 1893 in which she commented on the cases being treated by the department and described her work as a letter writer. She cited the cases of several people whose physical ills had been alleviated through the absent healing.[18]

Charles and Myrtle insisted on engaging in absent healing on a freewill offering basis only.[19]

They considered it improper to charge for this service. "Our work is not to be bought with a price," they indicated. "We make no bargain or ask any pay."[20] Freewill offerings, they had observed, were a well-established practice in religious circles in America, indicating that "the religious institutes of this whole country depend upon freewill offerings of the people for their support." It followed that since the Silent Unity Healing Department was engaged in the same work as the churches, the same methods to obtain financial support should be used.[21]

Charles and Myrtle were convinced of the value of their efforts and those of the Silent Unity healers in the Kansas City headquarters. They were forthright in pointing out the benefits of their work. Writing in 1907, when the Unity movement was almost two decades old, they explained:

> We are not giving out drugs, or anything that can be measured or seen, yet there is a constant outpouring of Spiritual Life Energy from this center, and all who put themselves en rapport with us get its effect. It has taken twenty years' constant work to get this current established, and we know that it is the greatest healing agent in the universe.[22]

Charles and Myrtle believed there should be a fair exchange between client and healer. "Spiritual reciprocity" was the name they gave this relationship, and they defined it as "the spontaneous reciprocal exchange of values between healer and patient." It was a concept they often referred to and wrote about: "The healer gives his time and the word of the Spirit just as fully as he knows how; this is his value. The patient is expected to give in return that which he counts valuable, be it money, jewels, books, goods or whatever."[23]

In January 1901, Charles and Myrtle summarized the work of the first twelve years of the Silent Unity Healing Department and commented on the status of the work. Describing both the activities at Unity headquarters in Kansas City as "The Silent Unity Center" and the progress made since the movement began, they said:

> This Center of the Silent Unity Society begins the new year and new century with a consciousness of great spiritual power. For over twelve years we have without interruption centered our hearts, our souls,

our minds, upon the one omnipresent God working in and through us, and in and through all people, until there has been established in our minds a consciousness of Spiritual Power having substance and mental tangibility. That God is Life and Substance is no longer a theory, but His presence has become to us a mental visibility, and we know and feel the power of the Divine Word as plainly as one having hold of the wires of a great battery.[24]

At the turn of the century, in addition to Charles and Myrtle, three others—Mr. and Mrs. Cassius Shafer and Jennie Croft—were engaged in absent healing at Unity headquarters. Society members were informed that the healers at Unity headquarters welcomed their requests for spiritual work and assured them that valuable help would be provided:

> We are ready to help you all to come into the Christ Presence and Power. The power is mighty in us, and we are assured that we can help others to realize it. . . . As a Spiritual Center we send forth the Christ Word for all members and for the friends of members. There is no limit to the power of the Divine Logos where there is a faith center in working order. If you have faith that God can reach your friends in their trials, mental or physical, send forth your spiritual word and God will prove it for you. If you have faith in Silent Unity, write or wire us, and our power will be joined with yours.[25]

In early 1905, the Fillmores began on a regular basis to actively encourage subscribers to write to them for healing work. It was the first time that they used a full page of *Unity* magazine to print an application form. They declared:

> We can help you in matters pertaining to health, finances, spiritual understanding, and, in fact, everything that is desirable, and for your highest good. . . . We put no limit on the power of the Holy Spirit, through which the work is done. Write us freely just what you most desire.[26]

Direct invitations produced more requests for prayer work than the more passive approach previously taken. While no statistics are available prior to 1907 on the number of letters and telegrams received or sent, the number of healers working at Unity headquarters rose from three to eleven from 1900 to 1906.[27]

In an effort to make it easier for those who wanted "healing and spiritual assistance," the October 1906 issue of *Unity* stipulated that applicants should "write short letters. A little silent prayer before you write concerning the question of what and how much is necessary to be told, will help you to tell us your needs clearly and concisely."[28] More detail was also provided to members regarding how prayer was used by the staff at Unity headquarters:

> Many write us that they feel the vibrations of love and life and strength carried by the letters received from us, and one who mentions it asks, "Do you treat the letters before you send them?" Yes. As soon as letters are received, The Word of help is sent forth, and the reply is written with prayer. The Word is spoken again and sent with them as they are sent out. Prayer characterizes all the Silent Unity work.[29]

It was also revealed that the Silent Unity healing work was done in privacy, on a floor of the building where only Silent Unity staff was allowed. The aforementioned report in *Unity* indicated:

> The Silent Unity Healing Department is on the top floor of the Unity Building where no one is allowed except the healers and the correspondents. Eight healers and seven correspondents now constitute the staff. This "upper room" is a great healing pool, from which flows a perpetual stream of health—giving life and substance to all who ask, in faith believing.[30]

In January 1907, the first report of Silent Unity Healing Department's workload was given. It was stated that about one hundred letters were being written daily.[31] In addition, *Unity* magazine now published extracts from letters "written by Silent Unity healers to patients." These extracts provided "excellent lessons" and therefore were "worthy of repeating to all our readers."[32] The Fillmores viewed these letters as presenting the teaching in a direct and accessible form.

In 1910, about a dozen workers constituted the staff and about 100 letters were received daily, suggesting that little growth had taken place since the size of the staff and the workload were first reported three years earlier in

January 1907.[33] One of the more detailed accounts of the work of the Silent Unity Healing Department (which by now was beginning to be called simply "Silent Unity") was written in October 1911 by Edna L. Carter. Carter, who had worked at Unity headquarters for almost a decade, reported in an article titled "Points From Silent Unity" that the workday began early and was punctuated by periods in which all the workers gathered for silent meditation:

> Every morning at ten o'clock the sixteen local workers of the Society of Silent Unity drop the letter writing, gather in the Silence room, and join in this word: "Christ is the head of the Movement." In the afternoon at three o'clock they again have a Silence, and then spend a half hour in discussing various points that come up in the letter-writing. . . . At five o'clock in the afternoon the regular healing silence is held.[34]

Between 1910 and 1915, the Silent Unity healing work grew rapidly. Several hundred letters were now being received daily, and the staff grew from twelve to thirty-five. Larger quarters were required, and space was designed in a new building specifically to meet Silent Unity's needs. Healers were available on a twenty-four-hour basis, including weekends, with someone available throughout the night to respond to telegrams. Details of the work were reported in the March 1915 issue of *Unity*. The workday began at 8 a.m. with a silent prayer that lasted fifteen minutes. "During the Silence," it was reported, "workers sit at their desks ready to begin on their letters as soon as they have prayed for Divine Guidance and help." Letter writing was interrupted for prayer and meditation at 10 a.m. At 3 p.m. each day, the workers met in the healing room "to take up some special feature of the work."[35]

Silent Unity continued the rapid growth that began in 1910, and at the time of Charles' death in 1948 Silent Unity had been for many years a major role player in the work of the Unity School of Christianity.

PUBLISHING

From the beginning of his public work in April 1889, Charles Fillmore sought to publish and distribute spiritual literature. Spiritual magazines were an important vehicle for presenting the Basic Unity Teaching. *Modern Thought* magazine was the first of those publications, followed in the 1890s by successor magazines, *Christian Science Thought, Thought*, and *Unity*. A very popular children's magazine, *Wee Wisdom,* edited by Myrtle Fillmore, was introduced in 1893. In pictures, poems, and stories *Wee Wisdom* presented "the knowledge that Jesus Christ is the objective spirit of every child."[36]

The Modern Thought Publishing Company, which began operating in April 1889, offered for sale about two hundred metaphysical books and pamphlets. Two pages of the magazine *Modern Thought* were devoted to advertising these works. The authors most valued by Charles and Myrtle were listed, including the essays of Ralph Waldo Emerson, *Isis Unveiled* by Madame Helena Petrovna Blavatsky, *Who Carry the Signs* by Emma Curtis Hopkins, *The Buddhist* by Emanuel Swedenborg, *Science and Health* by Mary Baker Eddy, and six books by Warren Felt Evans including *Esoteric Christianity, Divine Law of Cure, Primitive Mind-Cure, Mental Medicine,* and *Mental Cure.* Charles indicated his intention to make available a wide selection of books and pamphlets. He said, "Our object shall be to keep in stock everything in the line of advanced thought, and if a work does not appear in the list, we will use every means to procure it in the least possible time. Hence, do not hesitate to write us for any book you want."[37]

In the 1890s, Charles began publishing pamphlets and books specifically written from Modern Thought Publishing Company and its successor, the Unity Book Company. It is interesting to note that the name of the organization was changed in 1897 to the Unity Tract Society because the former names gave the appearance of a commercial venture. Charles wrote, "That people may more fully understand that there is no element of financial gain in our publications department we purposely adopted the word 'tract' which is synonymous with spiritual literature." Charles concluded by stating, "This is not a business but a ministry."[38]

H. Emilie Cady, a New York City homeopathic physician, was the author of the most successful work published by the Unity Tract Society. Her first piece, *Finding Christ in Ourselves*, was published initially as an article in *Thought* magazine. It was so well received by the magazine's readership that Charles decided to publish it in pamphlet form.

By August 1894, Charles was convinced that Cady possessed extraordinary spiritual insight. He told their readers, "We know that among all the Christian people on earth today none appreciate her writings more than we of the liberal science school."[39] Continuing positive reader response to Cady's writings, plus his own confidence in her abilities as a metaphysical teacher and writer, led Charles to ask her to prepare a series of twelve "lessons" in article form to be published monthly over the course of one year in *Unity* magazine.

The lessons, according to Charles, were popular with readers who needed encouragement and help and were "especially appreciated by beginners."[40] The lessons were in such demand that the Unity Tract Society began publishing them in booklet form. The first four lessons were ready by spring 1895, the second set of four by summer, and the third and final set of four by winter. The lessons were put in book form and titled *Lessons in Truth*. The book was characterized as "A Course of Twelve Lessons in Practical Christianity."[41] The book immediately became a Unity best seller. In 1903, *Unity* magazine declared that *Lessons in Truth* appealed to a broad audience of Christians, not just Unity students, observing that "The twelve lessons, written in a fascinating manner, appeal to every denomination of religion. The easy and logical steps with which she [Miss Cady] takes you along the road hunting your God are not only charming but glorious in their simplicity and clearness."[42] *Unity* magazine in June 1908 called the book "a marvel" and indicated that it was "causing thousands to rejoice in spiritual understanding and health."[43] *Lessons in Truth* continued to be a popular favorite within the Unity Movement throughout the twentieth century. By the year 2000, it had been translated into several languages, and sales totaled over 1.6 million copies.

The Unity Tract Society continued to publish a sizeable number of books and pamphlets, primarily by well-known metaphysical authors or by Unity students on the Kansas City staff or in Unity centers around the country. *Unity* magazine in July 1915 listed a total 125 tracts in print and in September 1917 reported that the number of copies printed between 1915 and 1917 was "nearly one million five hundred thousand, 1,478,250 to be exact." In April 1923, *Unity* reported that three million copies of tracts were published that year.[44]

During the first three decades of the twentieth century, several new magazines were introduced. *Weekly Unity,* begun in 1909 and edited by Lowell Fillmore, became a highly successful publication, ultimately outdistancing *Unity* magazine in circulation. By the 1920s, the magazine had over 100,000 subscribers. *Daily Word* was begun in 1924. Edited by Frank B. Whitney, a talented young Silent Unity worker, it was to surpass in readership all magazines published by Unity. By the time of Charles' death in 1948, *Daily Word* had several thousand subscribers.

The Christian Business Man was introduced in 1922 and presented short articles that taught the practice of Christian psychology in business. *Youth* magazine began publication in 1926 and was aimed at an audience of young readers who had outgrown *Wee Wisdom.*

Unity published all of Charles Fillmore's books, beginning in 1909 with *Christian Healing.* During his lifetime, eight other books written by him were published by the Unity School of Christianity including *Talks on Truth, The Twelve Powers of Mind, Metaphysical Bible Dictionary, Prosperity, Mysteries of Genesis, Jesus Christ Heals, Teach Us to Pray* (co-authored with Cora Dedrick Fillmore), and *Mysteries of John.* Two books were published posthumously, *Atom Smashing Power of Mind* and *Keep a True Lent.*

Spiritual Education

1. Classes in Kansas City

During the 1890s, classes and workshops in "Practical Christianity" were the primary means by which Charles and Myrtle educated Unity students. Charles and Myrtle taught the classes themselves as the Unity movement was not large enough to employ other teachers until after the turn of the century. In July 1896, the first class on Practical Christianity was offered by Charles for Unity students in Kansas City.[45] In June 1897, Myrtle joined him in teaching a class entitled "Practical Christianity and Christian Healing," a class that "covered all the ground of the higher courses in Metaphysics."[46]

In December 1902, Charles and Myrtle initiated a second and more in-depth class, which they called the "Advanced Course in Concentration."[47] With the development of the advanced course, Charles and Myrtle settled into a pattern of teaching that was to continue until 1909. In addition to the advanced course, a primary course consisting of twelve lessons was offered three or four times yearly on "Christian Living and Healing" with twelve evening sessions given over a two-week period. The course was open to the general public, and the focus was on both teaching and healing, with the latter being emphasized. It was promised that, "a practical demonstration of the way to heal is given at the close of each lecture by audibly treating someone in the audience who asked for help."[48] Charles believed that the primary class was of particular value for beginners on the path of spiritual development.[49]

2. *The Unity Correspondence School*

Classes taught in Kansas City were attended primarily by Kansas City residents with an occasional outsider traveling to Missouri for the fourteen-day course. In an effort to reach students outside Missouri, Charles and Myrtle in 1909 created a course in Unity teaching that could be taken by correspondence.[50] In April 1909 they announced that "in response to widespread demand we have arranged to give lessons in Christian Healing and the true science of Christianity by correspondence."[51] The content of the course was similar in most respects to the primary course described previously and taught in person by Charles and Myrtle. The course was presented, as were all the Fillmores' courses, in twelve lessons. Students received one lesson at a time. Printed copies of the lesson, usually eight to ten typewritten pages, were sent to the students who were instructed to copy the lesson verbatim, go over it until they felt certain they fully understood the material, and then request the questions on the lesson from the school. Upon completing the questions—which the Fillmores estimated may take about one month—students were instructed to return their answers to Unity headquarters for grading. It was explained, "If answers are not satisfactory we will point out the errors and require further study. This system will be continued until all the points in the twelve lessons are understood and can be set forth by the student in his own language."[52]

Charles and Myrtle saw important benefits for those taking the course: "These lessons will give every student a training in the demonstration of prosperity, as well as health, and with each lesson he will manifest the teaching in health, harmony and understanding."[53] The correspondence course was immediately popular with Unity students. By June 1909, 268 students were enrolled,[54] and by November, the total had risen to seven hundred;[55] at the end of the first year (March 1910), over nine hundred pupils were taking the course.[56] Many students wrote to headquarters expressing their belief in the value of the course.

By December 1910, the enrollment had risen to sixteen hundred; in addition to students throughout the United States, there were enrollments from Cuba, Brazil, England, Scotland, France, Germany, Russia, India, Japan, Australia, New Zealand, and South Africa. The Fillmores announced that "the course is especially recommended for all who wish to become teachers and healers."[57] In 1911, with enrollment rising to two thousand, potential students were advised that they should have read Unity literature for at least one year before enrolling.[58]

Within a short time, the correspondence course became the basic text for the teachings of the Unity School, or as the Fillmores described it, "the written instruction of the Unity School of Practical Christianity."[59] By 1913, the Fillmores were so convinced of the value of the correspondence course, they dubbed it as "the basis of the teaching,"[60] or as it was later called, "the recognized Unity course of study."[61] Announcements for classes in Kansas City beginning in 1912 stated that teachings would be based on the "lessons of the Unity Society Correspondence School."[62] All involved with Unity work were expected to complete it and receive a passing grade.

Periodically, Charles focused on the benefits from taking the correspondence course, indicating that it was helpful both for those who wanted to do healing work as well as for those who wanted an introduction to Unity teaching. In October 1923, the Fillmores provided a particularly clear statement of the rationale for enrollment:

> We have established a system of instructing Unity students in their homes so they may have the same advantage as if they were in personal attendance at the Unity meetings in Kansas City. It is our desire to have students develop into Unity teachers and healers so they may minister to their own families and to those in their communities. It is not necessary, however, for one to signify his intention of becoming a public healer or teacher in order to have our personal instruction. If you do not understand Truth well enough to demonstrate it, you will find those Lessons very helpful. Many religious and metaphysical questions which puzzle and confuse are clearly explained.[63]

3. *The Unity Training School*

Though the Unity Correspondence School was the focal point of Unity teaching in the first decades of the twentieth century, efforts were also made to expand the teaching undertaken in Kansas City. While Charles spoke or taught in the Kansas City training sessions, the organizing work was done by others. The Intensive Training School, which operated from 1919 to 1922, was the first of these organizations. From 1922 to 1931, Unity summer conferences were held annually at Unity Farm.

The Unity Training School was established at Unity Farm in 1932 for the purpose of providing leadership training for those serving in Unity centers. Ministerial training was begun in earnest in 1933. Sporadic attempts at ministerial training had been made as early as 1906 by the Kansas City Unity Society of Practical Christianity. In the early 1920s, the Intensive Training School gave courses that were useful to center leaders but, until the organization of the Unity Training School in 1932, no fully developed ministerial training program was in place. While Charles undoubtedly was involved in the decision making that led to its creation, the organization and administrative work was most likely handled by his sons Rickert and Lowell.

4. *Unity Centers*

Unity centers for teaching, healing, and weekly religious services began germinating in the mind of Charles Fillmore in the early 1890s. After being ordained by Emma Curtis Hopkins of the Theological Seminary of Chicago to the "Christian Science Ministry," Charles spoke periodically on Sundays in the early 1890s as a part of the "No Name Lecture Series" sponsored by the Christian Science Association of Kansas City.[64] He began organizing religious services on Sundays with Myrtle for the first time in 1894. These first meetings, referred to as "Unity meetings," were devoted primarily to Bible study. All meetings were open to the public.[65]

By 1896, these Sunday meetings were held in rooms adjacent to Unity headquarters in the Pythian Building on Walnut Street in Kansas City. The "order of exercises" contained many of the elements found in traditional Christian services of the Protestant variety—silent prayer, scripture reading, congregational singing, silent meditation, and Bible study.[66] In June 1897, the

Sunday meetings were held under the auspice of the Unity Society of Practical Christianity. It was the first time the society was identified in *Unity* magazine as the organizing group for these meetings, called "Sunday services."

Services were conducted, both on Sundays and during the week, in facilities that could hold about one hundred people.[67] The year 1902 marked the first time that Charles was listed as "Speaker" for the Sunday morning service, a title he was to hold until he retired from active church work in 1933. As speaker, he performed pastoral duties for the congregation and presided over the Sunday meeting.[68] In 1903, the Unity Society for Practical Christianity was incorporated "for scientific and educational purposes," under the laws of Missouri. The development of this first Unity center, which functioned much like a church, would not have been accomplished without Charles' leadership and organizational ability.

With the success of the Unity center in Kansas City, Charles began encouraging Unity students outside the city to emulate the local work and start Unity centers in their communities. Center leaders were provided with a variety of services that included helpful literature from Unity publications, course work by correspondence from the Unity Correspondence School, and publicity in towns and cities where Unity centers were located. In addition, potential center leaders were invited to come to Kansas City and take classes in Practical Christianity.

As Charles committed himself to supporting the development of Unity centers outside Kansas City, he realized that literature and course work in Practical Christianity alone would not provide all the necessary knowledge and information. If centers for Unity teaching were to be established across America, men and women thoroughly grounded in Unity teachings must be sent out to provide fledgling groups with counsel and advice: "There are calls for teachers and lecturers," it was noted in *Unity* in May 1906, "from all parts of the country coming in constantly."[69] Charles pledged himself to provide lecturers who were sufficiently trained to give the needed aid. "This school," it was stated, "will meet the demand."[70]

A few members of the Kansas City staff performed as field lecturers during the thirteen years before the Unity Field Department was established in 1919. Most, like LeRoy Moore, Henry Benson, and Sophia Van Marter, after touring the lecture circuit for a few months, accepted an invitation of a local

Unity group to found a center. The field lecture program gained momentum during the 1920s with the establishment of the new department.

In summary, Charles' contribution to the organization of Unity centers as spiritual ministries consisted of planning and organizing the first Unity center in Kansas City, initiating the work that established centers outside Kansas City at the turn of the century, and setting in motion the work that was ultimately performed by the Unity Training School, the Unity Ministers Association, established in 1946, and the Association of Unity Churches, founded in 1966.

UNITY SCHOOL OF CHRISTIANITY

As indicated above, during the early years of Unity work, the Unity ministries of publishing, prayer, religious services, and spiritual education were administered by Charles Fillmore under various organizational umbrellas. In 1903, under his leadership, the Kansas City Unity Society of Practical Christianity was incorporated, and Unity religious services ministry in Kansas City found a permanent home.

Charles recognized that, as an incorporated organization, the Kansas City Unity group was needed to manage the three other ministries—publishing, prayer, and spiritual education. In 1909, *Unity* magazine began referring to the "Unity Society" as the organizational designation for these ministries. No attempt was made to incorporate the Unity Society at that time, although the organizational purposes of the group suggested that not-for-profit corporation would be appropriate for its work. In answer to the question, "What is the object of the Unity Society?" *Unity* magazine in 1909 explained:

> The object of the Unity Society is to harmonize and unify the Christian religion with modern metaphysics. It sees in the pure doctrine of Jesus and the apostles the same truths that modern independent investigators claim as original discoveries. It teaches that all the modern discoveries of the constitution of man are set forth in the doctrine of Jesus and his apostles. . . . The literature published by the Unity Society explains in detail the Divine Law and however man can take advantage of it and be restored to health, prosperity and happiness.[71]

The Unity Society was featured in a large headline on the front page of *Weekly Unity* on July 3, 1909, in which the following announcement appeared: "The Unity Society is not the offshoot of any organization, but is an original and independent movement in religious study."[72]

The origins of the society were traced back to the beginning of the Fillmores' activities as spiritual teachers. "The Society has been in existence about twenty years," it was explained, "having been started by Mr. and Mrs. Fillmore." It was further pointed out that there were twelve departments in the Unity Society, "but all work as one."[73]

In March 1910, *Unity* magazine reported on the good work being done by the Unity Society:

> Our friends write that they are with us in the work of the Unity Society and are glad to see reports of progress every month. . . . People from all over the land are telling us that a very great work for humanity is being done by the Unity Society and that it should be generously supported.[74]

Though it had no official legal status, the "Unity Society" by 1910 had become the preferred organizational designation for the Unity movement. In a Sunday morning address on November 24, 1910, titled "What Has the Unity Society to Be Thankful For?" Charles emphasized the steady growth in all aspects of the work and the impact of the teaching:

> Other societies had outstripped us from the worldly point of view, but we are satisfied to know that there has been here planted a great Truth that shall never pass away, but shall grow and be given to the whole earth. We have established here a school which is founded on Principle.[75]

In April 1913, *Weekly Unity* referred to the Unity Society as a "school" rather than a religious organization, indicating that a new designation for Unity work was in the offing:

> The Unity Society is not a church, but a school for the training and discipline of all who would develop spiritually. It aims especially to prepare teachers for the work of spreading the Truth. In keeping, therefore, with our mission, every session should bear out the school

idea and each member of the various classes should enter heartily into his privileges as a student.[76]

By 1914, Charles had concluded that the name "Unity Society" did not accurately reflect the nature of the Unity work. Since Unity had become an institution with a major interest in spiritual education in a Christian context, the name "Unity School of Christianity" seemed to be a better fit for Unity work. The September 1914 issue of *Unity* described the purposes of the new organization:

> To establish and maintain a school, institute or college for the instruction and promotion of mental, moral, spiritual and physical principles and qualifications deemed best for the promotion of the harmony, health and happiness of mankind, and to apply such principles and qualifications to such purposes as healing diseases and ailments anywhere.[77]

The school, which was incorporated under the General and Business Corporation Act of Missouri on April 14, 1914, included within its organizational structure the Unity Tract Society, the Society of Silent Unity, the Silent Unity Healing Department, the Unity Correspondence School, the Silent-70, and the Unity Pure Food Company.[78] Fifty shares of stock were issued at that time, all controlled by members of the Fillmore family. The school was established as a commercial business, rather than as a nonprofit educational organization, because Charles had been led to believe that a business charter was necessary if the school was to engage in the publication of books and magazines.[79]

In an address on January 1, 1915, at the dedication of a new Unity building in Kansas City, Charles described the objectives of the school and the ideas upon which it was based:

> Every great work must have as its foundation a great idea. If the idea is not present the work will fail in attaining the object for which it stands. The great idea upon which the Unity work is founded is the right concept of God. Our God is not an enlarged man but the one Great Principle of Being. God is Spirit—the direct opposite of matter. God is Supreme Mind—the storehouse of all perfect ideas. God is the One Spirit-Mind in whom all ideas of life, love, substance,

intelligence, power, originate. Spirit-Mind is the indwelling idea at the center of everything that has real existence.[80]

He ended his address by claiming a broad scope for the school's work and making an optimistic prediction of its future:

> The object of this school is the redemption of the human race. It is a link in the great educational movement inaugurated by Jesus Christ, which not only taught the Truth, but demonstrated it also. . . . This is but the beginning of a work that will in due season encircle the earth. This vision of the future which the Lord has shown us is of a magnitude beyond present description. The New Jerusalem is not to be in Palestine, but in the heart of the American continent.[81]

With incorporation in 1914 of the Unity School of Christianity, the prayer, publishing, and spiritual education ministries, as well as supporting services for Unity centers outside Kansas City, were finally brought together under one organizational unit. At the fourth annual convention, held October 3–7, 1926, Charles felt it necessary to make sure Unity students knew how Unity School was owned and operated. In answer to the question "Who owns Unity Property?" it was reported:

> Unity School of Christianity is a corporation that was created on April 14, 1914, under the Business Corporation Law of Missouri. The Unity School of Christianity was incorporated as a business corporation because of the fact that it prints books and does other things that are considered business. However, it is organized for religious and educational purposes and not for profit. There is a paragraph in the Articles of Incorporation which reads as follows: "Provided that no dividend shall ever be declared or paid but all profits and property of this organization shall be used to carry out the purpose of the organization or some part thereof." The sole purpose of the school is to set forth in a practical way the teachings of Jesus Christ and to establish the kingdom of heaven here on earth.[82]

The nonprofit status of the Unity School remained unchanged throughout the remainder of the twentieth century. The Internal Revenue Service has continued to allow the school tax-exempt status based on the educational and spiritual nature of its work.

Chapter 9

MYRTLE PAGE AND
CORA DEDRICK

C harles Fillmore had a deep respect for women and valued them for their contribution, not just in the home but in the workplace as well. Every man's success, he indicated, depended upon the support of a marital partner: "A man unconsciously depends upon his wife for the vitality which he expresses. The success that a man has in business always comes forth from some woman's thought. Every man in the world who has been successful has had some woman as his backer."[1]

In his own life, two women played important roles: Myrtle Page, his first wife, and Cora Dedrick, his second.

MYRTLE

Myrtle Page grew up in an Ohio farm family, the seventh of Marcus and Lucy Page's eight children. She was born August 6, 1845, to parents who were devout Methodists, living by a puritanical moral code with its belief in a punishing God. Myrtle was a bright child and loved learning. At an early age she was repulsed by the fundamentalist leanings of her parents:

> I found my dear ones did not have an understanding of God, who ruled their lives, which satisfied me. . . . My mother was a very spiritual woman. She always kept the principles of right and wrong before us by her own example. But she accepted the church creed. And had such a devotional spirit that she felt that if her God saw fit to punish, or do any of the many things that were attributed to God, He must have reason for it and it was all right. I marveled that my wonderful

mother, who loved so devotedly, could have a God who might pun-ish, or take the lives of His children.[2]

Myrtle found unacceptable the puritanical Methodist teachings on sin and the nature of evil. "There was something in me that protested against the declaration that I was by nature evil and sinful."[3]

She was afflicted at any early age by tuberculosis and went through sev-eral bouts with the illness during childhood and youth. Nevertheless, she graduated from high school, attended Oberlin College for one year—long enough to get a teaching certificate—and at age 23 in 1868 accepted a teach-ing job in Clinton, Missouri. Except for one year in Denison, Texas, where she went to recover from a bout with TB, she spent the next thirteen years teach-ing in Clinton, Missouri. She met Charles Fillmore, nine years her junior, in Denison in 1878, and married him three years later in 1881.

During the next four years, before moving to Kansas City in 1885, the Fillmores lived in Colorado and Nebraska, where Charles pursued business interests. Their two eldest sons were born during this period, Lowell in 1882 and Waldo Rickert in 1884. Myrtle's strong interest in transcendentalism is indicated in the naming of her two sons—Lowell after James Russell Lowell and Waldo Rickert after Ralph Waldo Emerson.

Myrtle suffered from poor health during this period, as a result of recur-ring bouts with TB. She reported:

> I had all the ills of mind and body that I could bear. Medicine and doctors ceased to give me relief and I was in despair.[4] . . . Along with tuberculosis trouble in my lungs, I had disorders through the abdom-inal walls. At time hemorrhoids made life miserable.[5]

Kansas City in the mid-1880s had become a destination for teachers of mental healing based in Chicago who had learned Christian Science healing practices from Mary Baker Eddy. This group, which consisted among oth-ers of Joseph Adams, George B. Charles, Edward J. Arens, Eugene B. Weeks, Ursula Gestefield, and Emma Curtis Hopkins, was teaching a type of mental healing that differed in significant ways from traditional Christian Science. In Kansas City, the Chicago group was sponsored by Dr. J. S. Thacher, who was director of the Kansas City College of Christian Science.

Myrtle's first contact with teachers from this group came in the spring of 1886 when Eugene B. Weeks presented a course of lectures in Kansas City. She left with insights that changed her life. She explained their impact:

> I must have been fully ready for the initial lesson, for it filled and satisfied all the empty, hungry longings of my soul and heart. There is nothing in the human language able to express the vastness of my possibilities as they unrolled before me. . . . The physical claims that had been considered such a serious nature faded away before the dawning of this new consciousness, and I found that my body temple had been literally transformed through the renewing of my mind.[6]

In letters to friends, she gave a fuller explanation of the illumination that took place as a result of attending Weeks' lectures. To one friend, she wrote, "I remember with great joy the time when it dawned on me that God was my Father and that I need not be bound by human limitations. I had been laboring under the belief in inherited ill health, and the Truth of my divine parentage freed and healed me."[7]

Rather than engaging a practitioner of mental healing, Myrtle indicated that she healed herself from tuberculosis, using the healing practices she learned in the courses from Weeks. "I did most of the healing myself," she said, "because I wanted the understanding for future use."[8] She gave a detailed description of how she used affirmations until she fully recovered from tuberculosis:

> It flashed upon me that I might talk to the life in every part of my body and have it do just what I wanted. I began to teach my body and got marvelous results. I told the life in my liver that it was not torpid or inert, but full of vigor and energy. I told the life in my stomach that it was not weak or inefficient, but energetic, strong and intelligent. I told the life in my abdomen that it was no longer infested with ignorant ideas of disease, put there by myself and by doctors, but that it was all athrill with the sweet, pure, wholesome energy of God. I told my limbs that they were active and strong. I told my eyes that they did not see of themselves but that they expressed the sight of Spirit, and that they were drawing on an unlimited source. I told them that they were young eyes, clear, bright eyes, because the light of God shone right through them. I told my heart that the pure love

of Jesus Christ flowed in and out through its beating and that all the world felt its joyous pulsation. I went to all the life centers in my body and spoke words of Truth to them—words of strength and power. I asked their forgiveness for the foolish, ignorant course that I had pursued in the past, when I condemned them and called them weak, inefficient and diseased. I did not become discouraged at their being slow to wake up, but kept right on, both silently and aloud, declaring the words of Truth, until the organs responded.[9]

Myrtle was certified in 1887 as a practitioner of mental healing by Joseph Adams of the Chicago group after taking a course of instruction from him in Kansas City. She soon began working with clients in Kansas City and felt that she was on a mission:

> From the moment I perceived the healing law I could not let my neighbors alone. If there was anything the matter with them it had to be put aright; they had to know that there is a better way. I did not do this meddlesomely. No one objected if the pain left him and he became perfectly well; in fact, our neighbors got so interested in healing that they would not let me alone and our parlors were filled nearly every morning.[10]

Charles, who in 1887 had also been certified as a practitioner by Joseph Adams, began practitioner work with Myrtle, and soon both had a full load of clients. "We didn't ask for the work," she recalled. "It just came to our home. One would hear from another that we had something good to offer, and that one would come."[11] Reflecting on the quick success that she and Charles enjoyed she commented, "It was the thing which shone in our faces, and the results we got through our prayers, that drew others to us."[12]

The decade of the 1890s was a busy one for Myrtle. She now had three sons, with her eldest being only eight when the decade began. She was able to carry a full daily load as a mental healer because she had help from Charles' mother, Mary Georgiana Fillmore, who lived with the family. In 1893, Myrtle launched *Wee Wisdom* magazine, devoted to the spiritual needs of children. In 1896, she published *Wee Wisdom's Way,* a book based on her own healing experiences. In 1897, she began co-teaching with Charles a two-week course in Practical Christianity, which they presented in Kansas City three or four times annually. In addition, she co-led a Sunday service with Charles for the Kansas City Society of Practical Christianity.

During the first decade of the twentieth century, the nature of Myrtle's work remained much the same, except there was more of it. Silent Unity, the healing department of the Unity work, gained momentum as the decade progressed, with letters coming in from those who sought absent healing. Answering those letters comprised a significant part of her workload. As years passed, Myrtle saw her life's purpose as being "a torch-bearer to light the way for all sincere true followers of the Master Metaphysician Christ Jesus."[13]

In 1910, Myrtle was sixty-five years old. Retirement was not an option for her: it was something she never considered. She was convinced that men and women were ageless beings capable of living and contributing far beyond the normal life span. She told a Unity correspondent, "We consider seventy years a mere childhood! The soul is just getting a well rounded knowledge of the world in which it lives, and preparing to really live, after being here for seventy summers."[14]

Myrtle lived and worked another twenty-one years, going into the office every day. At age eighty-two in March 1928, just three-and-a-half years before she died, she told a friend, "We climb up and down six flights of winding stairs several times a day. Working all day and several times a week far into the evening, and going to bed happy, and eager for the next day." Myrtle Fillmore died on October 6, 1931. Active until the end, her last letter was dated October 5. While she had some ups and downs in health during her last years, she never encountered serious illness. Her family reported she died peacefully in the evening at her home at Unity Farm.

When Myrtle died, Charles was seventy-six years old. He lived for another seventeen years. His continued productivity as a writer and traveling lecturer was in part due to the support of Cora Dedrick, the woman who in 1933 became his second wife.

CORA

Cora Fillmore grew up as Cora Dedrick, a Kansan of German descent. Born December 15, 1876, into a family of six children in the small town of Osawatomie, she grew up in the rural Kansas town of Beagle and was given a strict Protestant upbringing. Her religious training, which was probably Lutheran, coupled with her German background, may have accounted for the orderliness and self-discipline that characterized her throughout life.[15] She moved to Kansas City as a young adult and was working in a fashionable jewelry store in the early 1900s when a woman friend, who attended Charles Fillmore's services at the Unity Society of Practical Christianity, suggested that she come to church with her.[16] "If you come," the friend told her, "you will be thankful for the rest of your life."[17]

During the two-plus decades she was involved with Unity before marrying Charles Fillmore in 1933, Cora Dedrick worked in several capacities. In 1908, she joined the Unity Guild, whose purpose was to draw together in social ways the young people of Kansas City Unity Society of Practical Christianity and put into practice and demonstrate the teachings of the Unity School. The group engaged in charitable works for the underprivileged of Kansas City and in raising money for the church building fund.[18] She was involved with Silent Unity as a letter writer, healer, and a worker in the file room. She served for a short time as director of Silent Unity, before May Rowland took over in 1916.[19] Cora was ordained by Charles Fillmore as a Unity minister in 1918, along with eighteen other Unity students.[20] For twenty years, she served as secretary to Myrtle Fillmore, and during the years before their marriage, she served as Charles Fillmore's secretary.[21]

Articles by Cora Dedrick began appearing in Unity publications as early as 1912 and appeared periodically over the next two decades. She was a capable writer. Her pieces reveal a sharp, disciplined mind that had absorbed the Unity teachings in depth. She was probably college educated, as her writing suggested, though there is no record of where or when she attended.[22] By the 1920s, she was articulating Unity principles as thoughtfully and clearly as any of *Unity* magazine's writers, including Charles Fillmore himself. In addition to writing, Cora Dedrick lectured and taught classes at Unity headquarters. *Unity News* listed several talks she gave during the 1920s.[23] In 1926, she taught classes at Unity headquarters on a topic that was central to the teaching of Charles Fillmore, "Following Jesus in the Regeneration."

Cora Dedrick studied dance and, according to Rosemary Fillmore Rhea (Charles' granddaughter), she was at one time a student of Isadora Duncan.[24] She was interested in interpretive dance and often interpreted prayers at Unity meetings. Those who knew her in later life described her as "tall, slender, and stately," while pictures of her as a young woman reveal a stylishly dressed, beautiful young lady.[25] In the years before she married Charles Fillmore, Cora spent vacation time on her Kansas farm. She loved to garden and grew carrots on forty acres of land she owned near Unity Village.[26]

Cora Dedrick was fifty-seven years old when she married Charles Fillmore. He was seventy-nine at the time, twenty-two years her senior. Despite the disparity in ages, it was a late-in-life marriage for Cora as well as for Charles. We have no information as to why Cora remained single for so many years. Many young people coming into Unity, as Cora did in her twenties, found partners within the growing Unity community. It's surprising, given Cora's personal attractiveness and mental gifts, that she waited so long to marry.

Ernest Wilson, a popular early Unity minister, a favorite of Myrtle, and successor to Charles in 1933 as speaker for the Kansas City Unity Society of Practical Christianity, indicated that, if Charles Fillmore was to remarry, Cora Dedrick was an obvious choice. She had credentials in the movement dating back for a quarter of a century. As Wilson noted, "She was deeply in sympathy with his most advanced teachings, such as the Twelve Powers, physical regeneration and bodily immortality."[27] Cora had been Charles' secretary and editorial assistant, and they had worked together in presenting commonly shared spiritual ideas. Through these contacts, they had obviously gotten to know each other well.

Wilson considered Cora to be more aware of Charles' needs than anyone in his life, including his family. "Perhaps, even more than his sons," observed Wilson, "she knew his spiritual and physical needs."[28] Wilson acknowledged that the marriage took place relatively soon after Myrtle died—a little more than two years after her passing—and that it was difficult to think of Charles Fillmore married to anyone other than Myrtle. Nevertheless, the marriage made sense. As Wilson stated, "Although the idea of anyone replacing Myrtle in his life came as a shock to most of us . . . it was the logical thing to do."[29]

According to Wilson, who performed the marriage ceremony, neither of Fillmore's sons, Lowell or Rickert, was pleased with their father's decision. Lowell did not think it a good idea for his father to marry his secretary but was less opposed than Rickert. The marriage took place in Lowell's home at Unity Village on New Year's Eve, December 31, 1933. According to the

Reverend Blaine Mays, who as a ministerial student became a close friend of Cora while rooming in her home near Unity Village in the early 1950s, Cora never received the approval of either Rickert or his wife Harriet or of Lowell's wife Alice. Rickert's opposition, according to his daughter Rosemary Fillmore Rhea, was based on the feeling that no one could replace his mother and that his father was wrong in attempting it.[30]

According to Mays, as time went on, Lowell became more accepting. While there was never an honoring of Cora as the woman his father had chosen to marry, Lowell in day-to-day contact was kind to Cora. In later years, Lowell apparently befriended her. Mays stated: "I have been with them when they had wonderful conversations. They got along just fine." Mays said that Cora loved Lowell and made him the executor of her will. Mays observed that Rickert and Lowell's wife Alice (his own wife Harriet was no longer living) were the ones who, as years passed, even after Charles died, continued to maintain their distance.

According to Rosemary Fillmore Rhea, Charles Fillmore found in Cora Dedrick someone who was "completely and utterly dedicated to him."[31] Two Unity ministers, L. E. Meyer and his wife Ethel, had the opportunity to observe the relationship of Charles and Cora at close range. They took a car trip with the Fillmores through Colorado and Montana during the summer of 1940. The trip began early on the morning of July 29. Food became an immediate preoccupation, as it was throughout the trip. Along with luggage, Cora had packed an ice chest full of vegetables and other nonmeat food products. Cora had "fixed ideas about what was good to eat and drink," recalled Meyer, and she wanted to make sure that Charles ate properly.[32] Charles went along with her up to a point but liked sugar and caffeine, which Cora felt were not good for him. Meyer described the gentle tug-of-war that went on around food:

> We had great fun along the way, deciding what we were going to eat and drink, sometimes at Cora's expense—she had very strict ideas about what was to be taken into the body, especially where Charles was concerned. For example, Charles liked Coca-Cola very much, but Cora did not feel that it was [a] proper drink for him. Frequently when we would stop for refreshments, Charles would take Ethel's arm and they would march off to find a soda fountain where they

could purchase Coca-Cola and ice cream. Cora would make suggestions to buy or to do something else, trying to distract Charles and Ethel from their goal of Coke and ice cream. Rarely was she successful. Finally she would give in, follow them, and order ice cream. Cora would laugh and say, "We must satisfy the little boy in him."[33]

Meyer also reported that Cora had a special brew she made called "alfalfa tea," and she was delighted when everyone in the party would agree to drink it. Before having some, Charles would say, "We must humor Cora." Once they were driving past an alfalfa field, and Charles asked Meyer to pull over to the side of the road. He said, "L. E., why don't you stop the car and let Cora out to graze a while."

Cora was a formal and proper person. Blaine Mays described her as "a stately woman who carried herself with pride and dignity." Because of the formality in her nature, L. E. Meyer observed, Cora found it difficult to call people by their first names. Though the Meyers were much younger than the Fillmores, she was reluctant to call him "L. E." She had the same problem with Charles. Meyer said that during the whole trip, he never heard Cora call Charles by his first name. "She always called him, 'Mr. Fillmore.'"[34] Blaine Mays observed the same formality during his four-year stay with Cora. "She called him 'Mr. Fillmore' with the greatest of reverence."[35] Both L. E. and Ethel Meyer were convinced that Charles Fillmore lived as long as he did because Cora watched over him so faithfully. Meyer saw her as "his nutritionist, nurse and secretary, as well as his wife and companion."[36] Rosemary Fillmore Rhea once made an apt comment about Cora as a marital partner when she said, "What man today wouldn't feel very lucky to have such a woman as his wife."[37]

Another person who had a close-up view of the Fillmores' day-to-day life together was Dorothy Pierson, a Unity minister who lived with Charles and Cora during her years in ministerial training at Unity School. Pierson remembered Cora with great tenderness because of how good Cora had been to her. Pierson acknowledged, however, that Cora had her idiosyncrasies. She was very dramatic, both in voice and gesture; she dressed formally and loved to ride her bicycle through the countryside in a long, flowing chiffon gown; she was a strict vegetarian, totally into health food, loved dandelion tea, drank potassium broth, wouldn't wear fur, fed Charles Fillmore goat's milk;

and called her husband, "Mr. Fillmore." "She was so good to him," recalled Pierson. "If he wanted strawberries in the middle of winter, she would have them flown in from the South. . . . I don't know how she kept so serene with the criticism that swirled around. She was not all that appreciated." Pierson was sorry that Cora was not accepted by members of the Fillmore family.[38]

Charles Fillmore, in the years before he married Cora, almost never ventured outside Kansas City. As the minister for the Kansas City Unity Society of Practical Christianity, he hardly ever missed a Sunday service from the time he was first appointed speaker in 1901 until he retired in December 1933. For five years immediately following his marriage to Cora, from January 1934 until the spring of 1939, he was on the go several months each year, making trips to almost every state in the Union, from New York to California. He visited Unity centers, spoke, met people, and saw the country. He remained in Kansas City during the war years but was off again to California in late 1945 and remained there off and on until returning to Kansas City in April 1948, just a few months before he died. Charles Fillmore was eighty years old in 1934 and in his nineties after World War II. All who knew him agree that he would have been unable to make these trips had he not had the support, both personal and physical, that Cora provided.

For several years during the 1930s and 1940s, Cora taught classes with Charles at the Unity Training School on the Twelve Powers. She handled the meditations for these classes and, in 1937, at the encouragement of Charles, published a book entitled *Christ Enthroned in Man.* The book was considered a companion to Charles Fillmore's *The Twelve Powers of Man.* Chapter by chapter, it followed his book, giving meditations and exercises for the purposes of bringing the Twelve Powers into full expression. Religious historian Marcus Bach, who knew Cora as well as Charles, gave her favorable marks as a teacher: "Cora's spirit, refinement and dedication to Unity's principles qualified her as a teacher no less than as the devoted wife of Charles."[39]

Dorothy Pierson once asked James Dillet Freeman whether he thought Charles and Cora had sex. Freeman responded, "Why, of course." To which Pierson rejoined, "I can't believe that."[40] Cora, who Blaine Mays said "was honest to the nth degree," told him that she and Mr. Fillmore had never had any kind of sexual involvement. Mays said that Cora "never had any kind of interest in sex or romance. Sexuality was in no way any part of her make-up."[41]

Choosing his words carefully, Mays said that Cora "worshiped Charles as a saint, and as a mystic . . . It was adoration on her part." She felt that being married to him "was a great honor for her." She was "a devotee of the Unity teachings and of him as a person." Mays gave the following overall assessment of their relationship:

> There was something working between them. It was not physical; it was not sexual; it was not a romance, except at a level that I can't explain. Companionship was a part of their relationship. His love would have been a recognition and appreciation of what he knew she felt toward him and the Unity work. . . . Her life was devoted to caring for him, seeing that he continued to live, and helping get his message out. For her, whatever he said or wrote was the truth. She was willing to give her life for him and the work.[42]

Cora was particularly good to Charles during his last illness. Hugh D'Andrade, in his biography of Charles, reported that she took exquisite care of him. "Read to me about the divine love," he would say to her. "I have always been a man of action. I need the comfort that comes from resting in love." Cora read to him much of the time, often from stenographic notes of his own talks or from his own manuscripts. "It was so wonderful," Cora was to say later, "to have him exclaim, 'That's good. I can see that!' or 'That's logical. Who wrote that?'" "Why you did, Charles," Cora would reply.[43] Night after night during this illness, Cora would sit and hold his head in her lap, stroke it, and affirm that light and wholeness and the goodness of God flowed in and through him. Blaine Mays praised her steadfastness and comforting support. "Dedication like that," Mays said, "I have not experienced with anyone else."[44]

Cora lived for seven years after the passing of Charles Fillmore. His death was a major blow to her. He had affirmed many times, "I am going to live forever in this body now," and Cora believed he would do it.[45] She was exhausted after he died, and, for almost three years, she stayed much to herself, a recluse in her home. She did not go out to shop or to Sunday service or to her office at Unity Village. She was still in seclusion when, in February 1951, she agreed to let Blaine Mays, then a ministerial student, room in her home. "I saw for myself a project," recalled Mays, who ultimately stayed four years with her.

Mays said that he saw in Cora Fillmore the strong desire to get all of Charles Fillmore's teachings out into the world and to circulate them as "widely and broadly and in their purest form as she possibly could." She felt his teachings held the key for healing nations, for peace on earth, and for wholeness and prosperity. Mays encouraged her to go back to Unity and begin work on the manuscripts that had not yet been published. She finally agreed to go in one day a week. It was soon increased to two, and then more often as she got into the work of editing *Keep a True Lent*. Cora eventually asked Mays to assist her in the work. He found it to be one of the most rewarding experiences of his years at Unity Village. Before she died in 1955, she had completed *The Revealing Word* and was at work on a third book.[46]

Cora Fillmore died early in the morning of January 29, 1955. She was seventy-nine years old. Her death came as a surprise to her friends since she had not been ill. Mays, who was still living with her, said that she was feeling better than at any time he had known her, "getting stronger and stronger." She told him she was getting ready for some change in her life. She was thinking of selling her property near Unity Village and moving to California. Mays recalled, "It was right in the peak of this energy, planning and thinking that change was going to come to pass that she died of a heart attack in her sleep."[47]

Despite the fact that she seemed to be gaining in health, believed in Charles Fillmore's most advanced teachings regarding regeneration, and had supported her husband in his efforts to overcome death, Cora Fillmore never affirmed as Charles did, "I am going to live forever in this body, now." She believed, according to Blaine Mays, that we are eternal beings and that the soul exists beyond death, but she made no attempt to regenerate her own body. Mays believed that she lost her desire to live after the death of Charles.[48]

Chapter 10

"HE HAD AN UNCOMMON LOT
OF COMMON SENSE"

A variety of valuable character traits came together in the person of
Charles Fillmore that enabled him to cofound and lead an important new spiritual movement in the United States at the beginning
of the twentieth century. Many friends and associates testified to the qualities
that enabled him to achieve greatness. These people found him to be inspirational as a speaker and a person; a gifted teacher; unpretentious, unassuming,
and genuine; a humorist and storyteller; playful and fun-loving, warm and
outgoing; and a dedicated, diligent worker.

INSPIRATIONAL AS A SPEAKER, TEACHER, AND PERSON

Of those who knew him personally, James Dillet Freeman captured the qualities that made Charles Fillmore an inspirational leader. Freeman, who wrote
at length about Charles in his book *The Story of Unity*, said:

> Charles Fillmore lighted many fires in many minds. He was a fire-
> bringer, a carrier of the Promethean spark. He was highly developed
> spiritually, yet his spirituality was salted by a sense of practicality.
> He was an original and creative thinker and moved boldly into new
> realms of thought, yet he never lost the common touch. He was
> always lighting fires in people's minds, but if the fire in the stove that
> warmed their bodies went out, he attended to that also. His head was
> in the clouds, but his feet were on the ground. He was gifted with
> uncommon sense, but he had an uncommon lot of common sense.[1]

One of the early Unity ministers, and one of the most successful, Richard Lynch, told how Charles inspired people to become a part of the Unity movement: "I want to testify to the greatness and universality of the mind and consciousness of Charles Fillmore. An institution is the lengthened shadow of the individual. This Unity movement, which is in various parts of the world, is part of the shadow (spirit) of Charles Fillmore."[2]

A Kansas woman, not a member of his congregation, who came to Kansas City to meet with him to get his opinions on a book, commented on how moved she was when she heard him speak:

> I went to the talk and sat in the front. When that "little man" walked on the rostrum I wondered at his power, but not for long, because as he gave his message or lesson for that day, I felt as though Christ himself was healing me. I can't begin to describe the uplift and peace which filled my body and soul.[3]

Retta Chilcott, a longtime Unity School worker, told Charles in a letter the benefits she received from listening to him speak:

> I always go away feeling that I have received a real spiritual baptism in addition to the helpful suggestions and real inspiration that you have given me in your talk, and that this spiritual blessing or substance, which I receive, stays with me through the days, weeks and years that follow. . . . There are many metaphysical teachers who give one helpful suggestions but it is not often that I receive the real satisfying spiritual substance from a teacher like I do from you.[4]

Silent Unity meant a great deal to Charles, and he spent a lot of time with Silent Unity workers. James Dillet Freeman described how Charles interacted with them and how it made a difference in the way they performed:

> Charles Fillmore knew how to call forth the talents of others. Many workers in Silent Unity remember an experience they had when they first came to work in that department: a difficult letter came to them that they did not know how to answer; they took it to Mr. Fillmore and asked him how to answer it. This happened perhaps three or four times, and he told them: "The Spirit that is in me is in you. Go back to your desk and ask that Spirit how to answer this letter. You can

answer it." At first, the letter writer might doubt that he could do it, but always in the end he discovered that he had the ability.[5]

Fillmore's way of encouraging people to be their best was described by his granddaughter Rosemary Fillmore Rhea, who said, "He had a way of making you feel good about yourself. He firmly believed that you could do whatever you wanted to do."[6]

Lowell Fillmore observed his father's impact on people, by the example he set, and by the way he lived and worked:

> My father was gifted with a keen power of perception and good judgment, as well as a love of Truth. . . . By applying the Christ healing power he was healed of a tubercular hip, which had made him lame since childhood. He began at once to spend much time in study and prayer and soon became a great strength to many who called upon him to help them find healing of mind, body and affairs.[7]

A Gifted Teacher

Those who studied with Charles Fillmore credited him with a well-developed capacity to communicate and encourage. May Rowland, the longtime head of Silent Unity, commented to James Dillet Freeman on the impact of Fillmore's teaching:

> He was a superb teacher. I do not mean because of his class merely. There was much more. He always gave his students faith—perhaps "gave" is not the word—I should say that being a man of faith, he imparted faith. Again and again I heard him say to someone, "You can do it." One got encouragement from Charles, not mere teaching.[8]

Vera Dawson Tait, who for many years was director of the Unity Correspondence School, observed how Charles was able to stimulate his students to think critically:

> The main aim of his teaching was to get students to think Truth through for themselves. By Socratic questioning, he would draw out his students' minds. He felt that Truth meant little as long as it was only words in a book. . . . He knew that only out of free discussion would his students arrive at an understanding of Truth that was in

their own language. This was his aim, for he knew that nothing means much to a person until he has made it part of his own experience.[9]

Tait further reported that Charles felt students learned best in the classroom when discussion was encouraged. He used the question-and-answer approach to elicit student response:

> They would sit around in a circle [and] Mr. Fillmore would ask one or another of them questions. Then the whole group would discuss the answers that were given. He loved to teach this way, freely and informally, with a group of students as sincerely interested in Truth as himself, gathered around him.[10]

Part of Charles' success as a teacher was due to his spontaneity. May Rowland reported:

> When he was teaching a class he used very few notes. As he spoke ideas would come to him. I have seen his eyes sparkle with light when an idea came to him, and then he would speak spontaneously, with a kind of inner fire, as it were. There was a great deal of spontaneity in his teaching.[11]

James Dillet Freeman indicated that Charles did not try to stuff Unity teaching down people's throats but presented the doctrine as suggestions for experimentation:

> All the Fillmores said in effect [was] "Here are some ideas that we believe to be true. Examine them. Study them; accept those that you can use in your life. For the rest, do not let what you cannot accept keep you from accepting what will help you now. The time may come when you can accept these other ideas too."[12]

Vera Dawson Tait also felt that Charles' goal in teaching was much broader than making converts to Unity teaching: "There is one thing of which I am certain and that is that the Fillmores really weren't trying to make Unity students. What they were seeking above all things was to have people go deep within and find their own way."[13]

Charles himself commented that the aim of his teaching was self-development. "The prime object," he said, "is to instruct students on how to overcome themselves, defects of mind, body and affairs."[14]

UNPRETENTIOUS, UNASSUMING, GENUINE

All who knew Charles Fillmore commented on his lack of affectation, his humility, and his kindness. James Dillet Freeman commented, "If there was anything that stood out about this man—and there were many things—it was the fact that he was a very genuine human being of deep humanity. He was easy to identify with. There wasn't a grain of pretension about the man."[15]

Richard Lynch saw the same sensitive, down-to-earth, what-you-see-is-what-you-get human being that others observed: "He was thoroughly genuine. I never found him otherwise. He had little vanity. If you praised him, he would move it over to Principle or Spirit. He did not court admiration."[16]

A Unity congregant, who for five years was connected with the work and observed Charles at close range, said, "His steadfast refusal to think or speak of himself as a person of any importance remains one of his outstanding characteristics in my thought."[17]

May Rowland indicated that Charles did not want to be looked up to or admired. It wasn't in his nature. She noted, "Charles never let anyone put him on a pedestal. He never encouraged an atmosphere of admiration. When he felt anything like that he would always change his manner. He would tell a humorous story and break the spell, so to speak."[18]

Fillmore's granddaughter Rosemary Fillmore Rhea, who remembered him as "a nice, warm human person," recalled how he disliked being admired:

> Never at any time would he let anyone offer him personal admiration. He would make a joke, change the conversation, tell a story, turn the admiration aside. . . . I would put it this way. He could never accept the "holy man" pedestal because he never thought that way. He never seemed self-conscious. He lost his self-consciousness before I knew him.[19]

Eric Butterworth, author of several books on the Unity teaching and who for many years was the speaker at the Unity center that met in Lincoln Center, New York City, recalled how Charles and Myrtle maintained a home-spun quality in the way they related to people, choosing not to set themselves apart. This was exemplified, he observed, by their deportment in the Unity cafeteria:

I was always impressed to see Charles and Myrtle in line at meal-times, like everybody else. They would take their place with trays and proceed step by step, no matter how long the line, and sometimes it was very long. Unless you knew who they were you would never imagine that those two people were the founders of Unity. . . . These two were simply being the warm, friendly, unostentatious human beings that they were at heart. They were simply being themselves, and that was that.[20]

James Dillet Freeman observed the same likeable qualities in both Charles and Myrtle, noting that these were people without large egos: "There was no pretense about these two. They never took a title to themselves, and they were such unassuming people that no one else felt like calling them by a title either. Among their workers and close friends, there was almost a family feeling."[21]

WARM AND OUTGOING

May Rowland also testified to Charles' warmth, openness, and his ability to connect with others. He had a natural interest in the lives of the people around him. She said, "There was a kind of wholesomeness about him that you could feel. And it was the kind of wholesomeness that made him interested in the human side of everything. He could see the human side in every situation. I never heard him criticize anybody."[22]

Sometimes on holidays or at other times when there were only a few workers in the office, Charles would invite the whole group into his office to have lunch. There he had a little hot plate. Sometimes all he had was soup and crackers. The workers would sit in his office, sip soup from cups or glasses, and any other kind of small container they could get.[23]

Rosemary Fillmore Rhea remembered that her grandfather also loved outings in the country with staff from Unity School:

After the farm was bought Papa Charles was always finding excuses to take people out there for a picnic. Again and again he would say, "Let's all go for a picnic out to the farm," and out to the farm we'd go. He enjoyed every moment of a picnic.[24]

At one of the Fillmores' evening programs at Unity Farm, an incident occurred that indicated his natural tendency to be engaging and hospitable.

The chapel was crowded, and everyone seemed to be enthusiastic about the evening session. When Charles concluded his remarks he said to the group, "When the program is over, you are all invited to come over to our place for a bite to eat." Myrtle rose to her feet and came forward. "If you do," she said, "there had better be another expression of the miracle of the loaves and fishes." Everyone knew Myrtle's dream house at the farm was without a kitchen.[25]

A FAMILY MAN

Charles' life centered around his family. From the time he was a young adult, his mother Georgiana, "Momsy" as she was called, lived with him and his family. He was in his seventies when she died at age 97. He worked closely with Myrtle for most of their fifty-year marriage. She was not only his wife but his closest companion and friend. His three sons, Lowell, Rickert, and Royal, all joined him in the spiritual work of the Unity movement.

He spent significant time with his three grandchildren, Charles R., Rosemary, and Frances, as they grew from children into adulthood. The family spent a good deal of time together, gathering on a weekly basis, both when they lived in the city and when they moved to Unity Farm. In her memoir, *That's Just How My Spirit Travels*, Rosemary Fillmore Rhea commented on how she looked forward to her grandfather's visits. "He would come to our home for Saturday night dinners. I would run down the back stone steps of the house to greet him. It was always such a joy to be in his presence. I liked to sit close to him and hold his hand."[26]

Whenever Rosemary was ill, her grandfather would come and sit by her bed, go into the silence, and pray. She would go to sleep and wake up well in the morning.[27] Rosemary delighted in the fact that her grandfather loved going places with his grandchildren. She recalled, "Even when he was in his late eighties and nineties, he was ready to go to the movies, shopping, or whatever. He especially enjoyed movies, westerns in particular. It was no problem getting him to take us to the little theatre in Lee's Summit."[28]

In an interview in 1995, Charles R. Fillmore recalled incidents about his grandfather and his great-grandmother. He particularly looked forward to his grandfather's weekly visits. While his grandmother, Myrtle, tended to take on the role of teacher and disciplinarian, his grandfather was more playful. Charles R. said:

> There was never a harsh word [from him]. He came out weekly to Unity Farm for dinner. We always looked forward to it because he was always in good humor. He liked nature and wildlife and encouraged that in me. As a child, each fish I caught in the lake at Unity Farm I took home to show him. I thought of him as a wonderful grandparent.[29]

The high school senior prom was a major event for Charles R. The family had only one car, and his father did not want him to use it, so Charles R. had a date and no transportation. His grandfather, who owned a new Dodge, saved the day by allowing him to use his car.[30]

Charles R. was particularly fond of his great-grandmother, Momsy, whom he viewed as a "very, very strong woman." She lived at Unity Farm and was the host of all the family's formal get-togethers. According to Charles R., she was "the focal point of the family when I was young."[31]

HUMORIST/STORYTELLER

Charles was a born storyteller. He loved funny stories and enjoyed telling them. He had the gift of all natural speakers to sense the moods of an audience; he could tell when they were getting restless, and he knew when to inject a story. "I don't mind you looking at your watches," he told his audience, "but when you look at them, then put them to your ear to see if they are running, that is too much."[32]

James Dillet Freeman indicated that he injected humor into all of his talks:

> I don't think he ever made a speech in his life that he didn't tell some kind of funny story. He believed that humor belonged in it. He would stop, especially if people were not paying attention, and introduce a funny story. . . . He was a man who wasn't afraid to poke fun at himself. He thought humor belonged in life.[33]

Ida M. Stuart, a Seattle women who heard him speak while on tour in Washington in the 1930s, reported how he used humor to get his message across:

Judging from Mr. Fillmore's pictures and his deep writings I had the impression that he must be very serious, if not a little grim. I had the surprise of my life when he opened the meeting by telling a series of funny stories each one more humorous than the rest and every one with a point to it, as sharp as a razor's edge. He kept this up till everyone in the audience was shaking with laughter, some losing their glasses, and many with tears streaming down their faces. Then he grew serious and said, quote, "Now you are relaxed and happy and ready for the message," and it was a wonderful message.[34]

Emma M. Henderson, a Texas woman who came to Kansas City for a New Thought convention, heard him give an impromptu talk. She reported how his use of humor enabled him to reach his audience:

I attended the New Thought Congress at Unity in 1919, I think, and met Mr. Fillmore for the first time. I had been reading his writing for several years and was delighted to see him in person. The first night of the banquet there was a program and they insisted that Mr. Fillmore make a speech. We expected a great talk and wished all the readers of Unity could be there to share it. Imagine our surprise when Mr. Fillmore said solemnly, "After eating so much at this great banquet, I was just a thinking, I hoped that I would not be like the little boy I read about the other day who had eaten too much the night before at Thanksgiving Dinner when he said (to himself), "What's the matter with you, stomach? Ain't you satisfied at all? I've done stuffed and stuffed you till you're hard just like a ball. Why, last night, I gave you more turkey, cranberries, pie and cake and all you could do to thank me was just to ache and ache. I've done make up my mind, stomach, that hereafter I don't intend to give you much to appreciate."[35]

Henderson said that Fillmore had the convention in the palm of his hand as the crowd "roared and roared."

Joyful, Playful, and Fun-loving

May Rowland recalled the joyousness Charles seemed to manifest in daily life:

I could describe Charles to you and yet the mere physical description would not suffice. There was a kind of gleam in his eyes—they were blue, but it wasn't so much the color in his eyes as the gleam of joy and life in them. But these are details. The essence of the matter is the impression of life that Charles gave. When you think of him an impression of life comes through—and joy, of course—always joy.[36]

Daily Unity magazine, the in-house Unity newsletter that was published for many years during Charles' tenure as president, printed a story that indicated that Charles was not the type of person who took himself too seriously:

Some of the Silent Unity members got real confidential the other day and began telling their boyhood ambitions. Mr. Fillmore started off by telling his. He wanted to go out on the wild prairies, wear leather breeches, break wild broncos, sing "Joe Bowers" until the natives all cried, and be an honest-to-goodness cowboy.[37]

Charles could also be outrageous and, on occasion, enjoyed letting his hair down. James Dillet Freeman indicated that Charles loved to playact. He would go into downtown Kansas City and pose as a hayseed. In Wolferman's, he would give girls dimes and act like a rube. "Here's a dime for you, Ma'am." Once in Emery Bird Thayer, he inquired about a rug that was rather expensive. He heard the price and decided he could get one. Then, to the clerk, he said, "We'll be back and get it when we sell our goats." "That's all right, Mr. Fillmore," said the saleslady. Evidently, Charles thought he was completely disguised and was taken aback when the young woman recognized him. "How did you know me?" he asked.[38]

Hard-working, Diligent, and Dedicated

Only a person of high energy could have performed the myriad of tasks that Charles Fillmore crammed into his workday. Writing in *Unity* magazine in 1903, using the third person to convey his message, Charles told of "the daily duties of the editor": "He writes numerous letters and articles for publication, he treats many patients, both present and absent, he teaches classes nearly every night in the week, and delivers a sermon on Sunday. This makes for a full day—and usually eats up most of the night."[39]

Fillmore tended to overwork, as this comment made in a piece in *Unity* magazine indicated:

I have undertaken more writing than I can well accomplish with my other duties. Yet I work twenty-one hours out of twenty-four, and have kept it up at this pace for several years. It is daylight every morning before I catch the few hours sleep that "knit up the ravelled sleeve." This three hours waste will eventually be overcome, and I shall work right through without a wink.[40]

A further indication of his crowded work schedule was communicated in a letter to Myrtle in August 1909. Myrtle had gone to Colorado to teach a course on Practical Christianity and had hoped that Charles would join her for a few days' vacation. Charles, who almost never took a vacation, wrote to tell her why he felt he couldn't join her:

I do not see any prospect of coming. The work is growing in every direction. The letters to Silent Unity are piling up—over 100 on hand tonight. *Unity* is to get out, meetings to look after—Wedding next Tuesday—Funeral Monday p.m. Mr. Smith who lives on Cypress back of us and who comes to our meetings died at the hospital yesterday, and left word he wanted me to conduct services. I could not refuse such a request, though I wanted to. Several new people here whom I have not seen. Kelly is oiling and washing both floors and it is causing us some inconvenience in Silent Unity.[41]

IDIOSYNCRASIES

Charles had his idiosyncrasies, habits you might not expect of someone who otherwise seemed so sane and predictable. James Dillon Freeman reported:

Stays up most of the night. Goes to bed around 4 or 5 in the morning. And a prowler. Always into anything available, opening and shutting drawers, closets, etc. Once visiting Cora's sister, Mary Darland in Pueblo, they went out to a show and left him home alone. Cora knew he would have been into everything. Late that night when they were in bed, he turned to her and in a whisper, "Cora, you know what?" "No. What is it?" "Mary doesn't keep her refrigerator any better than you do."[42]

He also viewed himself as the reincarnation of Paul the apostle and Napoleon Bonaparte. Charles on occasion reflected on his own past incarnations, believing he got accurate information while meditating in the silence. He believed that he was once incarnated as the apostle Paul. In a statement made in *Unity* magazine in October 1896, he wrote, "We happen to know Paul in his present incarnation and have his word for this." While he didn't specifically identify himself, he gave more detail when a *Unity* reader wrote to him asking for clarification. "Are we to understand that Paul reincarnated is now upon the earth, and an acquaintance of yours?"[43] the writer asked. Charles, who informed Charles S. Braden, a highly respected historian of religion,[44] that, in an earlier incarnation, he was the apostle Paul, was probably referring to himself when he responded to the Unity correspondent:

> He who once manifested as Paul the Apostle is now expressing himself through another form right here in America.[45] . . . Paul lived over thirty-eight years in his present form, a plain American citizen, before he knew that he was the same ego that had once expressed itself in the flesh as Saul the Jewish zealot; afterwards, Paul the Christian pioneer.[46] . . . He who once manifested as Paul is only now getting a practical understanding of the scientific laws underlying the so-called miracles of the religious world, and his aim is to so develop his own powers that he can demonstrate to materialistic science that there exists a connecting link between their world and the supernatural world of the church, which they have not understood for lack of that link. To do this successfully requires an extraordinary amount of silent work with physical, psychical, and spiritual powers.[47]

Contrary to what one might expect, Charles did not hold Paul in high esteem. Fillmore considered the apostle to have been deeply flawed, one whose work did more harm than good. Paul, according to Charles, failed to follow the instructions of the Holy Spirit and led Christianity away from the true teachings of Jesus:

> Paul, the chief Apostle, was a persecutor of women and children and a man-slayer, having been the ring leader and abettor of those who

stoned Stephen to death. Paul was by nature a fighter. He belonged to that class of irrepressibles that when fired by an idea cannot be hushed up. He just would talk about the subject that possessed his mind. He talked incessantly, argued and expostulated—an intellectual debater. In this day he would be called a wordy crank.[48]

In another issue of *Unity,* he once again wrote of Paul's limitations:

Paul was willful, according to his own admissions, and went contrary to the guidance of the Holy Spirit. For example the Spirit warned him not to go up to Jerusalem the second time. But his combativeness was up, and he was so determined to have a bout with those old Jews that he went anyway. The result was his imprisonment, appeal to Caesar, and long incarceration at Rome. Had Paul been more obedient and less ambitious to defend his religion, the history of Christianity would have been vastly different. To be successful in a spiritual work, we must not only be obedient to the leading of the Spirit part of the time, but *all the time.*[49]

Charles did not cite biographies or outside authorities as sources of information on his life as Paul. The information was revealed personally, presumably while in a meditative state. He considered Paul to be sincere but with grave defects:

In the history of his life, as revealed to me in the thought realms, I read that he died of consumption in a mountain town near Rome. The popular idea that the so-called saints were good and powerful enough to sit with Jesus in His power, will not bear close analysis. It is, in fact, a mere assumption. Paul in his own writings left a hundred admissions of his disobedience, weakness, ambition and double-mindedness. . . . Paul was a good man, and sincere, but he had his faults. He was possessed of a towering ambition. Ambition is a subtle mental force. . . . Paul, like Caesar, was ambitious, and that ambition was not converted when he turned his zeal from the Jews to the Christians; it was simply transferred. . . . During his lifetime his work did not come to fruitage, and he died in disappointment.[50]

Before incarnating as Charles Fillmore, the spirit that was in Paul the apostle, according to Charles, incarnated as Napoleon Bonaparte. Again,

Charles indicated he received this information while in a meditative state. In a sermon given in December 1902, which was published in *Unity* magazine, Charles explained:

> You may be surprised, and some of you may doubtless be shocked, if I tell you that Paul the Apostle and Napoleon Bonaparte were one and the same individual. Yet I know this to be a fact. I have gone deep into the subject of man and his subjective life, and I tell you that I have found his character, not as theory but as fact.[51]

Charles' identification of Napoleon as the reincarnation of Paul created a stir in the *Unity* readership, for Charles received several letters of inquiry and protestation. A Protestant minister declared he was "shocked and disappointed" by Charles' statement that "Paul the apostle and Napoleon Bonaparte were one and the same individual." The minister commented:

> It is the very essence of Christianity to teach that when men in whom the Christ-nature is distinctly formed, as it was in St. Paul, pass out of the limitations of the earthly life, they enter upon that life of glorified manhood into which Jesus was raised. . . . Such a supposition, as you make it, in the case of Paul is not only contrary to Scripture, and to all that Science teaches concerning the evolution of humanity; it is a backward and humiliating step in the Divine plan of human life.[52]

Charles responded by reasserting his belief in reincarnation and defending the means he used in uncovering the information. He indicated again his conviction that information which came to him in the silence was reliable objective data rather than subjective personal experience:

> Our good brother wishes me to reconsider my teaching in this matter of so-called reincarnation, as if it were a question that rested upon belief. I know that man does not die—that he lives right on, sometimes in a natural body, sometimes in an astral body, and sometimes in no body at all. I do not get this as a special revelation, but I have developed faculties that have enabled me to, in a measure, see behind the veil of sense. It is not a supposition on my part—I know the facts as I know about the events that have taken place and are taking place in the lives of myself and those with whom I come in contact.[53]

Moreover, the intuitive powers Charles was claiming for himself, he believed, could be developed by all who dedicated themselves to inner work. He explained, "This ability to see deeper than the sense consciousness may be developed by anyone who is willing to let go of the outer world, and patiently seek the inner."[54]

In responding to the minister, Charles again reasserted his position that Paul had reincarnated as Napoleon. Charles reported, "His [Paul's] ambition did not die." Charles further indicated that through the workings of divine law, the spirit of Paul was bound to reincarnate. "As a mental energy," he stated, "it was generating its force in the intellect, and under the law of mind action it must have a vent. That vent was found in the Napoleon incarnation."[55]

CHARLES FILLMORE—A MAN OF MANY GIFTS

Charles' special gifts as a human being were described in an unsigned piece in *Weekly Unity* magazine, which appeared shortly after his death and probably was written by Ernest Wilson:

> Charles Fillmore was gifted beyond most men with an inquiring mind, a creative imagination, a joyous spirit, and a steadfast faith in man's divinity. He was spiritual, yet his spirituality was salted by a divine simplicity that made him real and dear. He was an original and creative thinker and moved boldly in new realms of thought, and yet he never lost the common touch. There was a mixture in him of boy and mystic, jester and genius, businessman and saint. He was a man.[56]

During his lifetime, Charles Fillmore manifested qualities that are generally recognized as possessed by a person who had achieved a high level of spiritual attainment. Rosemary Fillmore Rhea described the attributes that led her to conclude that her grandfather was spiritually gifted:

> In the Bhagavad-Gita, Arjuna, the disciple, asks Krishna to tell him how he can recognize a man who knows the Truth; that is, how he can identify an illumined person. Krishna replies, "A man who is not affected by achievement or failure, who is free from emotions such as fear, anger, pride, vanity, jealousy, hate; a man who has disciplined his mind—he is wise; he is illumined." This is a good description of my grandfather, the man I called Papa Charlie.[57]

Appendix A

Emanuel Swedenborg

"The Largest of All Modern Souls"

In describing the origins of the Unity spiritual teachings, it is impossible to ignore the work of the Swedish spiritual philosopher Emanuel Swedenborg (1688–1772), even though only a few references are made to his works in Unity publications. J. Gordon Melton, author of *The Encyclopedia of American Religions,* includes Swedenborg as one of five authors who influenced the leaders of New Thought.[1] Others were Ralph Waldo Emerson, Warren Felt Evans, Phineas P. Quimby, and Emma Curtis Hopkins. In his *Religious History of the American People,* Sydney E. Ahlstrom recognized the impact Swedenborg's work had on religion and spirituality in nineteenth-century America:

> His influence was everywhere: In Transcendentalism and at Brook Farm, in Spiritualism and the free-love movement, in the craze for communitarian experiments, in faith healing, mesmerism, and a half-dozen medical cults, among great intellectuals, crude charlatans, and innumerable frontier quacks.[2]

Stephen Larsen, a Ph.D. psychologist and author of *The Shaman's Doorway*, credited Swedenborg with being an important catalyst for the nineteenth-century mental-healing movement of which Unity School of Christianity was a part: "Swedenborg's visionary worldview became seminal in a number of healing systems, from Christian Science to homeopathy, all of which emphasize the dependence of physical health on the inner or causal level of spiritual well-being."[3]

Ralph Waldo Emerson, in his book *Representative Men,* commented on the "genius of Swedenborg" and credited him with being "the largest of all modern souls."[4] Emerson observed:

Swedenborg styles himself in the title pages of his books, "Servant of the Lord Jesus Christ," and by force of intellect, and in effect, he is the last Father of the Church, and is not likely to have a successor. No wonder that his depth of ethical wisdom should give him influence as a teacher. To the withered traditional church, yielding dry catechism, he let in nature again, and the worshiper, escaping from the vestry of verbs and texts, is surprised to find himself a party to the whole of his religion. . . . The moral insight of Swedenborg, the correction of popular errors, the announcement of ethical laws, take him out of a comparison with any other major writer and entitle him to a place among the lawgivers of mankind.[5]

Charles Fillmore read the works of Swedenborg and found them "consistent with modern metaphysical teaching."[6] The works of Swedenborg were listed among recommended books in the first issue of *Modern Thought* magazine in April 1889.

The life and teaching of Emanuel Swedenborg will not be explored fully here. Rather, only those parts that lay the groundwork for transcendentalism, New Thought, and the Unity teachings will be presented.

Emanuel Swedenborg was brought up in a well-to-do, deeply religious Swedish household, one of seven children. His father Jesper Swedberg, a well-known Lutheran theologian, was a professor of theology and dean of Uppsala University before being appointed bishop of Skara. His mother, Sarah Behm, who died when he was eight, was an heiress of a mining family. Her personal wealth placed the Swedbergs among the Swedish aristocracy. Within a year after his mother's death, his father remarried. Emanuel's stepmother, who was childless, was devoted to her adopted children, particularly to Emanuel who was her favorite.[7]

As a youth, Swedenborg was not inclined to study theology or pursue a career in the ministry. He was deeply interested in science and math. After a university education, he spent over three decades pursuing a highly successful career as a scientist, scholar, and assessor of his country's Board of Mines. His many articles and books encompassed the disciplines of geology, anatomy, astronomy, and physics. He often traveled abroad to pursue his scientific studies and brought back to Sweden new concepts in mining, smelting, and ore processing, as well as new ideas in mathematics. He was not a churchgoer, and there was nothing in his diaries during his career as a scientist to suggest that he was inclined toward religion or that he would give up his career as a scientist or that he would spend the last twenty-five years of his life as a mystic and a seer.[8]

In 1745, at age 57, Swedenborg was living in Holland and studying anatomy at the University of Leiden when he had a powerful spiritual experience. Enjoying the quiet life of a scholar, he was unmarried and living singly, spending most of his time in libraries or in his rooms. For no apparent reason, his moods began fluctuating wildly from ecstasy to depression, and while sleeping he was having nightmares. On a crucial night in which he retired about 10 p.m., he was awakened by what he thought was a loud noise. He reported: "Straight away there came over me a shuddering, so strong from head downward over the whole body, with a noise of thunder, and this happened several times. I found that something holy was upon me."[9]

After sleeping for a while he was again awakened to find himself shuddering. He prayed, holding his hands together, when a hand came forth and squeezed his hands together. He identified the figure as that of the Lord, or Jesus, and declared:

> At that moment I sat in his bosom and saw him face to face; it was a face of holy mien and in all it was indescribable, and he smiled so that I believe that his face had indeed been like this when he lived on earth. He spoke to me and asked if I had a clean bill of health. I answered, "Lord, thou knowest better than I."[10]

From this experience and from visions thereafter, Swedenborg believed that the Lord had given him the task of disclosing the spiritual meaning of the scriptures.[11] He was forthright, asserting that God had given him a mission, commenting, "Lest men reject my statements as fables, I can testify in sacred earnest that I have been admitted into the spiritual world of the Messiah Himself."[12] Soon he was having open discourse with spirits and angels. He dropped his scientific studies and began a meticulous and ambitious project of biblical inquiry, using the same research techniques he used in his study of the physical sciences. Already knowledgeable in five languages, he learned Hebrew to facilitate his work. His first task was to construct a comprehensive index to the Old and New Testaments.[13]

Little by little, he developed what he believed were the Bible's hidden meanings. His information came in flashes of intuition as he meditated on passages of scripture. His diary explained how his insights were obtained. In one representative entry, he noted, "This morning it was clearly shown to me how spirits operate upon man, that is, how God Messiah leads man by means of spirits and angels."[14]

Swedenborg explained that his task was to make the spiritual world more real to humankind, giving testimony that it did, in fact, exist:

In Christendom to date, there is a thick fog about the existence of a spiritual world. To prevent ignorance of that world, and a consequent wavering of faith about heaven and hell, from making such fools of us that we become material atheists, the Lord has graciously opened the sight of my spirit. He has thus raised me into heaven and lowered me into hell and has shown me visually what each is like.[15]

Swedenborg wanted it understood that while he consorted with angels and spirits, his spiritual instruction came directly from God:

I have had discourse with spirits and with angels now for several years; nor has any spirit dared, nor angel wished, to tell me anything, still less instruct me, concerning things in the Word, or concerning any doctrine from the Word; but the Lord alone has taught me. Who has been revealed to me, and has since appeared constantly and does now appear before my eyes as a Sun in which He is as He appears to the angels, and has enlightened me.[16]

While he received spiritual instruction only from "the Lord," Swedenborg testified that he also made contact, in the spirit world, with the luminaries of history from all time. Included were renowned figures from Aristotle and Plato to Luther and Leibniz. He reported the encounters as well as the debates and dialogues on learned subjects in a matter-of-fact way, not claiming to be able to communicate with each and every spirit but only those with whom he had some kind of previous contact:

I cannot converse withal, but such as I have known in this world, with all regal and princely persons, with all renowned heroes or great and learned men, whom I have known either personally or from their actions or writings: consequently, of all of whom I could form an idea, for it may be supposed that a person whom I never knew or of whom I could form no idea, I neither could nor would wish to speak with.[17]

Swedenborg recorded these and many other communications with spirits, writing for several hours each day. His literary output in the twenty years of his life following his spiritual opening was prodigious. Below is a list of his theological works (thirty volumes in total). His writings, coupled with biographies and commentaries, today occupy a full library shelf. They include *Arcana Coelestia* (twelve volumes), *Apocalypse Revealed* (two volumes), *Apocalypse Explained* (six volumes), *The True Christian Religion* (two volumes), *Conjugal Love, Divine Love and Wisdom, Divine Providence, The Four Doctrines*, a collected volume titled *Miscellaneous Theological Works*, and *Posthumous Theological Works* (two volumes).

Swedenborg had no fear of death. Sometime before he died, he foretold the date of his death to his landlady and maidservant, and the latter remarked that he seemed pleased with the prospect "as if he was going to have a holiday, to go to some merry-making."[18] Swedenborg's views on dying were expressed in the following passage:

> If one is conjoined with the Lord, he has a foretaste of the eternal life in this world; and if he has this, he no longer cares so much about his transitory life. Believe me, if I knew that the Lord would call me to Himself tomorrow, I would summon the musicians today, in order to be once more really gay in this world.[19]

Appendix B

Ralph Waldo Emerson

"He was more a Quaker than anything else"

Ralph Waldo Emerson was born in 1803 in Boston into a family with deep roots in Massachusetts.[1] His mother was the daughter of a prosperous Boston distiller. His father was a liberal Boston minister from a family that had produced clergymen in eight previous generations. Though only eight when his father died, Emerson had the good fortune to be raised by and around women, including his mother, of notable intellectual and spiritual accomplishments. Emerson considered his aunt (his father's sister, Mary Moody Emerson, who deeply influenced him as he was growing up) to be one of the most brilliant women in New England.

Emerson attended the eminent Boston Latin School and, following in the family tradition, studied for the ministry and graduated from Harvard. He was ordained in 1826 at age twenty-three and was appointed the junior minister at the Unitarian Second Church in Boston. He quickly established himself as an eloquent, inspirational speaker. He was less successful, however, in fulfilling duties related to pastoral care, probably because of lack of interest. He resigned after six years, in 1832, because of disagreements with his parishioners over the administration of the sacrament of the Lord's Supper.

After leaving the ministry and traveling abroad for a year, he took up residence in Concord, Massachusetts. Emerson read widely in philosophical, literary, and religious literature. He also kept a daily journal and, in the early 1830s, began writing the essays that were to make him famous. "Nature," published in 1836, when he was age thirty-three, was the first that gained him notice. In a Harvard Divinity School address in 1838, he outlined the tenets of transcendentalism, the philosophical system that owes its beginnings to his work. In the Divinity School address, he disavowed many of the teachings of traditional Unitarianism, bringing him wide notoriety in New England.

The attention Emerson received set a pattern for the rest of his career. There were strong objections and attacks from one side and personal, witness-bearing praise, almost adulation, from another. His fame grew rapidly in the early 1840s with the publication of two volumes of essays, works that included the two that made his reputation, "Self-Reliance" and "The Over-Soul." During the course of his lifetime, his literary output, including journals, letters, lectures, and essays, was prodigious.

Along with writing, Emerson began working as a platform lecturer. He made a good living at it, and, by the time he was in his fifties, he was giving over sixty lectures a year, a total of approximately fifteen hundred during his forty-year career. Lecturing took him beyond New England, traveling to Minneapolis and St. Louis and even as far west as California. He was on the road four to six months of the year, most of the time in the winter. In the mid-nineteenth century, traveling was hard whether by stagecoach or slow train. Hotels and lecture halls were cold. Nevertheless, Emerson was undeterred by the difficult conditions and enjoyed the work. He was a captivating speaker, followed the work as a calling, was excited by the presence of a crowd, and loved the emotional bond that developed between lecturer and audience.

In 1847, Emerson traveled to England, where he gave sixty-seven lectures to audiences averaging 750 people. His most recent biographer, Robert Richardson, noted that, in England, people lionized him; hostesses gave dinners for him, while the Anglican clergy attacked him every Sunday from their pulpits. He met all the major English literary and public figures of the day: Tennyson, Macaulay, Disraeli, Palmerston, Wordsworth, Arnold, and Carlyle. His fame spread more widely in the United States after his English success.

By the late 1850s, Emerson was fast becoming an institution—a growing reputation now preceding him wherever he went. By the 1870s, he had become a fixture in American life. Moncure Conway, a religious commentator who met him in 1850, considered him to be a titanic iconoclast. "Emerson," Conway wrote, "has the distinction of being the first repudiator of sacraments, supernaturalism, biblical authority, and Christianity itself in every form, who suffered no kind of martyrdom."[2]

Emerson's formative years and his training, both philosophically and spiritually, were in the Unitarian tradition. Emerson, throughout his lifetime, continued to accept many of the defining statements of Unitarianism made by William Ellery Channing, the Boston minister and greatest of the defining figures of American Unitarianism. In his 1819 Baltimore address titled "Unitarian Christianity," Channing outlined the positions that Emerson and his fellow transcendentalists incorporated into transcendentalist doctrine.[3] These positions included believing in one and only one God; rejecting traditional Christian doctrines, including the doctrine of the Trinity as subverting the unity of God; considering Jesus to be distinct from and inferior to God; emphasizing the moral teachings of Jesus; rejecting the key elements of Calvinism, in particular the teaching regarding sin and salvation; championing individual responsibility; stressing the goodness in human nature; and embracing the discoveries of modern science.[4]

In his book *Representative Men*, Emerson had high praise for the teachings of the Swedish seer and mystic Emanuel Swedenborg. Emerson considered him to be "the largest of all modern souls . . . the person who *sees* all that the philosopher knows."[5] Emerson incorporated into his own teaching Swedenborg's famous "Doctrine of Correspondences" as well as ideas on the indwelling presence of God, and the importance of developing and using intuition.

After reading the works of the French philosopher Victor Cousin, Emerson developed a respect for the value and importance of the spiritual literature of India, particularly the Bhagavad Gita. He ultimately considered it to be a scripture of equal standing with the Gospels,[6] while his reading of Buddhist literature led him to value the importance and appeal of Buddhism as well.[7] As Emerson moved away from Unitarianism, he recognized that his belief in the reality of the Indwelling Presence was central also to the teaching of George Fox and the Quakers.

In 1839, in answering a question from his friend David Haskins regarding his religion, Emerson acknowledged his spiritual debt to the Quakers. Haskins reported that Emerson responded "with greater deliberateness and longer pauses between his words than usual, that he was more a Quaker than anything else." Haskins quoted Emerson as saying, "I believe in the 'still small voice,' and the voice is Christ within us."[8] Emerson's most recent biographer, Robert Richardson, surmised that Emerson was at heart Quaker. He explained, "Quakerism was thus for Emerson the ultimate Protestantism, the decisive locating of religious authority in the individual."[9]

Appendix C

EMMA CURTIS HOPKINS

L ittle is known about the life of Emma Curtis Hopkins before she met Mary Baker Eddy in 1883 and became involved in Christian Science. Born in 1849 in the farming community of Killingly, Connecticut, she was the eldest of nine children. Her father, Rufus Curtis, was a farmer and part-time realtor; her mother, Lydia Phillips Curtis, was a farmer's wife. Emma was raised in the Congregational Church and received a secondary school education at the Killingly high school. Afterward, she taught in local schools. She married at age twenty-four, in July 1874, to George Irving Hopkins, a high-school English teacher. A son, John Carver, was born in the summer of the following year. At the time of the 1880 census, the family was living in Nantucket, Massachusetts, and Emma was identified as a housewife. In the early 1880s, the family moved to Manchester, New Hampshire, where George Hopkins continued to work as a teacher.[1]

In October 1883, Hopkins met Mary Baker Eddy at the home of a mutual friend, Mary F. Berry of Manchester. Berry, a graduate of Eddy's Massachusetts Metaphysical College, had invited Eddy to give a talk on Christian Science healing. Hopkins was immediately attracted to the work and wrote to Eddy in December, telling her that the "beautiful theory" she had advanced had taken "a firm hold on my heart." Hopkins expressed an interest in coming to Boston to study with Eddy and told her that she was happily married and had "a sweet little son" but could not "command a single dollar" because of her husband's continued indebtedness for his college education. She asked if she could pay Eddy for the primary course, which was to begin on December 27, after graduating and working as a practitioner.

Eddy evidently agreed, since Hopkins came to Boston, completed the twelve lessons in the course, and qualified as a Christian Science practitioner.

In a letter to Eddy from Manchester in January, Hopkins testified to healing her husband of a throat infection and expressed her dedication to the work, stating, "I give myself and all my time to the Master's work wherever it lies, here, there and yonder."[2]

In April 1884, Hopkins contributed an article entitled "God's Omnipresence" to Eddy's *Christian Science Journal*; and, in August of that year, Eddy offered her the editorship of the publication, a job that did not pay a salary. Assuming she would make enough money to support herself from practitioner work, Hopkins left home in September, placed her son with surrogates, and took the job of editor. One month later, she expressed her loyalty to Eddy in a letter stating, "I am at your service," and signed it "lovingly, your disciple."[3]

Hopkins remained on the job until she was dismissed eleven months later in October 1885. The reasons for her firing are unclear, most likely due to disagreements over editorial policy. Hopkins evidently felt she had been wronged by Eddy for she wrote to a colleague on November 4, 1885, commenting, "I shall never serve a cause or a person without sharp business arrangements again, and shall hold strong guard over personal reference and worshipful feelings at every point."[4]

Shortly thereafter, Hopkins, again leaving husband and son behind, joined with Mary Plunkett, another Christian Science student who also had fallen out of favor with Eddy, and moved to Chicago. There they set up a Christian Science metaphysical college and teachers' association modeled after Eddy's organizations in Boston. Plunkett was the administrative president and Hopkins, the teacher. The first class, which was directed toward practitioner training, was graduated in June 1886. Shortly thereafter, Hopkins, though not an ordained minister herself, broadened the scope of the Chicago work and opened a seminary for the training and ordination of ministers.

Eddy, who was continually plagued by students who abandoned her, castigated Hopkins as one of "the unprincipled claimants," who was guilty of "dishonesty" and "fraud." Hopkins tried to conciliate Eddy, writing her in December 1886 from Chicago, assuring Eddy that she spoke highly of her in classes and used Eddy's *Science and Health* as a text. Eddy was not mollified and in an article in the April 1887 issue of the *Christian Science Journal* titled "Beware of False Teachers" charged Hopkins with "deluding the minds she was claiming to instruct," continuing, "Mrs. Plunkett and Mrs. Hopkins are traveling over the land, professedly teaching Christian Science, and deluding their victims. . . . Be it said that their journeying is done for the ducats, and not the interest of the cause."[5] When asked if Hopkins taught Mesmerism, Eddy responded, "She took the Primary Course at my college, but was not permitted to go farther. . . . She is not qualified to teach Christian Science and is incapable of teaching it."[6]

Unfazed by Eddy's criticisms, Hopkins continued to teach classes in Chicago and in other cities in the Midwest and far West, including Kansas City. When Mary Plunkett dissolved their partnership in 1888 and set up a rival Christian Science work on the East Coast, Hopkins found it necessary to both teach and administer. She continued her work until 1895, when she closed her seminary and moved to New York City. Although Hopkins enjoyed teaching and ordained 111 ministers during her stay in the Midwest, she did not enjoy administrative work. By 1895, she was apparently burned out.

From 1895 until her death in 1925, she taught students individually from her New York apartment, worked as a practitioner of mental healing, and spoke occasionally to metaphysical groups. In letters written to friends during her New York years, she told about her busy schedule. Appointments with her were apparently difficult to get. She evidently made a comfortable living from her work.

Hopkins, though a gifted teacher and practitioner of spiritual healing, was not an able writer. She wrote occasional articles for New Thought periodicals and her first book, *High Mysticism*, in 1907. A book titled *Scientific Christian Mental Practice* pulled together information from her classes. The writing in *High Mysticism* is disjointed and difficult to follow, moving precipitously from topic to topic with little or no follow-through. Only the most dedicated reader would stick with this work. The writing in *Scientific Christian Mental Practice* is much easier to follow. It appears that an editor helped pull this material together, as the writing style bears little resemblance to that in *High Mysticism*. It is understandable why the Fillmores, when looking for someone to present their work in book form in the 1890s, chose a gifted writer, H. Emilie Cady, rather than Hopkins.

While Hopkins was a gifted teacher, the content of her teaching, as presented in her two books, can be found in the works of Mary Baker Eddy, Warren Felt Evans, Ralph Waldo Emerson, and Emanuel Swedenborg. Hopkins' spiritual ideas—including her positions on the nature of the Divine and human; the teachings of Jesus; divine law; faith; the power of ideas, thoughts, and words; affirmations and denials; prayer; and metaphysical healing—are not original with her.

Like Charles Fillmore, Hopkins was an avid reader and a spiritual eclectic. She was acquainted with a wide literature, including the writings of Thomas Carlyle, Plato, Socrates, St. Paul, Jonathan Edwards, Henry Ward Beecher, Martin Luther, Francis Bacon, Thomas á Kempis, the Bhagavad Gita, Shakespeare, Agassiz, Bunyan, Dickens, Wordsworth, Confucius, the Buddha, Ibsen, and Zwingli, in addition to Eddy, Evan, Emerson, and Swedenborg. References to each can be found in *High Mysticism* and *Scientific Christian Mental Practice*.

Hopkins always acknowledged her intellectual and spiritual debt to Mary Baker Eddy. She never criticized in her writings or spoke disparagingly of Eddy and referred to her respectfully as "my teacher."[7] Though she broke with Eddy and established her own work, Hopkins was not among those former students of Eddy who accused her of plagiarizing the work of Phineas P. Quimby. In fact, she made public her view, long after she and Eddy had parted, that there was no truth in the argument being made against Eddy's "supreme originality." Eddy, she said, was "true to her own original inspiration."[8]

Gail Harley, in a PhD. dissertation on the work of Hopkins, indicated that she was also influenced by the transcendentalist thinking that permeated the cultural milieu of the mid-nineteenth century. According to letters Hopkins wrote to friends after she moved to New York, her lifelong role model was the transcendentalist writer and thinker Margaret Fuller. Hopkins also valued the work of Ralph Waldo Emerson, referring to his work several times in her writings and characterizing him as a "great man."[9]

Hopkins also respected the work of Warren Felt Evans. Referring to his abilities as a healer, she commented, "Dr. Evans, the great healer, could with inner vision see so plainly the action of the [disease] in sick people, that he could say with bold confidence, 'You are healed.' And they would hurry into health."[10]

Hopkins also referenced the work of Emanuel Swedenborg in passages of her writing, indicating a familiarity with his works. She reflected on his teachings regarding angels and was convinced of his deep spiritual nature.[11] She commented, "Swedenborg thought so much about God that his face shone so that sometimes his servants were afraid of him. Do you suppose he asked that his face might shine? No, he was thinking beyond faces."[12]

The Nature of God

Like Eddy, Hopkins was raised in a family of New England Congregationalists. Her writings indicate that she remained true to her spiritual roots. She considered the Protestant church to be "the most stalwart and vigorous religious body on earth."[13] She believed in the virgin birth and the doctrine of Incarnation. Jesus, according to this traditional Christian teaching, is the second person in the Trinity. As a part of the Godhead, he was incarnated in human flesh. "God sent forth his son," Hopkins said, "made of woman."[14]

Hopkins was a trinitarian and accepted the traditional Christian view of God as personal. She attributed personal qualities to Jesus as Savior, Redeemer, and Messiah:

> Some people are trying to show that Jesus of Nazareth did not claim to be the Promised Messiah, the Christ, the Savior, but he did. . . . They also declare that He did not teach the Trinity. But he did. Notice him saying, "I and my Father are one." The Holy Ghost whom the Father will send in my name shall teach you all things. . . . Go ye therefor and teach all nations, baptizing them in the Name of the Father, and of the Son and of the Holy Ghost.[15]

Hopkins considered Jesus to be "the Redeemer . . . who gave himself for our sins, that he might deliver us from this present evil world."[16] She described Jesus as "the Lord Jesus Christ . . . the vicarious bearer of all suffering . . . [and] the Savior of the world from disease and death, misfortune and decay."[17]

Appendix D

FRANZ ANTON MESMER

The mental healing movement that blossomed in the United States in the mid-nineteenth century grew, in part, out of the research and experimentation of an Enlightenment-era Viennese medical doctor, Franz Anton Mesmer (1734–1815). While the healing tradition was well established in Western and Eastern mysticism, Mesmer and his followers are credited with developing the first modern scientific method of mental healing.[1] Approaching their work from outside a religious or mystical context, they demonstrated the impact that one mind could have upon another for the purpose of restoring health.

Leaders of the mental healing movement in the United States (including Warren Felt Evans, Phineas P. Quimby, Mary Baker Eddy, Emma Curtis Hopkins, and Charles Fillmore, as well as the theosophists and the spiritualists) were indebted, in one way or another, to Franz Anton Mesmer. Modern twentieth-century psychotherapy is, in part, derived from his discoveries.[2] Charles Fillmore credited Mesmer with providing one of the proofs "that the mind can produce conditions in the mental world that ultimate in the material world."[3] Mesmer's theory of "animal magnetism," or "Mesmerism" as it was popularly labeled until the word *hypnotism* was substituted for it by medical science in the 1840s, can be defined as the healing power that suggestion, words, persuasion, and commands can be exerted for curative purposes, particularly for those illnesses that affect the mind-body interface.

Born on May 23, 1734, at Iznang on Lake Constance, Franz Anton Mesmer was the son of an Episcopal gatekeeper. He studied divinity and became a doctor of philosophy before moving to Vienna, where he studied medicine. At age thirty-three, he was granted the degree of doctor of medicine from the University of Vienna and went into private practice in Vienna.

By nature interested in research and experimentation, Mesmer was inspired by the work of the Swiss physician Paracelsus (1493–1541) and his disciples, who believed that magnets could be used to facilitate health by redistributing the body's magnetic fluids.[4] Using iron magnets in treating his patients, Mesmer, at the outset of his work, applied them to the throat, the heart, or whichever portion of the body needed relief. He assumed that health was restored as the body's fluids were brought into balance.[5]

As many of his clients reported amazing recoveries, news of Mesmer's successes spread. He was soon overrun with clients. People came from all over Austria to be touched by the miraculous magnet. Within a short time, hundreds of patients testified to the efficacy of his method in restoring health. Mesmer was so pleased with his initial success that he called magnetism the "invisible fire" of Hippocrates.[6] Further experimentation, however, led Mesmer to realize that the cure was not due to the lifeless mineral he held in his hand but to human touch itself. It was he himself, the magnetizer, he concluded, that restored health.[7] Like Van Helmut (1577–1644)[8] before him, Mesmer discovered that he could relieve symptoms by making passes over the afflicted parts of the patient's body with his hands alone.[9]

Mesmer now faced a dilemma: how would he explain that his popular theory of "magnetism" was still responsible for the cure when the mineral had nothing to do with it? He solved the problem by developing a strategy that further confused the matter. Instead of admitting that his theory of magnetism was untenable, he declared that magnetism issued forth from the fingers of the doctor or magnetizer. The mysterious energy was an "animal" energy. In 1776, he called his practice of laying on of hands "animal magnetism."[10]

Mesmer was now sure that a healer, through his or her presence and personal influence, could do more to cure the sick than any other remedy. He declared, "Of all bodies in nature, no one is so important on its influence upon man as the body of man himself."[11] Further research showed Mesmer that animal magnetism was most effective in cases of "nervous disorders," and that its impact on diseases of the organs was indirect.[12] Professor Roy Udolf, author of *Handbook of Hypnosis for Professionals*, indicated that, without knowing it, Mesmer was inducing a state of hypnosis, though the type of hypnotic reaction was different from that produced by the modern hypnotist.[13] Biographer Stephen Zweig maintains that, from 1776 onward, Mesmer's practice consisted entirely of suggestive and hypnotic treatment, and the fundamental secret of his success lay in his strong and impressive personality.[14]

While Mesmer was popular with clients in Vienna, the medical profession in the city found fault with his methods. Though he held impeccable medical credentials, his colleagues looked askance at his theories and considered him a quack. Articles in Austrian newspapers and periodicals ridiculed him.[15] In 1778, he moved to Paris, hoping that the medical profession in France would accept his discoveries. Soon after arriving, he tried to no avail to get the French Academy of Sciences to review his work. In an attempt to develop credibility for his research, he published in 1779 a report describing the discovery of animal magnetism.[16]

Mesmer became extremely popular in Paris in the early 1780s. The aristocracy, including members of the nobility, were attracted, and he treated patients from morning until night. He came to be revered by the people his methods cured. If he went for a stroll in the street, he would be beset by people. Princes and princesses invited him to visit them. Few medical men have risen so quickly to fame and fortune. His name and his work were the topics of drawing room conversations. "Everyone suffered," Stephen Zweig indicated, "from mesmermania."[17]

Because he was so successful, Mesmer found that it was necessary to develop group therapy techniques to accommodate all the patients seeking treatment.[18] Roy Udolf reported:

> He was quite a showman and during his group sessions wore flowing lilac robes and flourished a wand. The treatment room was dimly lit and had reflecting mirrors and background music. Patients were seated around a large oaken vat or baquet filled with chemicals and iron magnets, and they would hold hands in a circle very much like at a seance. Mesmer would then move about from patient to patient making passes with his hands and touching them with magnets.[19]

Queen Marie Antoinette became interested and attempted to secure for him an annual pension.[20] King Louis XVI, however, was skeptical and commanded in 1784 that a commission of inquiry composed of France's most renowned scholars from the Academy of Science assess the merits of animal magnetism. The academy concluded that magnets produced no cures unless the patients knew that they were being magnetized: hence, the effects were due to the patient's imagination or belief. The commission went beyond pronouncing Mesmer's methods worthless, denouncing them as potentially harmful because of the close contact between therapist and patient.[21] Following the report, Mesmer fell into disrepute in Paris.

In 1784, the same year the French Academy issued its findings, a student of Mesmer (a retired military officer, Marquis Armand de Puysegur) by accident discovered the phenomenon of artificially induced somnambulism. Working on his estate in France with the peasantry, he was alarmed when a shepherd boy, instead of responding to magnetic manipulations in the customary way, went off into a deep trance. Efforts to arouse him proved futile. Yet when ordered to stand and walk, the boy behaved as if awake. He answered questions in the dream state, and his replies were lucid and to the point. Puysegur experimented again and again with the shepherd boy and others and provided a written report of his findings.[22] Roy Udolf credited Puysegur with developing a technique that was more like that used by modern hypnotherapists: "By the hypnotist telling the patient and suggesting relaxation and calmness, the patient would develop a tranquil trance which he (Puysegur) referred to as artificial somnambulism, or a 'sleeping' trance. In this tranquil state the patient could talk and be given instructions."[23]

Observers have been surprised that Mesmer himself had not identified somnambulism in his own work, for he frequently noticed that, under his manipulations, certain people would get heavy-eyed, yawn, and appear to go to sleep. Stephen Zweig speculated that Mesmer was concentrating so thoroughly on effecting cures that he overlooked conditions that took place in the twilight state.[24]

Mesmer was outraged at the way somnambulism was soon being used by charlatans and amateurs. Persons called mediums, people who were amenable to suggestion in the dream state, were naively thought to possess extraordinary powers. Occult capacities were attributed to people with newly discovered powers of mediumship, including clairvoyance, telepathy, precognition, and the ability to communicate with the dead. Soon, people with no professional training took up the career of professional somnambulist, using mediums to diagnose illnesses and prescribe cures. Seances were held, and the twelve apostles were called upon for spiritual guidance.[25] By the early 1800s, mesmerists, or lay magnetizers, were speaking and practicing in cities, towns, and villages across Europe and the United States. The public halls were crowded with people seeking to be healed by what was coming to be known as "mind-cure."[26]

Mesmer was appalled that his work had been abused and his name misapplied. He had attempted to establish a new method for healing mental ills, but his work had resulted in his name's being associated with necromancers, pseudomagicians, and occultists. "Many a prejudicial judgment has been pronounced against me," Mesmer lamented, "on account of the reckless levity of those who are imitating my methods."[27] Stephen Zweig indicated that, for decades thereafter, Mesmer's name was under a cloud and his teachings further discredited.

In addition to his professional difficulties, Mesmer suffered fallout from the French Revolution. Having associated with the privileged classes, he was no longer welcome in Paris. His hospital was destroyed, his property scattered, and his livelihood taken away. He left Paris a poor man in 1792, as Robespierre was rising to power.[28] He returned to Vienna only to find that he was unwelcome because of supposed connections with French revolutionaries. He retired to Lake Constance and settled in Frauenfeld, a small town north of Zurich, where he established a medical practice. He spent his last two decades living quietly, out of the limelight. He died in 1815 at age eighty-two.[29]

Appendix E

WARREN FELT EVANS

A farmer's son, Warren Felt Evans (1817–1889) was born to Eli and Sarah Edison Evans at Rockingham, Vermont, on December 23, 1817, the sixth of seven children. Unlike Quimby, Evans was the recipient, by nineteenth-century standards, of an excellent education. Private schooling at Chester Academy was followed by one year at Middlebury College and a year and a half at Dartmouth. He left in the middle of his junior year to study for the Methodist ministry. He served in a variety of Methodist churches for over two decades. In 1840, he married M. Charlotte Tinker, a union that was to last until his death in 1889.

Evans' respect for Emanuel Swedenborg was made evident when, in 1863, he left Methodism and joined the Church of the New Jerusalem, the church established by Swedenborg's disciples. Evans indicated that one could find in Swedenborg's writings "all the truth there is in the various schools of mental cure"[1] and credited Swedenborg as having "thrown more light upon the subject of our inner self than any other writer,[2] characterizing him as "the pioneer and John the Baptist of the New Age."[3] Evans considered Swedenborg's spiritual philosophy to be "a reproduction and amplification of the ancient Hermetic and Kabalistic science."[4]

After leaving the Methodist ministry, Evans worked with his wife primarily in Boston, as a practitioner of mental healing. During this period, he saw patients, taught students the principles of mental healing, and wrote seven books on its theory and practice. They are *The New Age and Its Messengers* (1864), *Mental Cure* (1869), *Mental Medicine* (1872), *Soul and Body* (1876), *The Divine Law of Cure* (1881), *Primitive Mind-Cure* (1884), and *Esoteric Christianity* (1886). His books presented many of

the spiritual ideas and healing principles that Charles Fillmore incorporated into the Basic Unity Teaching. Charles characterized Evans as "the
Recording Angel of Metaphysics,"[5] an indication of the high regard he had
for him. Evans did not attempt to establish an organization to carry forward his teaching and healing work. As a result, after his death, his influence was confined to those who read his books. None of these works is
currently in print.

Evans' work as a healer and teacher was also built in part on the work of
Franz Anton Mesmer and his followers. Evans recognized the power of the
mind to heal and would use hypnosis if required, as well as hands-on healing.
The high regard he had for Mesmer is indicated in the following statement:

> The science of human magnetism ... is not a mere plaything ... but is
> one of the greatest gifts of God to man. Its intelligent employment as
> a curative agency will be fruitful in blessings to the world, in alleviat-
> ing suffering and curing disease of mind and body.[6]

Evans was aware of the healing abilities of Phineas P. Quimby, acknowledged his successes, and was generous in his praise but never indicated that he
personally became a patient of Quimby or a student of his work.

Quotes from Ralph Waldo Emerson appear throughout Evans' writings.
He viewed Emerson as both "poet and philosopher" who was able to reach
"the higher altitudes of thought."[7] The ideas of Emerson and the transcendentalists permeate Evans' writings and can be found in the following areas:
the divine inner self, divine law, manifesting the Christ Self, the role of intuition, the power of the mind, the mission of Jesus, and the role of traditional
Christianity. Evans' acknowledgment of the validity of transcendentalist ideas
was made clear when he stated, "The intelligent force that creates and governs
the world is transcendental, in that it is purely mental and is beyond the grasp
of sense, but is none the less real."[8]

Evans was concerned that the system of mental healing that he advocated
might be criticized for being "too transcendental." He asserted that the real
problem was with critics who were not "sufficiently unfolded spiritually to
practice it."[9] In several passages of *Primitive Mind-Cure*, Evans embraces transcendentalism, referring to it as "our transcendental philosophy" and as "our
transcendental medical science and practical metaphysics."[10]

Traditional Christianity

Evans did not have the same respect for the teachings of traditional Christianity, Protestant or Catholic. He felt the churches caused more harm than good, writing:

> We encounter at the outset of our instruction a great evil, and one that has served to hold humanity down and prevent its rising from the lane of sense to the life of faith. I refer to the fact that the Church, Catholic and Protestant, has claimed a monopoly of the principle of faith. They have connected it with dogmas, which are to many intelligent minds, unreasonable, absurd, and incredible.[11]

Evans took issue with traditional Christianity's view of human nature, asserting, "We are expected and taught by the pulpit and the Church to find our real self and view it as polluted by sin, from the crown of the head to the soles of our feet. But this is in direct opposite of the truth."[12]

One of the major weaknesses of traditional Christianity, according to Evans, was its unwillingness to follow the example of Jesus in healing the sick:

> The power of curing disease was conferred by the Christ upon the Church, not as a transient circumstance, attending the introduction of Christianity to the world, but as a perpetual inheritance. . . . The Protestant clergy, in order to excuse and account for their spiritual impotency, have strenuously argued that the gift was confined to the chosen twelve, or to the seventy-two disciples.[13]

Traditional Christianity, according to Evans, prepared men and women to die, but he believed that humanity's true purpose was everlasting life:

> It is a prominent intent of the current religious instruction of the day to prepare men to die. That string has been harped upon until it is well-nigh worn out. The philosophy which we advocate aims to prepare men never to die, to view death as an illusion, and to lead the disciple to the attainment of that knowledge of God, and our relation to him, which is eternal life.[14]

DIVINE NATURE AND HUMAN NATURE

Evans recognized God's all-encompassing power, yet he devoted little attention in his writing to the transcendence of God: "God is the First and the Last, the Alpha and Omega, the Beginning and Ending of All Finite Things. . . . The highest truth in the universe is that God is all, and all that truly exists is a manifestation of God."[15]

Appendix F

HELENA PETROVNA BLAVATSKY

From an early age, Madame Helena Petrovna Blavatsky felt a sense of mission. At nineteen, she told a friend, "I will bless mankind by freeing them from their mental bondage. . . . I know I was intended to do a great work."[1] Nevertheless, Blavatsky's personal history prior to her creating the written works that articulated the teaching gave little indication she had the background and ability to develop a complex and appealing system of spiritual beliefs and to cofound a worldwide movement. Born in 1831 into an upper-class Russian family, she was married at age seventeen to the forty-year-old Nikifor Blavatsky, the vice-governor of the province of Yerevan in Armenia. After a brief time, she abandoned her husband and, until her mid-forties, traveled in Europe, America, and the Middle East. She never remarried, although she had long liaisons with a Russian opera singer as well as several others.[2] She had a business relationship with Henry Steel Olcott that was apparently platonic.

In the 1860s, Blavatsky became involved with spiritualism, conducted seances, worked as a medium, and spelled out messages from invisible entities.[3] She claimed at the time she left Europe in 1873, sailed for the United States, and settled in New York City that she had been a Spiritualist for over a decade. In October 1874, she met Olcott, who was also deeply involved in spiritualism, at the Eddy brother's farmhouse in Chittenden, Vermont, where both had gone to observe spiritualist manifestations. They immediately became friends.[4]

In the spring and summer of 1875, Blavatsky conducted seances and hosted Spiritualist lecturers at gatherings in her New York apartment. Olcott attended, along with persons interested in Kabbalism, Rosicrucianism, and spiritualism. Olcott considered Blavatsky to be the most unusual medium he had ever met, observing that "instead of being controlled by Spirits to do their will, it is she who seems to control them to do her bidding."[5] At a meeting in Blavatsky's apartment on September 7, 1875, Olcott proposed that those in attendance form a society to pursue occult research. The seventeen present agreed, and, on the following evening, the group met and passed a resolution that formally established the Theosophical Society. In October, bylaws were approved and officers elected, with Olcott chosen as president.[6]

In his inaugural address, Olcott defined the purpose of the society as helping free "the public mind of theological superstition and a tame subservience to the arrogance of science."[7] One of the chief goals of the society was to transcend the cleavage between science and religion and to return to concerns of an ancient-wisdom tradition. Olcott distinguished theosophy from spiritualism, indicating that spiritualism was plagued by "imposture, tricky mediums, lying spirits, and revolting social theories."[8] He indicated that the primary task of the society was investigation. Its twice-monthly meetings would be devoted to "researches and experiments of our members and of eminent correspondents in this and other countries . . . [and to] tests, experiments, and practical demonstrations."[9]

Madame Blavatsky indicated that there were three major objects of the society: to form the nucleus of a universal brotherhood of humanity without distinction of race, color, or creed; to promote the study of scripture, particularly those of the East; and to investigate the mysteries of psychic and spiritual powers.[10] Like Olcott, she had become disenchanted with spiritualism, particularly concerning teachings about the afterlife. Blavatsky noted:

> According to their doctrine, unfortunate man is not liberated even by death from the sorrows of this life. Not a drop from the life-cup of pain and suffering will miss his lips . . . since he sees everything now. . . . The "gentle wafting to immortal life" becomes without any transition the way into a new path of mental suffering! And yet the columns of the "Banner of Light," the veteran journal of the American Spiritualists, are filled with messages from the dead, the "dear departed ones," who all write to say how very happy they are! Is such a state of knowledge consistent with bliss? Then "bliss" stands in such a case for the greatest curse, and orthodox damnation must be a relief by comparison to it![11]

The word *theosophy* was chosen to represent the society's philosophy because it expressed the esoteric truths the group sought to uncover.[12] Etymologically, the term *theosophy* means "wisdom about God."[13] It was not the first time the term was used in a spiritual context. The word appears in works of several church fathers, both Greek and Latin, as a synonym for *theology*.[14] *Theosophy* was also used from ancient to modern times to refer to a particular form of mysticism.[15]

The morning after the second meeting of the society, Madame Blavatsky traveled to Ithaca, New York, to visit friends and begin work on her first book, *Isis Unveiled*. Written when she was forty-five and published in 1877, it was a massive and comprehensive treatise of an ancient wisdom religion. It was divided into two volumes, the first titled "Science" and the second, "Theology." Included were chapters on modern science, psychic phenomena, spiritualism, Mesmerism, the kabbalah, the devil, and esoteric interpretations of Christianity.[16] The book has become a modern occult classic.

Madame Blavatsky claimed that the theosophical doctrines she presented were not her own but were obtained through a kind of thought transference from so-called Masters or adepts. She claimed that these personages, also called "Mahatmas," were highly evolved living beings who possessed the hidden truths of the universe and whose chief residence was Tibet.[17] Mahatmas were believed to live to a great age and were called "great-souled-ones" because of their moral development and intellectual attainment. Blavatsky claimed that entire passages were "entirely dictated by them and verbatim."[18] In other parts of her writing, the mahatmas inspired the ideas. "They are our teachers," she declared, "because from them we have derived all the Theosophical truths."[19] Blavatsky described the process by which thoughts were transferred, stating: "When two minds are sympathetically related, and the instruments through which they function are tuned to respond magnetically and electrically to one another, there is nothing which will prevent the transmission of thoughts from one to the other, at will."[20]

Bruce F. Campbell, who has written a balanced and thorough study of the work of the early theosophists, indicated that the existence of the masters is among the weakest of the theosophists' claims.[21] Blavatsky's importance is due in part to the fact that she was among the first to present Eastern philosophy in a popular way that was accessible to Western readers.[22]

Appendix G

MARY BAKER EDDY

The youngest of six children, Mary Baker Eddy was born into a family of moderately well-to-do New Hampshire farmers with English and Scots-Irish roots. Her father, Mark Baker, was a rock-ribbed Puritan and tightfisted Yankee. Religion, including theological disputation, was important to him, and his family was required on Sundays to attend lengthy forenoon and afternoon services at the local Sanbornton Bridge, New Hampshire, Congregational church.[1]

Eddy suffered from ill health during the first fourteen years of her life and, as a result, was kept out of school a good deal of the time. Nevertheless, she demonstrated a lively mind, even though she received an irregular education. She showed an early interest in religion, and her Congregational pastor considered her his brightest pupil, superior intellectually and spiritually to any other woman in the community.

She was married at age twenty-two to George Washington Glover, a New Englander eleven years her senior who had established himself successfully in business in Charleston, South Carolina. They moved to the South after the wedding. After losing all of his money in an unsuccessful business deal, Glover died of a tropical disease less than a year after their marriage. Mary returned to Sanbornton Bridge, penniless and pregnant, to live with her parents. Though talented, she was an untrained young mother seeking to support herself and her young son. Again plagued by ill health, she was often confined to bed with what was described as dyspepsia, liver complaint, and nervous disease. The occasional teaching and writing she did was insufficient to support herself and her son. During periods of ill-health she spent a great deal of time reading the Bible.[2]

A key turning point in her life came in 1862 when she went to Portland, Maine, to receive treatment from the renowned mental healer Phineas P. Quimby. She heard about Quimby through her second husband Daniel Patterson—a man whom she would soon divorce—who reported that Quimby was performing marvelous cures. She was treated by Quimby for the first time in October 1862 and improved with a rapidity that seemed like a miracle. Remaining in Portland for most of the next two years, she spent a great deal of time with Quimby. Not only did she receive treatment, but she learned from him, not as a student but by sitting in his room, observing his practice, talking with him, asking him questions, reading the manuscripts that he was writing, and offering editorial suggestions.[3] She last saw Quimby in April 1865, about nine months before he died. She ultimately concluded that work with Quimby provided only temporary relief, for symptoms returned when she was away from him.[4]

A serious fall on the ice in Lynn, Massachusetts, in January 1866 was a life-changing event. She believed that the spiritual efforts she made to heal herself led her to the discovery of divine healing. Gillian Gill, in her biography of Eddy, indicated that certain facts surrounding her fall and ultimate recovery are commonly agreed upon:

> The then Mrs. Mary Patterson in the company of some friends was on her way to a meeting at the Linwood Lodge of the Good Templars when she slipped on the ice just outside the Bubier house in the center of Lynn, hit her head and was knocked unconscious. She was sheltered for the night by Mr. and Mrs. Bubier who called in the busy and popular homeopathic doctor and surgeon, Alvin M. Cushing. . . .
>
> He considered the accident serious. She was then cared for by two women who reported that she had broken her back. A minister was urgently called. On Sunday, three days after the accident, she asked for her Bible and sent everyone out of her room, and then amazed everyone by getting out of her bed unaided. She got dressed and walked downstairs to meet incredulous friends.[5]

Eddy herself indicated, "I rose from my bed, and to the utter confusion of all, I commenced my usual avocations and notwithstanding displacements, etc., I regained my natural position and functions of the body."[6] She claimed that she was healed as a result of a direct experience of God and made the discovery that "God is the only healer and helping Principle, and that Principle is divine not human."[7] With that realization, she indicated that her healing occurred instantaneously: "It was what I saw, felt and knew," she testified, "that first saved my life."[8] She explained later that it all happened very quickly, stating, "That short experience included a glimpse of the great fact that I have since tried to make plain to others, namely, Life, in and of Spirit; this Life being the sole reality of existence."[9] After recovering from the fall, her overall health improved. She was transformed from an invalid who spent much of her life incapacitated and in a sickbed to a paragon of good health, continually resilient and energetic.

With the experience of having been divinely healed, Eddy believed she could facilitate others in having the same experience. She noticed that, when in the presence of a neighbor who was ill, the person got better if she, Eddy, entertained thoughts about the "Allness" of God, similar to those she had when she was healed from the fall. It was as a result of these experiences that she discovered how to give mental treatment. Eddy came to believe that God had chosen her for a special mission and that God's teaching regarding healing would be transmitted to the world through her.[10]

Biographer Robert Peel noted that, from 1866 onward, Eddy lived for only one thing—to carry out the mission she was sure God had given her. In 1868, she advertised for students in local newspapers. At about the same time, she began calling her work "Christian Science," which she defined as the never-ending search "to reveal man as God's image."[11]

Shortly after Quimby's death, Eddy began working on a book to facilitate the expansion of her work. The book was of large scope and was tentatively entitled *The Bible and Its Spiritual Meaning*. A friend called it Eddy's "version of the Bible." It was really her metaphysical comment on the Bible.[12] In 1875, the manuscript was published as *Science and Health*. In the first years after publication, the book sold poorly. Eddy revised *Science and Health* six times during the course of her long career, in 1878, 1881, 1883, 1886, 1891, and 1902.

From 1875 to 1882, Eddy continued to live in Lynn, Massachusetts, writing, teaching, and giving lectures. Her clientele was never large, and nothing indicated that her efforts were to expand beyond rural Massachusetts. In 1876, in an effort to gain personal support for her work, she married a student, Asa Gilbert Eddy. Ten years younger than she was, Mr. Eddy had been a Singer sewing machine salesman until studying Christian Science and becoming a practitioner. He proved to be a suitable companion and helper until his untimely death in 1882 of heart failure.

After the publication of *Science and Health* in 1875, inquiries came from around the country from people who had read the book, but few were ready to travel to Lynn to undertake the discipline of class study.[13] Still, by 1876 she had enough students to form an organization called the Christian Science Association. Membership was open only to those who had studied with her. Its weekly meetings focused on continuing education and metaphysical discussion.[14]

In 1882, Eddy moved her work from Lynn, which had a population of only thirty thousand, to the greater Boston area. Her adherents at the time numbered in the dozens rather than the hundreds. The press considered her a quotable crackpot rather than a serious religious leader.[15] In Boston, she opened a school, the Massachusetts Metaphysical College, which proved highly successful. Cosmopolitan Boston proved a much more fertile environment for Christian Science than had rural Massachusetts. Soon people from all over the country—mainly women, from Kansas to California—came to Boston to attend classes and return to their communities to do practitioner work and establish churches of Christian Science.[16]

A particularly distressing problem for Eddy was the charge of plagiarism made by Julius and Annetta Dresser, former students of Quimby. The Dressers, who studied with Quimby in the 1860s, left the field of mental healing after Quimby's death and took up unrelated work in California. In 1882, they returned to Boston to set up a mental-healing practice of their own. Julius Dresser charged Eddy with stealing Quimby's work and renaming it "Christian Science." He indicated that Eddy copied from Quimby's unpublished manuscripts in writing *Science and Health*. Former Quimby students A. J. Arens and Richard Kennedy joined in the attack, adding credibility to the charge and complicating matters for Eddy. The case against her was pressed forward by Annetta Dresser in her 1895 biography of Quimby and taken up by the Dressers' son Horatio, who attained academic respectability by studying at Harvard and associating with William James. Horatio authored several books and articles on mental healing and established himself as a theorist of New Thought. Part of his advocacy of New Thought was an effort to discredit Eddy and Christian Science.

Both Robert Peel and Gillian Gill conclude, after reading the Quimby manuscripts, that Eddy's spiritual teaching and her methods as a metaphysical practitioner work were different from those of Quimby, and it was a mistake to label her a plagiarist. My reading of the text of Quimby's writings indicates that, while both used mental argument in their practitioner work, their approach had few other similarities. There were basic differences in their spiritual teaching. Eddy's healing practices, for the most part, do not resemble those of Quimby.

Christian Science grew significantly in the 1890s. At the start of the decade the movement, though still small, had achieved the status of a minor religious denomination. By the end of the decade, Eddy claimed a following of three hundred thousand people.[17] *Science and Health* had become a bestseller, and Christian Science churches were popping up all over the country and in Europe. A large edifice was built in Boston's Back Bay area in 1895 to house the First Church of Christ, Scientist. Called "the Mother Church" because it was the headquarters for the movement, it was enlarged in 1905 to seat one thousand. Membership in the Boston church totaled thirty-six thousand in 1906. A total of thirty thousand Christian Scientists poured into Boston to attend its dedication on June 10, 1906.

By the turn of the century, Christian Science was sufficiently sizable and threatening to established Christian churches as to bring it under vigorous attack. Sermons, pamphlets, and denominational journals presented Christian Science as the work of Satan, a dangerous heresy, and a fraud. Her severest critics saw her as caring only for power and money, a shameless huckster.[18] Leading figures in the secular establishment joined in the attack. Charles Elliot Norton of Harvard called her "the ugliest figure in New England today."[19] *McClures Magazine* commissioned Mark Twain to write derogatory articles. A proponent of mind-cure and spiritual healing, Twain had nothing against the teachings of Christian Science. It was Eddy he targeted. "I am not combing Christian Science," he wrote. "I haven't a thing in the world against it. Making fun of that shameless old swindler, Mother Eddy, is the only thing

I take interest in."[20] William Dean Howells wrote Twain saying, "Read your Mrs. Eddy massacre just before I left home and gloated on every drop of her blood."[21]

Opposition to Eddy was due in part to her being a divorced woman. Robert Peel made the point succinctly when he commented:

> For a woman to preach, write for the newspapers, challenge the doctors, and the clergy, claim a new religious revelation and a new scientific discovery—all of this was in itself enough to make her an object of suspicion to cautious Yankees. But for a divorced woman to do these things clearly put her outside the pale of provincial acceptability.[22]

During her declining years, Eddy suffered from painful kidney stones. As with all disease, she attempted to relieve her distress through prayer. On other occasions, when prayer did not relieve her suffering, a doctor was called to administer morphine. On most occasions, Eddy did not allow the doctor to be called until she had gone through mortal agony. Morphine to Eddy was considered an analgesic since the drug, in and of itself, could not remedy kidney stones. At the time of her death at age eighty-nine in 1910, there were a reported eight hundred thousand Christian Scientists worldwide.[23]

PHINEAS P. QUIMBY

B orn February 16, 1802, in Lebanon, New Hampshire, Phineas P. Quimby grew up in Belfast, Maine. The son of a blacksmith of modest means, he was one of seven children. He had little formal education, attending the local Belfast school only on a part-time basis. He was apprenticed at a young age to a clockmaker and eventually took up the trade.[1] As a young adult he was told by a medical doctor that he was "fast wasting away from consumption," that his liver and kidneys were diseased, and his lungs "nearly consumed." No cure was available for his ailments. Working with a psychic, he became convinced that he had been deceived by doctors into believing he was mortally ill. His symptoms had been the result of false beliefs. "My troubles," he concluded, "were of my own making."[2] After restoring himself to health by changing his beliefs, he developed a lifelong distrust of allopathic medicine.

A major turning point in his life came in 1838, when, at age thirty-six, he attended a lecture and demonstration of Mesmerism by a traveling mesmerist by the name of Charles Poyen. It was at a time when a wave of interest in hypnotism and somnambulism, which Anton Mesmer's name had become identified with, had been spreading through the eastern United States.[3] Quimby became very interested, traveling from place to place to hear Poyen lecture and demonstrate the techniques. The two became acquainted, and soon Quimby learned how to work as a hypnotist and somnambulist. Whenever he could find someone who was willing to allow him to experiment, he would attempt to put the person into a mesmeric sleep.[4]

During the course of these endeavors, he met a young man of nineteen with well-developed psychic abilities named Lucius Burkmar.[5] Soon they began working together, traveling through Maine and New Brunswick

(Canada) assisting physicians who were treating the ill. Quimby, in the presence of a patient and the physician, would hypnotize Burkmar.[6] He would do this by sitting opposite him holding both hands while looking intently into his eyes. With Quimby and the doctor standing by, Burkmar, from the sleep state, would diagnose the patient's ailment and prescribe a medicinal remedy.[7]

At some point, Quimby came to doubt the efficacy of this practice. He became convinced that Burkmar was reading the mind of both the patient and the physician and prescribing the medicine the doctor felt right for the ailment. He suspected that patients got well because of the suggestive power associated with a "subject" speaking out of the trance state. Sometime in the 1840s, Quimby abandoned Mesmerism. He came to consider the practice as doing more harm than good. Years later he wrote, "It is more than twenty years since I first embarked upon the greatest humbug of the age—mesmerism."[8]

After parting with Burkmar and giving up his practice as a mesmerist, Quimby pursued a career as a counselor to those victimized by the medical profession. He then expanded his practice to include those who suffered from problems with their health, either physical or psychological. Quimby apparently had a large clientele. During the last decade of his life, he reported that he saw between three hundred and five hundred patients annually.[9] Testimonials of patients indicate that many benefited from his work. Annetta Dresser recorded her observations of those who sought his help, reporting:

> The most vivid remembrance I have of Dr. Quimby is his appearance as he came out of his private office ready for the next patient. That indescribable sense of conviction, of clear-sightedness, of energetic action . . . made an impression never to be forgotten. . . . There was something about him that gave one a sense of perfect confidence and ease in his presence—a feeling that immediately banished all doubts and prejudices, and put one in sympathy with that quiet strength or power by which he wrought his cures.[10]

Dresser considered Quimby to be a man of high character and spoke of him with great appreciation:

> It has always seemed strange to me that anyone who knew him and was taught by him could ever forget his loving sympathy and kindness of heart. He was one that inspired all honest souls with a conviction

of his own sincerity. He had nothing to gain nor lose; for his own life was a constant out flowing of the spirit of truth in which he lived.[11]

During the last five years of his life (1861–1865), Quimby used the short personal essay to present his ideas on issues related to mental healing. Many were dictated or written in rough draft and then copied by students. Quimby's lack of formal education is apparent in these writings. Within the context of one essay, he rambles from one topic to another, seldom fully exploring a theme or subject. He constantly leaves the reader in midair, failing to follow through, complete a point, or fully develop an idea. Only the most dedicated reader will stick with his work.

Given the disjointed nature of his writing and its lack of focus, it is not surprising that none of it was published during Quimby's lifetime. It was not until 1921, several decades after his death, that the first group of his works appeared in print under the title the *Quimby Manuscripts*. In 1988, a comprehensive three-volume compilation of his writings was published by DeVorss and Company, titled *Phineas Parkhurst Quimby: The Complete Writings*.

Charles Braden believed Quimby was either consciously or subconsciously influenced by the teachings of the transcendentalists. Braden held this view even though he acknowledged that Quimby never referred to their teachings, including those of Ralph Waldo Emerson, whose work was widely available in his lifetime.[12] In an article in the *New England Quarterly,* titled "Phineas P. Quimby, Scientist of Transcendentalism," a Methodist writer, Stewart W. Holmes, argues that in Quimby's work with patients he demonstrated "the operational validity of Emerson's hypothesis."[13]

Quimby's untimely death at age sixty-four came probably as a result of overwork. His son George reported, "The last five years of his life were exceptionally hard. Overcrowded with patients and over-worked, he could not or would not take opportunities for relaxation." Quimby was apparently worn out by the incessant labor of attempting to bring health to others.[14]

CHRISTIAN METAPHYSICAL:
CHARLES FILLMORE AND PHINEAS P. QUIMBY

The practice of metaphysical healing as taught and practiced by Charles Fillmore differed significantly from the practices of Phineas P. Quimby. As a metaphysical practitioner, Charles did not find it useful or necessary to employ rational analysis to convince clients of the falsity of their beliefs, religious, spiritual, or otherwise. The Quimby method lacked the essential elements used by Charles including:

- going into the silence for spiritual nourishment and power;

- using an inner knowing or intuition to connect with the Divine within;

- manifesting the Christ within, or the divine Indwelling Presence through spiritual practice;

- maintaining a strong belief or conviction that healing would take place if the Inner Power or Presence was activated;

- acknowledging the power of the word, as expressed through affirmations and denials.

TRANSCENDENTALISM AND PHINEAS P. QUIMBY

Charles F. Braden and Stewart W. Holmes both indicated, after acquainting themselves with the writings of Quimby, that the influence of transcendentalism was apparent in his work.[15] Horatio Dresser takes an opposing view indicating that Quimby "was not a reader of philosophy or theology."[16] Dresser indicates that Quimby was not "in any sense a borrower," leading to the conclusion that he independently developed ideas such as "God is in us, even in our speech,"[17] and "The Christ is the God in us all."[18]

Quimby himself indicated a longtime interest in religion. Late in his life, he said, "I have been trying all my life ever since I was old enough to listen, to understand the beliefs of the world."[19] In another passage in his writing, he indicated that "from time immemorial the subject of the mind has been a theme of ancient and modern philosophers."[20] His awareness of their writings is implied in that statement. In another part of his written work, he indicated that he was aware of the conflict between Unitarianism and traditional Christianity. In referring to their theological disparities, he asked, "How long is it since the Unitarians were admitted as Christians? Even now the Universalists are scarcely admitted within the pale of Christianity."[21]

In light of the above information, it seems that Braden and Holmes, rather than Dresser, had a better understanding of Quimby's religious or spiritual underpinnings. Quimby confessed to not having a religion or a creed. Yet he continually confronted traditional Christians regarding their beliefs. Did he do it by presenting the positions of an atheist or agnostic? Probably not. It is more likely that he countered with transcendentalist ideas, ideas that were becoming increasingly popular with those who were disaffected from traditional Christianity. Though his writing does not so indicate, it is likely that he was also one of the disaffected ones.

Notes

Introduction

1. May Rowland, "Reminiscing about Charles Fillmore," undated manuscript, but most likely written in 1948. Charles Fillmore papers, Unity Archives.

2. *Modern Thought*, April 1889, 10.

3. *Unity*, August 1894, 7.

4. Rowland, "Reminiscing."

1. From Businessman to Spiritual Teacher

1. U.S. Bureau of the Census, "Inhabitants in Sauk Rapids District in the County of Benton (Minnesota)," 1850; "County of Stearns (Minnesota)," 1860; and "3rd Ward of the City of St. Cloud (Minnesota)," 1870.

2. Dana Gatlin, *The Story of Unity's Fifty Golden Years* (Kansas City, MO: Unity School of Christianity, 1939), x–xi.

3. Ibid.

4. *Unity*, September 1896, 262.

5. Charles Brodie Patterson, "Charles Fillmore: A Biographical Sketch," *Unity* (August 1902): 69.

6. Gatlin, *Fifty Golden Years*, x–xi.

7. "Unity Religion Founder Tells What It Means," unidentified New York City newspaper article (photocopy), 1934, Charles Fillmore Collection, Unity Archives.

8. Ibid.

9. Gatlin, *Fifty Golden Years*, xi.

10. *Denison (TX) Daily News*, July 11, 1880. In a piece entitled "Finds Regrets at Gold Trail End," the editor printed a letter from Charles to K. Murphy, who apparently was a resident of Denison.

11. Gatlin, *Fifty Golden Years*, xi.

12. Ibid.

13. "Not an Answer, But an Opportunity," *Unity*, February 1894, 6.

14. Ibid.

15. Gatlin, *Fifty Golden Years*, xii.

16. James Dillet Freeman, *The Story of Unity* (Unity Village, MO: Unity Books, 1978), 27.

17. Charles Fillmore, *Biographical Sketch of Charles Fillmore: A Questionnaire*, 1927, Charles Fillmore Collection, Unity Archives.

18. *Modern Thought*, April 1889, 10.

19. Ibid., 6.

20. *Modern Thought*, June 1889, 8.

21. Ibid.

22. *Unity*, December 1891, 6.

23. *Unity*, August 1891, 6.

24. *Modern Thought*, September/October 1889, 9.

25. *Modern Thought*, February 1890, 8.

26. *Christian Science Thought*, March 1891, 5–6.

27. *Modern Thought*, March 1890, 8.

28. Ibid., 9.

29. *Thought*, September 1891, 248.

2. Co-creator of the Basic Unity Teaching

1. *Unity*, August 1895, 9.

2. Freeman, *The Story of Unity*, 60–61.

3. *Unity*, September 1920, 212.

4. *Thought*, January 1894, 405.

5. *Unity*, June 1904, 336.

6. Ibid.

7. *Unity*, November 1, 1895, 9.

8. *Modern Thought*, June 1889, 9.

9. *Unity*, March 1, 1896, 4.

10. Ibid.

11. *Thought*, February 1894, 10.

12. *Thought*, December 1894, 376–78.

13. *Thought*, July 1894, 157.

14. *Modern Thought*, September/October 1889, 9.

15. *Unity*, March 1, 1896, 4.

16. *Unity*, August 1895, 3.

17. *Thought*, July 1895, 153.

18. *Unity*, October 1894, 12.

19. *Unity*, February 1, 1896, 3.

20. Ibid.
21. *Thought*, January 1895, 244.
22. *Unity*, February 1, 1896, 3.
23. *Unity*, February 1, 1897, 89.
24. *Christian Science Thought*, September 1891, 242–43.
25. Ibid.
26. *Unity*, December 1891, 6.
27. *Christian Science Thought*, September 1891, 240.
28. Ibid.
29. *Unity*, January 1, 1896, 2.
30. *Modern Thought*, June 1889, 6.
31. *Christian Science Thought*, June 1890, 9.
32. *Unity*, October 15, 1895, 4.
33. *Unity*, June 1893, 13.
34. Ibid.
35. *Thought*, July 1894, 213.
36. *Thought*, March 1895, 532.
37. *Modern Thought*, April 1889, 10.
38. *Modern Thought*, November 1889, 9.
39. *Modern Thought*, September/October 1889, 9.
40. *Weekly Unity*, December 13, 1911.
41. *Unity Magazine*, August 1938, 6.
42. *Modern Thought*, May 1889, 3.
43. Ibid., 12.
44. *Christian Science Thought*, June 1890, 9.
45. *Christian Science Thought*, October 1890, 10–11.
46. *Unity*, October 15, 1895, 11.
47. *Christian Science Thought*, June 1890, 9.
48. Ibid.
49. *Christian Science Thought*, November 1890, 8.
50. *Christian Science Thought*, August 1890, 4.
51. Ibid., 8.
52. *Unity*, August 1901, 84.
53. *Unity*, July 1908, 4.
54. *Thought*, January 1894, 404.
55. *Christian Science Thought*, July/August 1890, 4.
56. *Unity*, August 1901, 84.
57. *Thought*, November 1894, 348.
58. Ibid.

59. Charles Fillmore, *Prosperity* (Kansas City, MO: Unity School of Christianity, 1936) 26.

60. *Thought*, September 1895, 248.

61. *Modern Thought,* December 1889, 8.

62. *Thought,* July 1894, 158.

63. *Christian Science Thought*, November 1890, 9.

64. Ibid.

65. *Christian Science Thought*, March 1891, 11.

66. *Christian Science Thought*, September 1890, 12.

67. *Christian Science Thought*, September 1891, 243.

68. *Thought*, October 1893, 308.

69. *Christian Science Thought*, November 1890, 9.

70. *Thought*, November 1894, 346.

71. *Unity*, December 1891, 4.

72. *Thought*, July 1894, 243.

73. *Thought*, June 1892, 103.

74. *Christian Science Thought*, June 1890, 8.

75. *Christian Science Thought*, April 1890, 8.

76. *Christian Science Thought*, September 1891, 243.

77. *Unity*, June 1891, 3.

78. *Unity*, December 1891, 2.

79. *Modern Thought*, September/October 1889, 12.

80. *Unity*, October 1, 1896, 376.

81. *Unity Magazine*, May 1941, 5.

82. *Modern Thought*, May 1889, 8.

83. *Unity*, May 1942, 4–5.

84. *Modern Thought,* September/October 1889, 12.

85. *Unity*, January 1942, 8.

86. *Thought*, July 1894, 216.

87. Ibid.

88. *Thought*, January 1894, 405.

89. *Unity*, January 15, 1897, 51.

90. *Unity*, November 1902, 273.

91. *Modern Thought*, May 1889, 10.

92. *Unity*, August 1895, 13.

93. *Unity*, December 1893, 7.

94. *Unity*, November 15, 1896, 481.

95. Ibid., 490.

96. *Unity*, December 1903, 321–23.

97. *Unity*, November 15, 1896, 485.
98. *Unity*, November 1946, 2–3.
99. *Christian Science Thought*, April 1890, 4.
100. *Unity*, March 1896, 10.
101. *Thought*, April 1894, 11.
102. *Christian Science Thought*, September 1891, 243.
103. Ibid.
104. *Modern Thought*, April 1889, 10.
105. *Christian Science Thought*, May 1890, 8.
106. *Unity*, May 1905, 276.
107. Ibid.
108. Ibid.
109. *Unity*, October 1903, 220.
110. *Unity*, August 1894, 213; *Unity,* August 15, 1897, 143.
111. *Thought*, April 1894, 7.
112. *Modern Thought*, November 1889, 8–9.
113. Ibid.
114. *Thought*, April 1894, 7.
115. Ibid.
116. *Modern Thought*, November 1889, 8–9.
117. *Modern Thought*, February 1890, 8.
118. *Thought*, December 1891, 362–63.
119. *Christian Science Thought*. November 1890, 8; June 1890, 9.
120. *Unity*, January 1903, 38–39.
121. *Modern Thought*, December 1889, 8–9.
122. Ibid., 8.
123. *Modern Thought*, February 1890, 5.
124. *Unity*, January 1, 1897, 4, 5.
125. Ibid., 4.
126. Ibid., 14.
127. *Thought*, January 1894, 409.
128. *Thought*, January 1895, 336.
129. *Unity Magazine*, November 1938, 7.
130. *Thought*, April 1894, 14.
131. Ibid.
132. Ibid.
133. *Unity*, October 1896, 377.
134. *Modern Thought*, April 1889, 8; August 1889, 4; September/October 1889, 9.
135. *Unity*, May 15, 1897, 422.

136. *Thought*, December 1894, 379.

137. *Unity*, March 1938, 8.

138. *Unity*, March 1943, 3.

139. *Thought*, July 1894, 210.

140. Charles Fillmore, *Christian Healing* (Kansas City, MO: Unity School of Christianity, 1909), 67.

141. *Modern Thought*, April 1889, 9.

142. *Unity*, July 1931, 6–7.

143. *Christian Science Thought*, November 1890, 10–11.

144. Charles Fillmore, *Talks on Truth* (Kansas City, MO: Unity School of Christianity, 1926), 101.

145. Charles Fillmore, *Jesus Christ Heals* (Kansas City, MO: Unity School of Christianity, 1939), 63.

146. *Thought*, January 1895, 444.

147. *Thought*, February 1895, 479.

148 *Unity*, May 1, 1897, 353.

149. *Modern Thought*, April 1889, 9–10.

3. CO-CREATOR OF THE DOCTRINE OF THE TWELVE POWERS

1. *Thought*, October 1894, 284.

2. *Thought*, June 1895, 114.

3. *Unity*, August 1895, 12.

4. *Unity*, February 1, 1896, 2.

5. *Unity*, November 15, 1896, 482–83.

6. *Unity*, January 15, 1897, 52.

7. *Unity*, June 1897, 518

8. *Unity*, February 1898, 116–17.

9. Charles Fillmore, *Christian Healing* (Kansas City, MO: Unity School of Christianity, 1909). 98.

10. Ibid., 118.

11. Ibid., 117.

12. Ibid., 110.

13. *Unity*, April 1920, 374–75.

14. *Unity*, February 1920, 103.

15. Charles Fillmore, *The Twelve Powers of Man* (Kansas City, MO: Unity School of Christianity, 1930), 23.

16. Ibid., 3.

17. Ibid., 117.
18. Ibid., 172.
19. Ibid., 170.
20. *Unity*, March 1907, 187.
21. *Unity*, May 1908, 284.
22. *Unity*, July 1929, 1.
23. *Thought*, June 1895, 114.
24. *Unity*, June 15, 1897, 52.
25. Fillmore, *Twelve Powers*, 155.
26. Ibid., 93
27. Ibid., 84.
28. Ibid., 91
29. *Unity*, March 1900, 388.
30. *Unity*, February 1902, 75.
31. Fillmore, *Christian Healing*, 91.
32. Fillmore, *Twelve Powers*, 58–59.
33. *Unity*, October 1903, 209.
34. *Unity*, August 1908, 65; Fillmore, *Christian Healing*, 96.
35. *Unity*, February 2, 1902, 75.
36. *Unity*, August 1920, 103
37. Ibid.
38. Ibid.
39. *Unity*, January 1902, 25.
40. *Unity*, March 1930, 13.
41. *Unity*, April 1908, 244.
42. Ibid.
43. *Christian Science Thought*, April 1890, 4.
44. *Unity*, June 1920, 504.
45. *Unity*, February 1, 1896, 3.
46. *Unity*, August 1920, 111.
47. *Unity*, July 1908, 20.
48. *Unity*, March 1920, 204.
49. *Unity*, February 1920, 104.
50. *Unity*, June 1929, 6, 4.
51. *Unity*, September 1908, 139.
52. *Unity*, April 1930, 2, 4.
53. *Unity*, January 1896, 10.
54. *Christian Science Thought*, April 1890, 4.
55. *Unity*, February 1902, 75.

56. *Unity*, September 1, 1896, 287.
57. Fillmore, *Christian Healing*, 91.
58. Ibid., 67.
59. *Thought*, January 1894, 404.
60. Ibid., 349-350.
61. Fillmore, *Twelve Powers*, 166.
62. Ibid., 107
63. Ibid., 5.
64. Ibid., 107.
65. Ibid., 93.

4. Sources of Charles Fillmore's Spiritual Teaching

1. *Unity*, August 1895, 9; *Unity*, October 1923, 203.
2. Two important early scholars are J. Stillson Judah, *The History and Philosophy of Metaphysical Movements in America* (Philadelphia: The Westminster Press, 1967), and Charles S. Braden, *Spirits in Rebellion: The Rise and Development of New Thought* (Dallas: Southern Methodist University Press, 1963).
3. *Thought*, December 1894, 415.
4. *Modern Thought*, April 1889, 8.
5. *Thought*, November 1891, 303.
6. Robert D. Richardson Jr., *Emerson: The Mind on Fire* (Berkeley: University of California Press, 1995), 197.
7. Carl Bode and Malcolm Cowley, eds., *The Portable Emerson* (New York: Viking Penguin Inc., 1981), 225.
8. Ibid., 172.
9. Catherine S. Albanese, ed., *The Spirituality of the American Transcendentalists* (Macon, GA: Mercer University Press, 1988), 78.
10. Richardson, *Emerson*, 158.
11. Albanese, *Transcendentalists*, 42–43.
12. Bode and Cowley, *Portable Emerson*, 217.
13. Albanese, *Transcendentalists*, 78.
14. Ibid., 76.
15. Ibid., 107.
16. Richardson, *Emerson*, 215.
17. Ibid., 564.
18. Albanese, *Transcendentalists*, 112.
19. Ibid., 104.

20. Ibid., 120.

21. Ibid.

22. *Thought*, October 1893, 281.

23. Bode and Cowley, *Portable Emerson*, 77.

24. *Unity*, November 1898, 224.

25. *Modern Thought*, April 1889, 15.

26. *Modern Thought*, November 1889, 12.

27. *Modern Thought*, January 1890, 8.

28. *Christian Science Thought*, April 1890, 13.

29. *Christian Science Thought*, October 1890, 10.

30. Emma Curtis Hopkins, *Scientific Christian Mental Practice* (Marina del Rey, CA: DeVorss & Co., Publishers, n.d.), 53. This book was originally published by the High Watch Fellowship, Cornwall Bridge, Connecticut.

31. Emma Curtis Hopkins, *High Mysticism* (Marina del Rey, CA: DeVorss & Co., Publishers, n.d.), 106. This book was originally published in 1907 by the High Watch Fellowship, Cornwall Bridge, Connecticut.

32. Ibid., 33.

33. Ibid., 327.

34. Ibid., 223.

35. Ibid., 198.

36. Hopkins, *Scientific Christian Mental Practice*, 12, 252.

37. Ibid., 178.

38. Ibid., 174.

39. Ibid., 47.

40. Ibid., 56.

41. Ibid., 145.

42. Ibid., 168.

43. Ibid., 239.

44. Ibid., 226.

45. Ibid., 81.

46. Gail T. Parker, *Mind Cure in New England: From the Civil War to World War I* (Hanover, NH: University Press of New England, 1973), 50.

47. Horatio W. Dresser, *A History of New Thought* (New York: Thomas Y. Crowell Co., 1919), 75.

48. Charles S. Braden, *Spirits in Rebellion: The Rise and Development of New Thought* (Dallas: Southern Methodist University Press, 1963), 126.

49. Ibid., 90.

50. *Christian Science Thought*, September 1890, 16.

51. Warren Felt Evans, *Esoteric Christianity and Mental Therapeutics* (Boston: H. H. Carter & Karrick, 1886), 17.

52. Ibid., 67.

53. Ibid., 140.

54. Ibid., 35.

55. Ibid., 58.

56. Ibid., 31.

57. Ibid., 76.

58. Ibid., 17.

59. Ibid., 16.

60. Warren Felt Evans, *The Primitive Mind-Cure, or Elementary Lessons in Christian Philosophy and Transcendental Medicine* (Boston: H. H. Carter & Karrick, 1884), 11.

61. Evans, *Esoteric Christianity*, 75.

62. Ibid., 140.

63. Warren Felt Evans, *The Mental-Cure: Illustrating the Influence of the Mind on the Body Both in Health and Disease* (Boston: William White and Company, 1869), 296.

64. Evans, *Primitive Mind-Cure*, 132.

65. Evans, *Esoteric Christianity*, 128.

66. Ibid., 142.

67. Ibid., 94.

68. Ibid., 140.

69. Warren Felt Evans, *Mental Medicine* (Boston: H. H. Carter, 1872), 24.

70. Ibid., 214.

71. Evans, *Esoteric Christianity*, 108–9.

72. Ibid., 77.

73. Evans, *Primitive Mind-Cure*, 16.

74. Evans, *Mental Medicine*, 207.

75. Evans, *Esoteric Christianity*, 150.

76. Evans, *Primitive Mind-Cure*, 103.

77. Evans, *Esoteric Christianity*, 133, 137.

78. Ibid., 129.

79. Evans, *Primitive Mind-Cure*, 163.

80. Evans, *Esoteric Christianity*, 123.

81. Ibid., 123.

82. Evans, *Mental Medicine*, 185.

83. Evans, *Esoteric Christianity*, 132.

84. *Unity*, February 1894, 6–7.

85. *Thought*, July 1894, 155.

86. *Modern Thought*, January 1890, 12.

87. Cokky van Limpt, "Hermes Conquers Europe," *Trouwon*, September 12, 2002, www.ritmanlibrary.nl/c/p/lib/pre/pre-01.html.

88. Ibid.

89. *Thought*, February 1894, 457.

90. van Limpt, *Trouwon*, 1.

91. John Baines, *The Secret Science* (New York: The John Baines Institute, Inc., 2004), 16.

92. *Modern Thought*, June 1889, 15; *Thought*, February 1894, 11.

93. *Unity*, October 1, 1896, 357.

94. *Unity*, June 1891, 4.

95. *Christian Science Thought*, October 1890, 8.

96. Ibid.

97. Ibid.

98. Ibid.

99. Ibid.

100. Jessica Rosemischer, "The Transmission of Consciousness: Reviving the Role of the Spiritual Master," *What Is Enlightenment?* December–February 2005/06, 97.

101. Baines, *Secret Science*, 58.

102. Ibid., 28.

103. Ibid.

104. Ibid.

105. Ibid., 62.

106. Ibid., 61.

107. Ibid., 99.

108. Ibid., 19.

109. Ibid., 59.

110. Ibid., 205, 139.

111. Ibid., 61.

112. Ibid., 164.

113. Ibid., 33–34.

114. Ibid., 36.

115. Ibid.

116. Ibid., 59.

117. Ibid., 98.

118. Ibid., 63.

119. Ibid., 149.

120. Ibid., 87.

121. Ibid., 95.

122. Ibid., 91.

123. Ibid., 131.

124. Ibid.

125. Ibid., 71.

126. Ibid., 116–17.

127. *Modern Thought*, April 1889, 9–16.

128. *Thought*, December 1892, 358.

129. Bruce F. Campbell,. *Ancient Wisdom Revived: A History of the Theosophical Movement* (Berkeley: University of California Press, 1980), 14.

130. Ibid., 40.

131. Ibid., 48.

132. Helena Petrovna Blavatsky, *The Key to Theosophy* (Pasadena, CA: Theosophical University Press, 1972), 60.

133. Ibid., 221.

134. Ibid., 63.

135. Ibid., 64.

136. Ibid., 67.

137. P. Pavri, *Theosophy Explained* (Adyar, Madras, India: Theosophical Publishing House. 1930), 186.

138. Blavatsky, *Key to Theosophy*, 10.

139. Pavri, *Theosophy*, 122.

140. *Thought*, December 1892, 359.

141. Blavatsky, *Key to Theosophy*, 161.

142. Ibid., 140.

143. *Modern Thought*, May 1889, 12.

144. Ibid.

145. *Modern Thought*, June 1890, 9.

146. *Christian Science Thought*, March 1891, 4.

147. Robert Peel, *Mary Baker Eddy: The Years of Trial, 1876–1891* (New York: Holt, Rinehart and Winston, 1971), 203.

148. *Thought*, September 1891, 254.

149. *Unity*, July 1900, 38.

150. *Unity*, July 1907, 10–11.

151. *Modern Thought*, July 1889, 12.

152. *Unity*, May 1, 1896, 2.

153. Mary Baker Eddy, *Science and Health with Key to the Scriptures* (Boston: First Church of Christ, Scientist, 1994), 2. Originally published in 1875.

154. Ibid., 166.

155. Ibid., 234.

156. Robert Peel, *Mary Baker Eddy: The Years of Authority, 1892–1910* (New York: Holt Rinehart & Winston, 1977), 3:354.

157. Eddy, *Science and Health*, 55.

158. Mary Baker Eddy, *Miscellaneous Writings* (Boston: First Church of Christ, Scientist, 1924), 42–43.

159. Eddy, *Science and Health*, 146.

160. Ibid., 497.

161. Eddy, *Miscellaneous Writings*, 22.

162. Peel, *Years of Authority*, 3:332. This was written in a letter.

163. Eddy, *Science and Health*, 30.

164. Ibid., 223.

165. Ibid., 36.

166. Ibid.

167. Ibid., 174.

168. Ibid., 179.

169. Horatio W. Dresser, *The Quimby Manuscripts* (Hyde Park, NY: University Books, Inc., 1961), 23; Gillian B. Gill, *Mary Baker Eddy* (Reading, MA: Perseus Press, 1998), 144.

170. Judah Stillson, *The History and Philosophy of Metaphysical Movements in America* (Philadelphia: The Westminster Press, 1963), 25.

171. Charles S. Braden, *Spirits in Rebellion: The Rise and Development of New Thought* (Dallas: Southern Methodist University Press, 1963), 84.

172. Ralph W. Major, *Faiths That Healed* (New York: Appleton-Century Co., 1940).

173. *Unity*, July 1895, 163.

174. Ibid.

175. Ibid.

176. Ibid., 9.

177. Gill, *Mary Baker Eddy*, 313–16, 146; Robert Peel, *Mary Baker Eddy: Years of Discovery, 1821–1875* (New York: Holt, Rinehart & Winston, 1966), 1:170–83.

178. William J. Leonard, "Warren Felt Evans, M.D.," *Practical Ideals* 10, no. 3 (Nov. 1905): 13.

179. A. J. Swarts, "The Work Gain—Dr. Evans Revisited," in *Mental Science Magazine* 4, no. 6 (March 1881): 137.

180. William J. Leonard, "Warren Felt Evans, M.D.," *Practical Ideals* 10, no. 2 (Sept.–Oct. 1905): 1.

181. Ibid., 14.

182. Ibid., 13–14.

183. John H. Teahan, "Warren Felt Evans and Mental Healing," *Church History* 48 (March 1979): 64.

184. Robert C. Fuller, *Mesmerism and the Cure of Souls* (Philadelphia: The University of Pennsylvania Press, 1982), 146–47.

185. *American National Biography* (New York: Oxford University Press, 1999), 622.

186. Cited in Leonard, *Practical Ideals*, Nov. 1905, 6.

187. Ibid., 7.

188. Ibid., 8.

189. Ibid., 10.

190. Gill, *Mary Baker Eddy*, 312.

191. Ibid., 313–16.

192. Swarts, *Mental Science Magazine*, 137.

5. Charles Fillmore, the Jesus Christ Standard, and New Thought

1. J. Stillson Judah, *The History and Philosophy of Metaphysical Movements in America* (Philadelphia: The Westminster Press, 1963), 172; Catherine L. Albanese, *America: Religions and Religions* (Belmont, CA: Wadsworth Publishing, 1981), 181.

2. Charles S. Braden, *Spirits in Rebellion: The Rise and Development of New Thought* (Dallas: Southern Methodist University Press, 1963), 140; J. Gordon Melton, "New Thought's Hidden History: Emma Curtis Hopkins, Forgotten Founder" (paper presented at the 1987 annual meeting of the American Academy of Religion, Boston, Dec. 5–8, 1987); Gail M. Harley, "Emma Curtis Hopkins, Forgotten Founder of New Thought" (PhD diss., Unity-Progressive Theological Seminary, Clearwater, FL, 1991).

3. Judah, *The History and Philosophy of Metaphyical Movements in America*, 11.

4. Ibid.

5. Included were the Bahá'ís, Chicago Truth Center, The Circle of Light, College of Freedom, Englewood Spiritual Union, Esoteric Extension, The Higher Thought, Illinois Metaphysical College, The Mental Advocate, Mental Science Institute, Prentice Mulford Club, Sara Wilder Pratt Rooms, Stockholm Publishing Company, Suggestions Publishing, and Universal Truth Club. See *Unity*, December 1903, 126–27.

6. *Unity*, December 1903, 326–27.

7. Ibid., 327.

8. Ibid., 333.

9. *Unity*, November 1904, 275.

10. Ibid.

11. *Unity*, November 1904, 307.

12. *Unity*, March 1905.

13. *Unity*, October 1905, 238.

14. Charles Fillmore, "New Thought: A Second Explanatory Lesson," *Unity*, October 1905, 195.

15. Ibid.

16. Ibid.

17. Ibid.

18. Ibid.

19. *Unity*, January 1906, 47.

20. Ibid.

21. Charles Fillmore, "About the New Thought Convention in Chicago," *Unity*, December 1906, 384.

22. Ibid.

23. Ibid.

24. Ibid.

25. Charles Fillmore, "Editorial Note," *Unity*, January 1907, 63.

26. Ibid.

27. *Weekly Unity*, April 30, 1913, 8.

28. Ibid.

29. *Unity*, April 1916, 292.

30. *Unity*, November 1919, 471.

31. Ibid.

32. Ibid.

33. Ibid.

34. Ibid.

35. *Unity*, November 1920, 473.

36. Ibid.

37. Ibid.

38. Charles Fillmore, "About the International New Thought Convention," *Unity*, October 1921, 275.

39. Ibid.

40. Ibid.

41. Ibid.

42. *Unity*, May 1922, 49.

43. *Unity*, July 1922, 49–52.

44. Ibid.

45. Ibid.

46. Ibid.

47. Ibid.

48. Ibid.

49. Ibid.

50. *Unity*, October 1923, 305.

51. Letter from Myrtle Fillmore to Mrs. Kramer, May 15, 1928, Myrtle Fillmore Collection, Unity School Archives, Unity Village, MO.

52. Board of Directors meeting, Unity School of Christianity. Lowell Fillmore, Secretary, no date listed, but presumably the late 1930s. Lowell Fillmore Collection, Unity School Archives, Unity Village, MO.

53. Ibid.

6. Regenerating the Human Body

1. *Unity*, August 1905, 71.

2. *Unity*, February 1894, 7.

3. Charles Fillmore, radio interview, 1936, as reported in "Master Way Shower," Unity School pamphlet, September 1974, Charles Fillmore Collection, Unity Archives, Unity Village, MO. All further references in the chapter to this radio interview are referred to within the text.

4. Dana Gatlin, *The Story of Unity's Fifty Golden Years* (Kansas City, MO: Unity School of Christianity, 1939), xii.

5. Charles Fillmore, radio interview, 1936.

6. Ibid.

7. *Unity*, November 1898, 227.

8. Charles Brodie Patterson, "Charles Fillmore: A Biographical Sketch," *Unity*, August 1902, 69; reprinted from *Mind* magazine.

9. Ibid.

10. *Unity*, May 1903, 301.

11. *Unity*, July 1907, 104–5.

12. *Unity*, July 1913, 68–69.

13. *Unity*, October 1920, 354–55.

14. *Unity*, October 1924, 410–11.

15. Letter from Myrtle Fillmore to William Ray, October 31, 1928, Myrtle Fillmore Collection, Unity Archives, Unity Village, MO.

16. Letter from Myrtle Fillmore to Mary Eaglehoff, November 9, 1929, Myrtle Fillmore Collection, Unity Archives, Unity Village, MO.

17. *Unity*, August 1929, 5–6.

18. James Dillet Freeman, *The Story of Unity* (Unity Village, MO: Unity Books, 1978), 167–68.

19. James W. Teener, "Unity School of Christianity" (PhD diss., University of Chicago, 1939).

20. Marcus Bach, *The Unity Way of Life* (New York: Prentice Hall, 1962), 4–5.

21. Hugh D'Andrade, *Charles Fillmore: The Life of the Founder of the Unity School of Christianity* (New York: Harper & Row, 1976), 125.

22. Charles Fillmore, *Atom-Smashing Power* (Unity Village, MO: Unity Books, 1949).

23. *Unity*, September 1948, 10.

24. D'Andrade, *Life of the Founder*, 130.

25. Freeman, *Story of Unity*, 212.

7. Metaphysical Healer

1. *Unity*, February 1894, 7.

2. *Christian Science Thought*, October 1890, 10–11.

3. *Thought*, December 1893, 4.

4. Ibid.

5. *Thought*, July 1892, 164.

6. Dana Gatlin, *The Story of Unity's Fifty Golden Years* (Kansas City, MO: Unity School of Christianity, 1939), 8.

7. *Thought*, February 1895, 480.

8. *Unity*, November 1898, 226.

9. Ibid.

10. *Thought*, January 1894, 410.

11. *Unity*, December 1, 1895, 2.

12. *Unity*, July 1892, 163.

13. *Unity*, August 1894, 7.

14. Ibid.

15. *Unity*, July 1892, 163.

16. *Unity*, September 1896, 268.

17. *Thought*, July 1893, 178.

18. *Christian Science Thought*, September 1891, 243.

19. *Thought*, January 1894, 407.

20. *Unity*, August 1894, 7.

21. Ibid.

22. *Modern Thought*, April 1889, 2.

23. Ibid.

24. *Christian Science Thought*, August 1890, 9.
25. *Christian Science Thought*, March 1891, 5–6.
26. *Unity*, October 1, 1896, 376.

8. Organizer of Spiritual Ministries

1. *Unity*, June 1891, 2.
2. *Unity* magazine in the period 1891 to 1895 was published solely for the purpose of presenting Truth principles to members of the Society of Silent Unity.
3. *Unity,* June 1891, 2–3.
4. *Unity,* December 1896, 386.
5. *Unity*, November 1891, 6.
6. *Christian Science Thought*, April 1890, 9.
7. Ibid.
8. *Unity*, June 1894, 14.
9. Ibid.
10. *Christian Science Thought*, April 1890, 9.
11. *Unity*, June 1891, 1.
12. *Unity*, August 1894, 216.
13. *Christian Science Thought*, February 1891, 11.
14. *Unity*, August 1905, 104.
15. *Unity*, November 1894, 349.
16. *Unity*, October 1896, 375; *Unity*, August, 1896; *Unity*, January 1907, 52; *Unity*, September 1909, 148.
17. *Thought*, July 1892, 177.
18. *Unity*, July 1893, 10.
19. *Unity,* January 1902, 371.
20. *Unity,* December 15, 1897, 517.
21. *Unity,* December 1, 1897, 463–64.
22. *Unity*, April 1907, 261.
23. *Unity*, January 1902, 37.
24. *Unity*, January 1901, 27.
25. Ibid., 28–29.
26. *Unity*, June 1905, published on the last page of the issue as an ad.
27. *Unity*, March 1906, 166.
28. *Unity*, October 1906, 311.
29. Ibid.
30. Ibid.
31. *Unity*, January 1907, 54.

32. Ibid.

33. *Weekly Unity*, February 19, 1910, 11.

34. *Unity*, October 1911, 332.

35. *Unity,* March 1915, 225–27.

36. *Unity*, September 1894, full-page ad in an unnumbered back page of the magazine.

37. *Modern Thought*, April 1889, 11.

38. Quoted in James Dillet Freeman, *The Story of Unity* (Unity Village, MO: Unity Books, 1978), 71.

39. *Unity*, August 1894, 9.

40. *Unity,* October 1895, 16.

41. *Unity*, July 1895, 16.

42. *Unity*, November 1903, 320.

43. *Unity*, June 1908, 380.

44. *Unity*, July 1915, 88; *Unity*, September 1917, 272; *Unity*, April 1923, 381.

45. *Unity*, August 1, 1896, 207.

46. *Unity*, January 1, 1899, 325.

47. *Unity,* December 1902, 371–72.

48. *Unity*, September 1903, 179.

49. *Unity*, June 1903, 375.

50. *Unity,* December 1920, 582.

51. *Unity*, April, 1909, 263.

52. Ibid.

53. Ibid.

54. Figures taken from *Weekly Unity*, June 5, 1909.

55. *Unity*, November 1900, 366.

56. *Unity*, March 1910, 277.

57. *Unity*, December 1910, 544–45.

58. Gatlin, *Unity's Fifty Golden Years*, 73.

59. *Unity,* December 1917.

60. *Unity*, December 1913, 533.

61. Ibid.

62. *Weekly Unity*, December 11, 1912, 6.

63. *Unity*, October 1923, 283.

64. *Unity,* December 1891, 1.

65. *Thought*, December 1894, 414.

66. *Unity*, August 1, 1896, 200.

67. *Unity*, June 1, 1898, 113; Unity, June 15, 1898, 416, 427.

68. *Unity*, May 1902, 199.

69. *Unity*, May 1906, 319, 341.

70. Ibid.

71. *Unity*, July 1909, 29.

72. *Weekly Unity*, July 3, 1909, 1.

73. *Weekly Unity*, October 30, 1909.

74. *Unity*, March 1910, 273.

75. *Weekly Unity*, November 24, 1910, 1.

76. *Weekly Unity*, April 13, 1913, 5.

77. *Unity*, September 1914, 254.

78. *Unity*, June 1914, 529.

79. "Findings of Fact About Unity School of Christianity," United States Board of Tax Appeals, Appeal of Unity School of Christianity. Docket No. 1799, Submitted February 4, 1926. Decided April 23, 1926, before Sternhagen, Lansdon, and Arundell. Corporate Documents, Unity Archives.

80. *Unity*, February 1915, 1.

81. Ibid.

82. Convention program, Fourth Annual Convention, October 3–7, 1926, 8, Unity Archives, Unity Village, MO.

9. Myrtle Page and Cora Dedrick

1. *Unity,* January 1908, 53.

2. Letter to Grace Norton, August 9, 1928, Myrtle Fillmore Collection, Unity Archives, Unity Village, MO.

3. "Report of Midweek Services," *Unity*, July 1899, 28.

4. Myrtle Fillmore, "How I Found Health." *Unity,* August 1899, 68.

5. Myrtle Fillmore, *How to Let God Help You*, selected and arranged by Warren Meyer, Unity Village, MO: Unity School of Christianity, 1957, 197–98.

6. Myrtle Fillmore, "Health in the Home," *Unity*, October 1911, 323.

7. Letter to Jennie Koerner, December 3, 1929, Myrtle Fillmore Collection, Unity Archives.

8. Myrtle Fillmore, "How I Found Health," 68.

9. Ibid.

10. *Weekly Unity*, August 18, 1923, 8.

11. Letter to Minnie Goodbred, September 18, 1928, Myrtle Fillmore Collection, Unity Archives.

12. Ibid.

13. Letter to Herbert Fry, January 22, 1931, Myrtle Fillmore Collection, Unity Archives.

14. Letter to Mrs. Tracy, August 1, 1928, Myrtle Fillmore Collection, Unity Archives.

15. Blaine Mays, telephone interview with the author, Mill Valley, California, September 18, 1995.

16. One source indicates that Cora came to Unity between 1900 and 1905. Cora herself indicates that she was there as early as 1908. See Cora G. Dedrick, "The Unity Guild," *Weekly Unity*, January 20, 1915, 3.

17. James Dillet Freeman Papers, Unity Archives.

18. *Weekly Unity*, January 15, 1915, 3.

19. Ernest C. Wilson, *If You Want to Enough*, comp. and ed. Ronald and Beverly Potter (Kansas City, MO: Unity Temple, 1984), 160.

20. Record of Ordinations, Unity School of Christianity, September 18, 1918, Unity Archives.

21. Biographical data, Cora Fillmore Papers, Unity Archives and *Kansas City Times*, February 1, 1951.

22. Blaine Mays, telephone interview with author, September 18, 1995. Mays stated, "I assumed that she had received some type of college education." Mays did not remember her mentioning attending college, yet she had the attributes of someone who had received college training. "She was interested in things being right, of people being qualified and knowledgeable."

23. *Unity News*, June 19, 1920; and December 9, 1929.

24. Rosemary Fillmore Rhea, personal interview with author, October 18, 1994, Unity Village, Missouri.

25. Blaine Mays, "Cora Fillmore's Role in Unity," audiotape, 1995, Unity Archives.

26. Mays, telephone interview.

27. Wilson, *If You Want to Enough*, 160.

28. Ibid.

29. Ibid.

30. Mays, "Cora Fillmore's Role in Unity"; Rhea, interview.

31. Rhea, interview.

32. L. E. Meyer, "A Vacation with the Fillmores," *Unity*, January 1973, 21.

33. Ibid.

34. Ibid.

35. Mays, "Cora Fillmore's Role in Unity."

36. Meyer, "A Vacation with the Fillmores."

37. Rhea, interview.

38. Dorothy Pierson, personal interview, October 15, 1995, Sacramento, California.

39. Marcus Bach, *The Unity Way of Life* (New York: Prentice Hall, 1962), 122–23.

40. Dorothy Pierson, personal interview, October 15, 1995, Sacramento, California.

41. Mays, telephone interview.

42. Mays, "Cora Fillmore's Role in Unity."

43. Hugh D'Andrade, *Charles Fillmore: The Life of the Founder of the Unity School of Christianity* (New York: Harper & Row, 1976), 99.

44. Mays, "Cora Fillmore's Role in Unity."

45. Pierson, interview.

46. Blaine Mays, "Cora Fillmore's Role in Unity."

47. Mays, telephone interview.

48. Ibid.

10. "He Had an Uncommon Lot of Common Sense"

1. James Dillet Freeman, *The Story of Unity* (Unity Village, MO: Unity Books, 1978), 9.

2. Richard Lynch, "My intimate acquaintance with Charles Fillmore," Unity School of Christianity, Field Department memorandum, July 22, 1958, Unity Archives, Kansas City, Missouri.

3. Letter from Mrs. Floyd Doan to Charles Fillmore, November 22, 1948, written after Charles' death.

4. Letter from Rhetta Chilcott to Charles and Cora Fillmore, February 26, 1934, Charles Fillmore Collection, Unity Archives.

5. James Dillet Freeman, *Story of Unity*, 152.

6. Rosemary Fillmore Rhea, *That's Just How My Spirit Travels: A Memoir* (Unity Village, MO: Unity House, 2003), 44.

7. Lowell Fillmore, "Things to Be Remembered." *Weekly Unity*, May 1954, 5.

8. Freeman, *Story of Unity*, 9.

9. Vera Dawson Tait, "The Fillmore Message," unpublished manuscript from talk given at Unity on the Plaza, Kansas City, Missouri, Sunday, January 14, 1973.

10. Ibid.

11. Quoted in D'Andrade, *Charles Fillmore: The Life of the Founder of the Unity School of Christianity* (New York: Harper & Row, 1976), 184.

12. Freeman, *The Story of Unity*, 184–85.

13. Tait, "The Fillmore Message."

14. *Unity*, February 1899, 377.

15. James Dillet Freeman, "The Story of Unity," talk given at Unity on the Plaza, January 7, 1973, unpublished manuscript, Unity Archives.

16. Lynch, "My intimate acquaintance with Charles Fillmore."

17. Unsigned letter from a congregant who lived near Unity School of Christianity in Kansas City, no date, James Dillet Freeman Papers, Unity Archives.

18. Quoted in D'Andrade, *Charles Fillmore*, 103.

19. Quoted in ibid., 129.

20. Quoted in ibid., 71.

21. Freeman, *The Story of Unity*, 14.

22. Quoted in D'Andrade, *Charles Fillmore*, 106.

23. Freeman, *The Story of Unity*, 149.

24. Quoted in D'Andrade, *Charles Fillmore*, 126

25. Ibid., 90.

26. Rhea, *That's Just How My Spirit Travels*, 36.

27. Ibid., 42.

28. Ibid., 43.

29. All reminiscences are from Charles R. Fillmore, personal interview with author, Unity Village, Unity School of Christianity, October 17, 1995.

30. Ibid.

31. Ibid.

32. Freeman, "The Story of Unity," unpublished manuscript, James Dillet Freeman Papers, Unity Archives.

33. Ibid.

34. Letter from Mrs. Ida M. Stuart, Elk, Washington, to Lowell Fillmore, February 25, 1949, Lowell Fillmore Papers, Unity Archives.

35. Letter from Emma M. Henderson, 1828 Albans Road, Houston, Texas, to Unity School of Christianity, November 20, 1949, Lowell Fillmore Papers, Unity Archives.

36. Quoted in D'Andrade, *Charles Fillmore*, 103.

37. *Daily Unity*, July 11, 1916, 1.

38. Freeman, unpublished manuscript, Freeman Papers, Unity Archives.

39. *Unity*, September 1903, 182.

40. *Unity*, July 1905, 38.

41. Letter from Charles Fillmore to Myrtle Fillmore, August 20, 1909, Myrtle Fillmore Collection, Unity Archives.

42. Freeman, unpublished manuscript, James Dillet Freeman Papers, Unity Archives.

43. *Unity*, January 1, 1897, 3.

44. Charles S. Braden, *Spirits in Rebellion: The Rise and Development of New Thought* (Dallas: Southern Methodist University Press, 1963), 260.

45. *Unity*, January 1, 1897, 4.

46. Ibid., 5.

47. Ibid., 14.

48. *Unity*, May 1903, 282.

49. *Unity*, June 1901, 258.

50. *Unity*, January 1903, 35.

51. *Unity*, December 1902, 329.

52. Ibid.

53. Ibid.

54. Ibid.

55. Ibid.

56. *Weekly Unity*, August 22, 1948, 3.

57. Rhea, *That's How My Spirit Travels*, 55.

Appendix A: Emanuel Swedenborg

1. J. Gordon Melton, "New Thought's Hidden History: Emma Curtis Hopkins, Forgotten Founder," unpublished paper, 198, Unity Archives, Unity Village, MO.

2. George F. Dole, ed., *Emanuel Swedenborg: The Universal Human and Soul-Body Interaction* (New York: Paulist Press, 1984), back cover.

3. Ibid.

4. Harry W. Barnitz, *Existentialism and the New Christianity: A Comparative Study of Existentialism and Swedenborgianism* (New York: Philosophical Library, 1969), 198.

5. Ibid., 201.

6. *Modern Thought*, November 1889, 11.

7. Dole, *The Universal Human*, 3–5. Swedenborg did not retain his father's family name "Swedberg."

8. Ibid.

9. Ibid., 10.

10. Ibid., 11.

11. Cyriel O. Sigstedt, *The Swedenborg Epic: The Life and Works of Emanuel Swedenborg* (New York: Bookman Associates, 1952), 207.

12. Ibid., 213.

13. Ibid., 207.

14. Dole, *The Universal Human*, 11.

15. Ibid. (back cover).

16. Emanuel Swedenborg, *Angelic Wisdom Concerning Divine Providence* (New York: Houghton Mifflin, 1907), 113. First published in Amsterdam in 1764.

17. Dole, *The Universal Human*, 21.

18. George Trowbridge, *Swedenborg: Life and Teaching* (New York: Swedenborg Foundation, 1955), 275.

19. Ibid.

APPENDIX B: RALPH WALDO EMERSON

1. Information on the life and teachings of Ralph Waldo Emerson was taken from Robert D. Richardson Jr., *Emerson: The Mind on Fire* (Berkeley: The University of California Press, 1995). Richardson, a faculty member at Wesleyan University, has written a superb biography of Emerson, the product of eight years of research and writing. Richardson consulted the vast written works of Emerson, including his essays, letters, lectures, addresses, sermons, and journals. The result is a work that gives highly useful information on Emerson's life and in-depth coverage to his philosophical and spiritual ideas and teaching.

2. Ibid., 254.

3. Ibid., 47; William Ellery Channing, "Unitarian Christianity," in the *Collected Works of William Ellery Channing*, rev. ed. (Boston: American Unitarian Association, 1886), 384.

4. Ibid., 249–50; Ralph Waldo Emerson, "The Transcendentalist," in *Current Works, Vol. I, Nature, Addresses and Lectures*; Catherine L. Albanese, ed., *The Spirituality of the American Transcendentalists* (Macon, GA: Mercer University Press, 1988), 5.

5. Richardson, *Emerson*, 415.

6. Ibid., 214.

7. Ibid., 393.

8. Ibid., 158; David Green Haskins, *Ralph Waldo Emerson: His Maternal Ancestors* (Boston: Cripples, Upham & Co., 1887), 118.

9. Richardson, *Emerson*, 162.

APPENDIX C: EMMA CURTIS HOPKINS

1. Information for this biographical sketch was taken from Gail Harvey, "Emma Curtis Hopkins: 'Forgotten Founder' of New Thought," PhD diss., Florida State University, 1991, 14.

2. Ibid., 19.

3. Ibid., 21.

4. Ibid., 21–22.

5. Ibid., 29.

6. Ibid., 36.

7. *Christian Science Journal,* April 1887, 61.

8. Ibid.

9. Ibid., 62.

10. Harvey, "Emma Curtis Hopkins," 142.

11. Ibid., 143.

12. Ibid., 591.

13. Ibid., 33.

14. Ibid., 46.

15. Ibid.

16. Emma Curtis Hopkins, *High Mysticism,* Marina del Rey, Calif.: DeVorss & Co., n.d. Originally published by the High Watch Fellowship, Cornwall Bridge, Conn., 281.

17. Emma Curtis Hopkins, *Scientific Christian Mental Practice,* Marina del Rey, Calif,: De Vorss & Co., n.d. Originally published by the High Watch Fellowship, Cornwall Bridge, Conn., 105.

Appendix D: Franz Anton Mesmer

1. Stephen Zweig, *Mental Healers: Franz Anton Mesmer, Mary Baker Eddy, Sigmund Freud* (New York: Frederick Unger Publishing Co., 1932), 96.

2. Ibid.

3. Charles Fillmore, *Jesus Christ Heals* (Unity Village, MO: Unity School of Christianity, 1939), 46.

4. Roy Udolf, *Hypnosis for Professionals* (New York: Van Nostrand Reinhold Co., 1981), 2.

5. Zweig, *Mental Healers*, 18.

6. Ibid., 19.

7. Ibid., 27.

8. Udolf, *Hypnosis*, 2.

9. Ibid., 3.

10. Zweig, *Mental Healers*, 28.

11. Ibid., 31.

12. Ibid., 36.

13. Udolf, 3.

14. Zweig, *Mental Healers*, 31.

15. Ibid., 35.

16. Ibid., 47–48.

17. Ibid., 53, 57.

18. Ibid., 54–55.

19. Udolf, *Hypnosis*, 3.

20. Zweig, *Mental Healers*, 52.

21. Udolf, *Hypnosis*, 4.

22. Zweig, *Mental Healers*, 71–73.

23. Udolf, *Hypnosis*, 4.

24. Zweig, *Mental Healers*, 77.

25. Ibid., 82–85.

26. Ibid., 66.

27. Quoted in ibid., 85.

28. Ibid., 86.

29. Ibid., 87, 91.

Appendix E: Warren Felt Evans

1. Warren Felt Evans, *Esoteric Christianity and Mental Therapeutics* (Boston: H. H. Carter & Karrick, 1886), 134.

2. Warren Felt Evans, *The Primitive Mind-Cure: or Elementary Lessons in Christian Philosophy and Transcendental Medicine* (Boston: H. H. Carter & Karrick, Publishers, 1884), 50.

3. Warren Felt Evans, *Soul and Body: The Spiritual Science of Health and Disease* (Boston: Colby & Rich, Publishers, 1876), 32.

4. Evans, *Esoteric Christianity*, 134.

5. *Unity*, May 1908, 283.

6. Warren Felt Evans, *Mental Medicine* (Boston: H. H. Carter & Karrick, Publishers, 1872), 16.

7. Evans, *Primitive Mind-Cure*, 45.

8. Evans, *Esoteric Christianity*, 169.

9. Ibid.

10. Evans, *Primitive Mind-Cure*, 5.

11. Ibid., 10.

12. Evans, *Primitive Mind-Cure*, 16.

13. Ibid., 187.

14. Evans, *Mental Medicine*, 12.

15. Evans, *Esoteric Christianity*, 108–9.

Appendix F: Helena Petrovna Blavatsky

1. Bruce F. Campbell, *Ancient Wisdom Revived: A History of the Theosophical Movement* (Berkeley: University of California Press, 1982), 6.

2. Ibid., 2–6.

3. Ibid., 22.

4. Ibid., 20–22.

5. Ibid., 26.

6. Ibid., 27–28.

7. Ibid., 29.

8. Ibid.

9. Ibid.

10. Helena Petrovna Blavatsky, *The Key to Theosophy* (Pasadena, CA: Theosophical University Press, 1972), 39.

11. Ibid., 146–47.

12. Ibid., 28.

13. Mircea Eliade, ed., *The Encyclopedia of Religion* (New York: Simon & Schuster, 1995), 465.

14. Ibid.

15. Jonathan Z. Smith, ed., *The HarperCollins Dictionary of Religions* (San Francisco: HarperSanFrancisco, 1995), 1071.

16. Campbell, *Ancient Wisdom*, 35.

17. Ibid., 53.

18. Blavatsky, *Key to Theosophy*, 290.

19. Ibid., 280.

20. Ibid., 291.

21. Campbell, *Ancient Wisdom*, 61.

22. John R. Hinnels, ed., *Who's Who in World Religions* (New York: Simon & Schuster), 57.

Appendix G: Mary Baker Eddy

1. Robert Peel, *Mary Baker Eddy: Years of Discovery, 1821–1875* (New York: Holt, Rinehart & Winston, 1966), 24. Information on Mary Baker Eddy's early years as presented in the opening pages of this chapter were taken from Peel.

2. Ibid., 127.

3. Gillian Gill, *Mary Baker Eddy* (Reading, MA: Perseus Books, 1998), 137. This fine biography, written by a woman with solid academic credentials from outside Christian Science, is a comprehensive, balanced, and insightful work. Gill, who writes from a feminist perspective, views Eddy's work as the result of a resilient

and determined woman's attempt to insert unconventional spiritual ideas into a culture dominated by paternalism and traditional Christianity. Though attracted to her subject, Gill is not blind to Eddy's many foibles.

4. Peel, *Years of Discovery*, 188.

5. Gill, *Eddy*, 161, 167.

6. Quoted in Peel, *Years of Discovery*, 259.

7. Quoted in ibid., 205

8. Quoted in Robert Peel, *Mary Baker Eddy: The Years of Trial, 1876–1891* (New York: Holt, Rinehart and Winston, 1971), 196.

9. Quoted in Peel, *Years of Discovery*, 197.

10. Ibid., 220, 227; Gill, *Eddy*, xxiii.

11. Gill, *Eddy*, 470.

12. Ibid., 204.

13. Peel, *Years of Trial*, 9.

14. Ibid., 11.

15. Gill, *Eddy*, 295.

16. Peel, *Years of Discovery*, 288.

17. Gill, *Eddy*, 451.

18. Ibid., 297.

19. Peel, *Mary Baker Eddy: The Years of Authority, 1892–1910* (New York: Holt Rinehart & Winston, 1977), 322.

20. Gill, *Eddy*, 453–54.

21. Peel, *Years of Authority*, 322–23.

22. Peel, *Years of Trial*, 4.

23. Gill, *Eddy*, 513–15.

Appendix H: Phineas P. Quimby

1. Charles S. Braden, *Spirits in Rebellion: The Rise and Development of New Thought* (Dallas: Southern Methodist University Press, 1963), 47.

2. Erwin Seale, ed., *Phineas P. Quimby: The Complete Writings* (Marina Del Rey, CA: DeVorss and Company, 1988), 175–78. From the nineteenth century onward, the material in *The Complete Writings* has been referred to by historians as well as students of New Thought as the "Quimby Manuscripts." They are referenced in this way below.

3. Zweig, *Mental Healers: Franz Anton Mesmer, Mary Baker Eddy, Sigmund Freud* (New York: Frederick Unger Publishing Co., 1932), 118.

4. Annetta Dresser, *The Philosophy of P. P. Quimby* (Boston: Geo. H. Ellis, 1899), 12.

5. Seale, who wrote the introduction to the "Quimby Manuscripts," indicates that Burkmar was both clairvoyant and clairaudient.

6. Dresser, *P. P. Quimby*, 13.

7. Seale, "Quimby Manuscripts," ix.

8. Ibid.

9. Ibid., 350.

10. Dresser, *P. P. Quimby*, 4.

11. Ibid., 49.

12. Braden, *Spirits in Rebellion*, 73.

13. Quoted in ibid., 85.

14. Quoted in ibid., 83.

15. Braden, *Spirits in Rebellion,* 73. "He [Quimby] was probably either consciously or unconsciously being affected by the religious ferment of this time represented by Transcendentalist thinkers." Braden on page 85 quotes from an article by Steward H. Holmes, a Methodist, in the *New England Quarterly* Vol. 17 (no date provided) in which Holmes writes, "Dr. Quimby may be called the scientist of Transcendentalism because he demonstrated visibly on human organisms the operational validity of Emerson's hypothesis."

16. Horatio W. Dresser, The Quimby Manuscripts (Hyde Park, NY: University Books, Inc. 1961), 20.

17. Ibid., 225.

18. Ibid., 303

19. Ibid., 81.

20. Ibid., 235.

21. Ibid., 239.

INDEX